THE CHRISTIAN PHILOSOPHY
OF WILLIAM TEMPLE

THE CHRISTIAN PHILOSOPHY OF WILLIAM TEMPLE

by

JACK F. PADGETT

MARTINUS NIJHOFF / THE HAGUE / 1974

TO KITTY

ISBN 90 247 1610 1

PRINTED IN THE NETHERLANDS

TABLE OF CONTENTS

PART II

A CHRISTIAN PHILOSOPHY OF PERSONALITY: HUMAN AND DIVINE

PART III

A CHRISTIAN PHILOSOPHY OF PERSONAL AND SOCIAL MORALITY

PART V

EVALUATION AND RECONSTRUCTION OF TEMPLE'S CHRISTIAN PHILOSOPHY

ACKNOWLEDGMENTS

For their discerning criticisms and continued support, special gratitude is due to Professors Peter A. Bertocci and Richard M. Millard, my dissertation advisors, and to Edward C. Cell and John H. Lavely. Also, I am indebted for help from students in seminars in Christian philosophy at Simpson College and Albion College, and from Presidents William Kerstetter, Robert Lisensky, and Louis Norris. My wife, Kitty, has the unusual ability to be at once critical and supportive and her assistance has been immeasurable.

Numerous other persons have contributed much to my understanding of William Temple. D. Elton Trueblood first directed me to Temple and helped me to appreciate the depth of his work. It was under the wise tutelage of G. Wayne Glick at Juniata College that I first read *Nature, Man and God.* The most systematic and stimulating study of William Temple was provided by Joseph Fletcher in a seminar at Episcopal Theological School; his witty and insightful commentary on Temple whetted my appetite for further research culminating in a dissertation, "The Concept of Personality in William Temple's Philosophy" (unpublished Ph. D. dissertation, Boston University, 1959). The present volume is the result of numerous revisions and a continual updating of the material on Temple, especially in terms of recent developments in philosophy. My debt to other scholars is evident in the pages that follow.

I am grateful to *The Personalist* for permission to include, with some minor changes, as part of chapter 1 my article, "Did Archbishop Temple Alter his Christian Philosophy after 1939?" (Vol. 43, No. 4. Autumn, 1962); and to Macmillan, London and Basingstoke for permission to quote extensively from William Temple's three major works: *Mens Creatrix* (1923), *Christus Veritas* (1924) and *Nature, Man and God* (1934).

Albion College
November 5, 1973

Jack F. Padgett

CHAPTER I

INTRODUCTION

A. PURPOSE AND PLAN

William Temple was trained as a philosopher and lectured on philosophy at Oxford (1904), but his concern for labor, education, journalism, and the Church of England led him away from philosophy as a profession. Enthroned in 1942 as Archbishop of Canterbury, Temple persisted in applying his Christian position to the solution of the problems of the day. He will be remembered for his contributions in many areas of life and thought: his work in the ecumenical movement, and his writings in theology and social ethics attest to the variety and depth of his concern, but of special significance is his contribution toward the construction of a distinctly Christian philosophy relevant to the twentieth century.

Although Temple did not work out a systematic formulation of his Christian philosophy, the bases for a Christian philosophy are nevertheless evident in his position. It is the purpose of the present work to enter sympathetically and critically into the major facets of Temple's position and to weave together, as far as is legitimate, the separate strands of his thought into a meaningful, even if not a completely unified, Christian philosophy. The intent is not simply to present Temple's conclusions on a variety of philosophical and theological issues; rather, Temple's position is developed systematically, and the arguments for the conclusions at which he arrived are carefully expounded. This procedure should provide an adequate basis for evaluating the consistency, the justifiability, and the relevancy of Temple's Christian philosophy. Since the focus is on Temple as a philosopher of the Christian faith, his theological views are considered wherever relevant to an understanding of his Christian philosophy but no attempt is made to provide a systematic account of Temple's theology.[1]

Three aims may be noted: (1) to expound sympathetically and systematically the Christian philosophy expressed by Temple in his many books, essays, and addresses; (2) to evaluate critically the adequacy of his position; (3) to tender an estimate of Temple's contribution to the construction of a Christian philosophy and the use he made of his time and talents. The divisions and chapters are designed to execute these aims so as to make increasingly evident the source, the content, and the rationale of Temple's Christian philosophy. By examining the Table of Contents, the reader can see the overall structure and plan of the book, as well as the specific facets of Temple's position that are expounded and evaluated. The first fifteen chapters are primarily of a descriptive nature; Temple's position is argued as sympathetically and systematically as possible. Critical comments are inserted whenever doing so facilitates the interpretation of particular issues and clarifies ambiguities in Temple's position. However, extensive critical comments are reserved for Part V.

Three theses that are implicit in the exposition of Temple's position should be made explicit: (1) Temple's philosophical and theological views are best understood from the perspective of his own Christian theism; (2) there is a unity to his position throughout all of his writings; (3) personality is the central concept in Temple's Christian philosophy and serves as the unifying principle of his thought. The development of, and the justification for, the first and third theses should be evident from an examination of the table of contents. Thus, in Part I, the Christian faith as Temple interpreted it is shown to supply what is needed both for the philosophical and the theological enterprises. The dominant role of personality as a principle of explanation in Temple's thought becomes apparent throughout the remaining chapters, and in Chapter 18 the central place of the concept of personality in his philosophy is explicitly argued and its philosophical legitimacy evaluated.

The second thesis claims that there is a unity that pervades all of Temple's thought. However, since this unity is held to reside in Temple's own formulation of a Christian theistic philosophy, the first and second theses merge together and support one another. There is value, therefore, in dealing directly and somewhat extensively with

[1] An excellent theological portrait of Temple that supplements the predominantly philosophical portrait offered in the present work can be found in Joseph Fletcher, *William Temple: Twentieth Century Christian* (New York: The Seabury Press, 1963).

the issue of the unity of Temple's thought based upon the claim that his position is best understood as a venture in Christian philosophy.

B. THE UNITY OF TEMPLE'S CHRISTIAN PHILOSOPHY

Temple's commitment to the task of implementing a Christian civilization provided unity to the diverse activities of his life, but is there a similar unity to his thought as well? The incompleteness of his thought has already been acknowledged and has led some interpreters of Temple to claim that his philosophy altered significantly in the course of his life.[2] The problem is, indeed, posed by Temple himself. Writing in 1939 with a second World War in progress, Temple looks back with misgivings on some of his earlier writings, particularly his aspirations as a Christian philosopher. Two sentences he had written in the "Preface" to *Christus Veritas* (1924) are singled out for comment. Taking note that the dominant theistic position of 1924 conceived of God as the source of everything but as never doing anything in particular, Temple had stated:

> *I believe that a very slight touch to the intellectual balance may make the scales incline the other way .... What is needed is the exposition of the Christian idea of God, life and the world, or, in other words, a Christo-centric metaphysics.*[3]

Regarding these comments, Temple writing in 1939 states:

> The two sentences I have italicised seem very remote to-day. The estimate expressed in the earlier was probably mistaken in 1924, when that sentence was written; it has no relevance to the situation to-day. The later sentence expresses what I believe to be a permanent need and the supreme task of theology; but it is a task of which we now see the impracticality in anything less than many generations.[4]

Even earlier in the "Preface" to *Doctrine in the Church of England*,[5] Temple had felt the need for a different emphasis in theological writing

[2] See, e.g., Randolph Crump Miller, "Is Temple a Realist?" *Journal of Religion* XIX (January, 1939); John P. McGarvey, "Modernism in Archbishop Temple's Metaphysics and Value Theory" (unpublished Ph. D. dissertation, School of Theology, Temple University, 1951), Eugene Skelton, "The Problem of Evil in the Works of William Temple" (unpublished Ph. D. dissertation, School of Theology, South-Western Baptist Theological Seminary, 1951). The material that follows in Section B has been published as an article, "Did Archbishop Temple Alter His Christian Philosophy After 1939?" and is reprinted by permission of *The Personalist* (Vol. 43, No. 4, Autumn, 1962), pp. 539–545.

[3] Quoted in "Theology To-day" reprinted in *Thoughts in War-Time* (London: Macmillan & Co., Ltd., 1940), p. 98.

[4] *Ibid.*, pp. 98–99.

[5] See William Temple and Others, *Doctrine in the Church of England* (London: Macmillan and Co., 1938).

from that which he had been making. The times were out of joint; not simply was an intellectual map of the world from a Christian perspective needed, but there was an urgent demand to convert men to the Christian faith. Thus a Christocentric metaphysics, though a perennial need, was held to be less urgent than a theology of redemption. Indeed, Temple in 1939 even despaired of the possibility of constructing a coherent Christian world view. Individual sin, manifested in pride, and social evil reflected in war, must first be overcome *in fact* and not merely reconciled in principle with a Christian philosophy as he had tried to do in his earlier writings. He states: "The world of to-day is one of which no Christian map can be made.... Our task with this world is not to explain it but to convert it."[6]

The Christian theologian must strive to recover the essence of the Gospel and to make clear its message for the war-torn world. Summing up the task which confronts theology, Temple states:

> We have to face this tormented world, not as offering a means to its coherence in thought and its harmony in practice, but as challenging it in the name and power of Christ crucified and risen. We shall not try to "make sense" of everything; we shall openly proclaim that most things as they are have no sense in them at all. We shall not say that a Christian philosophy embraces all experience in a coherent and comprehensive scheme; we shall declare that in the Gospel there is offered to men deliverance from a system of things – "the world" – which deserves the destruction which is coming upon it, a deliverance offered to all so that "the world" itself may receive it if it will. We proclaim, not general progress, but salvation to them that believe.[7]

However, despite his despair over the world situation in 1939 and particularly the ineffectiveness of the Christian Church to avert war, Temple did not relinquish in principle the significance of working out a coherent Christian philosophy, though it should not, and could not, be done in his generation.

> One day theology will take up again its larger and serener task and offer to a new Christendom its Christian map of life, its Christo-centric metaphysic. But that day can hardly dawn while any who are now already concerned with theology are still alive.[8]

The tenor of this writing by Temple is certainly quite different from the mood which prevails in his three major works and throughout the majority of his writings. Does the emphasis on redemption represent a fundamental shift in Temple's position – that is, in his Christian

[6] "Theology To-day" reprinted in *Thoughts in War-Time*, p. 101.
[7] *Ibid.*, pp. 105–106.
[8] *Ibid.*, p. 107.

philosophy? Or, does it mean instead a shift in emphasis and in strategy for one who was by position at the time an important representative of the Christian Church, actively engaged in presenting the message of Christ to a divided and disillusioned world?

No definitive answer can be given. Temple himself is ambiguous as to the extent of the change in position. Some of his assertions seem to repudiate his previous efforts to formulate a Christian philosophy. But he also suggests that the emphases on redemption and conversion are formally contained in *Mens Creatrix* and *Christus Veritas*, in which a Christian world view is expounded.[9] The problem is further complicated by the fact that no major books on Christian philosophy by Temple appear after 1939. One might infer from this fact that a significant change has occurred, since his writings center on the relevance of the Gospel for the personal and social issues of the day. However, his concern with these same issues throughout his life, the responsibilities of his positions and the world crisis at the time, equally justify inferring that only a change in emphasis has occurred.

That there is a shift in emphasis, at least, from a theoretical formulation of a Christian philosophy to practical implementation of specific doctrines of the Christian faith is apparent. But such a shift could be made within the framework of Temple's position. He had already acknowledged that only a philosophy which makes the deliverances of religion central was adequate. Furthermore, in the formulation of his own position he gives central place to the person of Christ and strives to construct a metaphysics of the Incarnation. The practical concerns of the Christian believer also play a prominent role in Temple's position. As the following analysis of Temple's position makes apparent, the practical resolution of issues is of primary importance to Temple. Thus the resolution of the problem of evil, though of a formal nature – which he seems to lament in the comments noted above – is rooted in the believer's relation to God and the new life of love which even suffering, when gladly endured, makes possible. This is certainly more a practical than a theoretical solution of the problem of evil; evil is to be overcome and not simply understood.

The Gifford Lectures are concluded with a chapter entitled "The Hunger of Natural Religion" in which Temple suggests that it is the actual, not theoretical, justification of evil which man needs, and if evil is not conquered in practice, then theism is false in theory. But

[9] See *ibid.*, p. 102.

man cannot overcome evil himself, and what he needs most of all is to be redeemed. The redemption of man so as to transform his entire being and not merely the gradual improvement of certain aspects of his nature is what is required and desired. "Man cannot meet his own deepest need, nor find for himself release from his profoundest trouble. What man needs is not progress, but redemption."[10]

The need of man for conversion and not merely intellectual enlightenment is fundamental to the solution proposed by Temple to the practical problem of ethics. In one of his earliest books, Temple stressed that though man can recognize the good and his duty independently of religion, he needs the example of Christ's love and sacrifice to effect a change in will in order to be able to love as commanded.[11]

Also, no shift has been made by Temple from an attempt to construct a philosophical system based on reason and experience to one rooted on faith in God. Temple's assurance of the adequacy of his view was from the start founded on faith and not knowledge: "Security is of Faith and not of Knowledge; it is not won by intellectual grasp but by personal loyalty; and its test is not in logic only, but in life."[12]

Nor is the emphasis on the world's unintelligibility, as it is and apart from God's redeeming love manifested in Christ, absent from Temple's major writings at all periods of his life. In affirming that love is sovereign in history he explicitly states that this does not mean that everything is made clear as it is in the world.[13] The meaning and fulfillment of history is in the Kingdom of God beyond history.[14]

What, then, can legitimately be concluded regarding a shift in Temple's Christian philosophy? No fundamental change seems to have occurred despite the contention on the part of some interpreters that Temple was more a metaphysical idealist in earlier writings and gradually moved closer to realism. What does seem to have taken place is that certain Christian concepts received increasing emphasis in Temple's thought and that in some instances the concepts become dominant in his presentation of the Christian message. Such is the case with the emphasis on the redemption of man and the created world by converting both to Christ, as opposed to explaining the world

[10] *Nature, Man and God* (London: Macmillan and Co., Ltd., 1934), p. 513.

[11] See *Kingdom of God* (London: Macmillan and Co., Ltd., 1912), pp. 56–66, 101–103.

[12] *Mens Creatrix* (London: Macmillan and Co., Ltd., 1917), p. 4. Though this book was published in 1917, it was planned while Temple was an Oxford don in 1908; see p. vii.

[13] See *Christus Veritas* (London: Macmillan and Co., Ltd., 1924), pp. 190–191.

[14] See *Nature, Man and God*, p. 513.

and man by reference to the God revealed in Christ. However, as noted above, the redemption of man through conversion to Christ is prominent in Temple's earlier writings, including his major works. The point is, therefore, that a shift is made *within* the framework of his Christian philosophy. It is not a shift from philosophical theism to Christian theism or from Idealism to Realism. Christian theism is affirmed from the start, though expressed more in the language of metaphysical idealism in earlier writings and more in the language of metaphysical realism in later writings. But always it is Temple's own Christian philosophy which is being expressed.[15]

Further, it may be that Temple was not fully aware before 1939 of the importance he had given to practical guidance and redemption in the solutions he offered to philosophical problems. If so, then what happened is that in 1939 he became more clearly aware of the centrality of these concepts in his thought; it was a case of making explicit what before that time was more implicit in his own thinking. He had come to the realization that for him only a practical resolution can be made of the crucial problems faced by a Christian believer and that a theoretical formulation is deceptive.[16]

However, to suggest that Temple gave up completely the task of formulating a Christian philosophy is to exaggerate the shift in emphasis within his position; rather he came to recognize the necessity of postponing the task and was, perhaps, reflecting a certain amount of misgiving for having taken so long to come to this awareness.

Temple the philosopher cannot be dissociated from Temple the man. He constantly strived to make his thought relevant to coping with the problems of actual living. Most of his writing grew directly out of the responsible positions he held in education, in journalism, and in the Church of England. It is important, therefore, to consider the dominant influences on his life and thought.

[15] The essential unity of Temple's position is confirmed by Fletcher at one point, but challenged at another point; cf. *William Temple: Twentieth-Century Christian*, pp. 231, and 295–296; Temple is viewed as a Christian philosopher by Owen C. Thomas, *William Temple's Philosophy of Religion* (Greenwich, Connecticut: The Seabury Press, 1961), pp. 77–80, 167–168; for a mediating position on this issue, see Robert Craig, *Social Concern in the Thought of William Temple* (London: Victor Gollancz, Ltd., 1963), pp. 9, 18–22, 122–124, 128–129.

[16] Criticizing Hobbes' system of thought, Temple states in *Christianity and the State* (London: Macmillan and Co., Ltd., 1928), p. 61: "When a finite intelligence offers a perfectly neat and tidy scheme to cover all human experience, there is good ground for supposing that many of the facts have been ignored."

C. THE MAJOR INFLUENCES ON TEMPLE'S LIFE AND THOUGHT

Since the biographical details of Temple's life and statements on the theological and philosophical background of his thought have been presented by other writers,[17] they need not be repeated in detail here. What does seem appropriate is a brief analysis of the immediate context of Temple's life and thought in order to discover the major influences on the formation of his Christian philosophy.

It was to his parents that William Temple turned more than to anyone else for his inspiration and guidance. Though his father, "the old Archbishop," does not seem to have been well liked by his peers, in his own home quite the opposite was true. Iremonger reports that Frederick Temple "won from his children their complete devotion, their unaffected reverence, and a confidence that was absolute: 'Father says so' clinched every argument."[18] William himself made the following statement at the time ot his own enthronement concerning his father: "He was and is, among men, the chief inspiration of my life."[19] Moreover, the entire atmosphere of the palaces in which the Bishop and Archbishop resided played their roles in relating young William to the tradition of the church. His love for, and devotion to, his mother was likewise deep and abiding. In 1902, when William was twenty-one years old, his father died, and mother and son were joined together in even closer bonds until her death in 1915. Home for him was where his mother resided; and when he became Headmaster of Repton, and later Rector of St. James', his mother moved in with him and took charge of his home.

Academic preparation was well-founded in the best that Britain had to offer through her so-called Public Schools. First, there was Colet Court Preparatory School in 1891, followed by Rugby in 1894 and Balliol, Oxford, in 1900. By the time William was ready to leave

[17] There is a growing body of literature on Temple as a man, as a thinker, and as a churchman, including some unpublished doctoral dissertations. These works are considered at the appropriate places, but some of them should be mentioned at this point. In W. R. Matthews and Others, *William Temple: An Estimate and An Appreciation* (London: James Clarke & Co., Ltd., 1946), is to be found a brief but perceptive critical evaluation of Temple's varied life and work. F. A. Iremonger's, *William Temple, Archbishop of Canterbury: His Life and Letters* (London: Oxford University Press, 1948), provides the most thorough biography of Temple. Significant biographical information, some of which is not available in the other two works, as well as a sympathetic presentation of Temple's theological views are to be found in Fletcher's work. For brief statements on the theological and philosophical background of Temple's thought, see the books by Thomas, pp. 5–12, and by Craig, pp. 9–22.

[18] Iremonger, p. 3.

[19] "Enthronement" reprinted in William Temple, *The Church Looks Forward* (New York: The Macmillan Company, 1944), p. 6.

Rugby at the age of nineteen, the outlines of his personality, as well as his purpose in life, had taken shape. To his fellow classmates a clear picture of Temple could be constructed:

They recall the stout vigorous boy with a striking and intelligent face; walking with a deliberate stride, a little uncertain what to do with his hands – but quite sure of himself in all else .... Quick to absorb, ready to talk on all subjects and to laugh about most; with an insatiable thirst for knowledge, and an intense zest in life; enjoying keenly everything lovely and of good report, from cream buns to classical music. Very friendly to the smaller boys .... Above all unswervingly loyal to his father, his school, and his friends; already possessed by a sense of strenuous purpose, and with at least the outline of a philosophy of life.[20]

Upon graduation from Balliol (1904) he was presented with many alternatives but decided to accept the offer of Queen's College to become a fellow and lecturer in philosophy. During the first year of his fellowship he had no official duties; later his responsibilities consisted of lecturing three hours a week for one term on Plato's *Republic*, for one hour a week the second term on such subjects as "A Theory of Society," "A Theory of Knowledge," and "The Nature of Personality," and during the third term he did not have to lecture at all. With ample leisure time at his disposal, Temple made a careful study of the classical and English philosophers. Also during his tenure he visited Germany twice and sat in on lectures at Jena by Hilgenfeld and Ernst Haeckel, Rudolph Eucken, and Hans Heinrich Wendt. The years at Queen's (1904–1910) are considered by his biographer to be "in some respects the happiest, certainly the most formative and decisive years, of Temple's career."[21]

With philosophical idealism dominating the academic life of England (and of America) in the latter part of the nineteenth and the early part of the twentieth century, Temple's philosophical tutelage was in the idealistic tradition. F. H. Bradley was the acknowledged master in England, but more directly influential on Temple were Edward Caird, Bernard Bosanquet and the American philosopher, Josiah Royce. Books which contributed much to the formation of his general philosophical position were Royce's, *The World and the Individual*, and the Gifford Lectures of Bosanquet, *The Principle of Individuality and Value* and *The Value and Destiny of the Individual*.[22] However, it was from Edward Caird, his teacher at Balliol, that he learned the most.

[20] Iremonger, pp. 34–35.
[21] *Ibid.*, p. 61.
[22] See *Thoughts in War-Time*, p. 97.

How great Temple's respect was for Caird is shown by the fact that his major intellectual contribution to philosophy and religion, the Gifford Lectures, was dedicated to Caird. It was from him that Temple acquired the dialectical process of reasoning which he never forgot.[23] Caird's influence was social and spiritual as well as intellectual. In a statement that applies equally to himself Temple wrote: "Caird's efforts for social reform were the natural outcome of his philosophical convictions."[24]

Thus, to philosophical idealism Temple acknowledged a great debt, not least of which a dialectical method of thought in which he sought for unifying principles by means of which he could attain a synthesis of opposing views. The unifying principles, as we have seen, came from the tradition of the Christian faith for Temple; but when applied to the solution of major philosophical, especially metaphysical problems, led him, as he readily conceded, to "a position which in its positive content is almost identical with such Idealism as that of Edward Caird or of Bernard Bosanquet."[25] The impact of Idealism on Temple's own philosophical outlook is therefore real and permanent despite the fact that his writings span the years from 1910 to 1944, a period in which a reaction set in against the idealist tradition from a variety of sources – e.g., realism, naturalism, pragmatism, and positivism.

However, other philosophical influences on Temple are evident, including some of the reactions against idealism. Although the positivistic movement between the two world wars seems not to have affected Temple's thought, the epistemological reactions against idealism by G. E. Moore and Bertrand Russel did have an effect. In metaphysics the writings of Samuel Alexander and of Alfred North Whitehead were of obvious significance to Temple, particularly in regard to the notions of the levels of reality and the relations among world-process, mind, and value. The most important historical figures whom Temple recognized as making a major impact on his thought were the author of the Fourth Gospel, Plato, and Robert Browning.[26] Evidence of their significance is the fact that Temple produced published studies of their views.[27]

[23] See *Nature, Man and God*, p. x.
[24] Quoted in Craig, p. 11; See also Iremonger, p. 42.
[25] *Nature, Man and God*, p. 498.
[26] See *Mens Creatrix*, p. vii.
[27] *Plato and Christianity* (London: Macmillan and Co., Ltd., 1916); *Readings in St. John's Gospel: First and Second Series* (London: Macmillan and Co., Ltd., 1945).

The major influence on Temple's theological position, apart from the pervasive influence of his father, was the Church of England. Indeed, being both a Christian and an Englishman were significant facts in his development: "I am, as I hope a Christian Englishman; but then I am only an English Christian, and my character is moulded not only by the Spirit of Christ but also by the spirit of contemporary England, which is not the same."[28] Within the Anglican tradition the views of liberal catholicism as manifested in the volume *Lux Mundi* (1889) are worth noting.[29] The concern of the volume with "The Religion of the Incarnation" indicates a dominant theme of Anglican theology, at least during the period from 1889 to 1939, which Temple shared.[30] Specific points of emphasis and of doctrine with which Temple came to agree may also be noted: (1) the "attempt to put the Catholic faith into its right relation to modern intellectual and moral problems";[31] (2) the use of the category of personality to clarify man's status in a world under the rule of God; (3) the view of God as both transcendent and immanent; (4) the interpretation of revelation.[32] A mixture of philosophical idealism, particularly as espoused by T. H. Green, and of Christian orthodoxy is evident in *Lux Mundi*, as it is in Temple's thought. In the "Preface" to *Mens Creatrix* Temple indicates the impact on his views by the authors of *Concerning Prayer*, who include B. H. Streeter, E. Bevan, L. Hodges, N. Micklem, and R. G. Collingwood, and by the Augustinian, Father Kelley (of the Society of the Sacred Mission.)

Of all the men who influenced him theologically, Temple paid the highest tribute to Charles Gore, describing him as one "from whom I have learnt more than from any other now living of the spirit of Christianity and to whom more than to any other (despite great differences) I owe my degree of apprehension of its truth."[33] As the reference to "great differences" makes clear, Temple was not a slave to any

[28] William Temple, "The Church" in *Foundations, A Statement of Christian Belief in Terms of Modern Thought: By seven Oxford Men* (London: Macmillan and Co., Ltd., 1912), pp. 355–356; see also *The Kingdom of God*, p. 73.

[29] Charles Gore (ed.), *Lux Mundi* (New York: John W. Lovell Company, 1889).

[30] See Arthur Michael Ramsey, *An Era in Anglican Theology: From Gore to Temple* (New York: Charles Scribner's Sons, 1960).

[31] "Preface" to *Lux Mundi*, p. vii.

[32] Cf. the following statements: "Either God is everywhere present in nature, or He is nowhere." (Aubrey Moore in *Lux Mundi*, 5th ed., p. 82) "Either all occurrences are in some degree revelation of God, or else there is no such revelation at all." (Temple in *Nature, Man and God*, p. 306); See also Ramsey, pp. 3–4, 151.

[33] Statement of dedication, *Studies in The Spirit and Truth of Christianity* (London: Macmillan and Co., Ltd., 1914).

particular Christian position. "There was in his thinking," Canon Baker observes, "a notable balance between traditionalism and independence, the former stemming from his sensitive awareness of the value of fellowship, the latter expressing his profound conviction of Christ's careful respect for each individual soul and its value and freedom."[34]

If the "persistent traditions in English Theology" have been correctly analyzed by W. M. Horton as Catholic, Protestant, and Liberal, then Temple's position, as distinguished from these groups, is properly classified as part of the central tradition. According to Horton, the central party has its roots in Bishop Wilberforce and a group of "Good Churchmen" who, developing out of a group of High Churchmen, refused to join the Tractarian movement and have been represented by A. C. Headlam, O. C. Quick, and W. R. Matthews.[35] More recently Fletcher has written: "The plain truth is that Temple was every inch an Anglican, standing in between Romanism and Protestantism in the *via media* or bridge-church position."[36] Thus, if a label is necessary to describe Temple's theological position, it may perhaps best be categorized as critical classicism.[37]

Notably absent from the list of theological thinkers who influenced Temple is any reference to "such European 'architects' of modern Christianity as Schleiermacher, Kierkegaard, Ritschl, Troeltsch, Schweitzer, or of such later ones as Barth, Brunner, and Bultmann."[38] Part of the reason no doubt for the absence of wide references to contemporary theologians, Roman Catholic and Orthodox, as well as continental Protestant, and for the absence of clearly marked stages or periods in the development of Temple's thought can be attributed to his early and whole-hearted acceptance of the mainstream of the Christian tradition. "He once told his wife that his highest wish was 'to master the great stream of classical theology' not the polemics of the Reformers and the Counter-Reformers."[39] Hence, once Temple's

[34] A. E. Baker in William Temple, *Religious Experience and Other Essays and Addresses*, collected and ed. with an Introduction by A. E. Baker (London: James Clarke & Co., 1958), p. 3.

[35] See W. M. Horton, *Contemporary English Theology: An American Appreciation* (New York: Harper and Brothers, 1936), pp. 140, 148.

[36] Fletcher, p. 286, n. 10.

[37] See *ibid.*, p. 230.

[38] *Ibid.*, pp. 286–287, n. 10. This seems to have been true of most of Anglicanism up through World War II; see Robert J. Page, *New Directions in Anglican Theology* (New York The Seabury Press, 1965), p. 143. Page also notes that Paul Tillich has until quite recently been neglected in British theological circles; see *ibid.*, p. 151.

[39] Fletcher, p. 287.

own version of the classical Christian tradition was formulated – evidently by 1908, the year when *Mens Creatrix* was planned – changes in his position, particularly in exposition, may be noted, but they seem to represent changes of emphasis within his Christian philosophy rather than a radical departure from it.

As an example of this point it is worth recalling the story of Temple's ordination since the account is usually cited as evidence of Temple's switch from liberal to orthodox. The decision to become ordained was made by Temple early in life,[40] but when the time came (1906) he found that he could only support tentatively the virgin birth and bodily resurrection. Bishop Paget refused him orders, but two years later Archbishop Randall Davidson, satisfied of Temple's orthodoxy, ordained him deacon and then priest (1909). Though the incident illustrates real doubt and struggle on Temple's part with some specific *doctrines* of orthodoxy, it does not justify the conclusion that before ordination Temple was unorthodox in basic outlook and commitment and only afterwards became orthodox. What seems to have bothered Temple were particular problems arising from his faith in Christ as Lord and Savior, but *not* doubt about his own faith in Christ.[41] The point is instructive for an understanding not only of Temple's theological development but, more fundamentally, of the inner workings of his personality. More significant than any of the formal influences on his thought were the basic attitudes toward the meaning of life developed early under parental and church influence and confirmed and deepened by his own experience and reflection. To gain a fuller understanding of these broader and more subtle forces operating on his life and thought we need to take a closer look at Temple, the man.

Temple's interests were varied. He knew and enjoyed good music and he read widely. While at Oxford he developed a concern for social and educational reform which were to remain a part of the burden of his life's work. He joined the Workers' Educational Association in 1905 and served as its president from 1908 to 1924. Temple's direct affiliation with the labor movement and party in England, and his concern for their causes never ceased. This commitment to social issues

[40] See Iremonger, p. 96.

[41] Temple's autobiographical comments on this point are revealing; see "Some Implications of Theism" in J. H. Muirhead (ed.), *Contemporary British Philosophy*. First Series (New York: The Macmillan Company, 1924), p. 413. At issue here, of course, is the meaning of faith, that is, whether faith consists of specific beliefs about God, Christ, the Bible, etc., or in a relationship of trust with the God revealed in Christ. In principle, Temple's view is clearly the latter (see *Nature, Man and God*, p. 322); in practice his position, as we shall see, is more ambiguous.

was fully shared by his wife, the former Frances Anson, as evidenced by the circumstances of their meeting. She served as secretary for the Westminster branch of the Christian Social Union, while he was the chairman. They were married in June, 1916, at St. James's, Piccadilly, where Temple was Rector. Their marriage, Baker reports, "was a romance and an affectionate and understanding partnership"; sharing her husband's interests, Mrs. Temple "gave herself with complete selflessness, carefulness and efficiency ... to ensuring that the wheels of his work moved without hitch or interruption or mistake."[42] Numbered among Temple's friends were many of the most prominent leaders of his day in all areas of life. Charles Gore, whose impact on Temple has already been noted, and Hastings Rashdall of the older generation and R. H. Tawney and Sir Walter Moberly of his own age were among those whose guidance he sought and friendship he prized.

After serving as Headmaster of Repton for four years (1910–1914), Temple turned his energies to active and full- time church work. From this time on the demands on Temple's time and energy continued to increase. But all the while his intellectual productivity was not diminished as evidenced by the lectures and sermons he had already published[43] and by his editorship of the *Challenge* from 1915 to 1918.[44] *Mens Creatrix,* Temple's first major efforts in the area of theological philosophy, was published in 1917 and is considered by some to be his finest work.[45] A sequel was published in 1924, developing further Temple's Christian philosophy and entitled appropriately, *Christus Veritas.* These two volumes together with his Gifford Lectures published under the title, *Nature, Man and God* (1934), are generally considered to constitute the basic sources for Temple's Christian philosophy. G. K. A. Bell aptly summarizes the reception which Temple's Gifford Lectures received upon publication: "They were generally welcomed as work of a very high order, admirable if they had come from a University Professor, astonishing when the magnitude of the author's activities in public life was remembered."[46] Altogether,

[42] A. E. Baker, "William Temple – The Man" in Matthews, p. 96; see also Fletcher, p. 253.

[43] E. g. *The Faith and Modern Thought* (London: Macmillan and Co., Ltd., 1910); *The Nature of Personality* (London: Macmillan and Co., Ltd., 1911); *Repton School's Sermon: Studies in the Religion of the Incarnation* (London: Macmillan and Co., Ltd., 1913).

[44] The *Challenge* was a weekly newspaper taking as its stand the tenets of the Church of England with the aim of interpreting religious, political, and international issues by the standard of Christian conduct.

[45] See Iremonger, p. 218. However, one of the dissenters states: "*Mens Creatrix* is the most disjointed and poorly constructed of Temple's work." (Fletcher, p. 325, n. 169).

[46] G. K. A. Bell, "Memoir" in *William Temple and His Message*, collected and ed. by A. E. Baker (Harmondsworth, Middlesex: Penguin Books, 1946), p. 26.

thirty-four books and twice that many pamphlets, symposia, and articles were somehow produced by Temple in the midst of his amazingly active career.[47]

The productivity of Temple's intellectual and ecclessiastical work offer a clue both to his tremendous talent and to the use he made of it. Not a few of his writings were prepared in the interstitial moments between pressing church duties. "As a writer in the *Church Times* said, the minutes that smaller men fritter away in gossip or a cigarette he used to write *Mens Creatrix* and *Christus Veritas*."[48] Credit must also be given to the depth and breadth of his mind and the amazing integration of his knowledge. Temple possessed what is commonly referred to as a photographic memory. Thus, though he read everything at the same, slow pace, pronouncing each word as he read, he was able to quote long passages of prose and poetry at will.[49] At his disposal for quick and ready recall were all the rich resources of his mind so that he could easily arrange his thought and express them with clarity such that he was able, as one writer graphically puts it, "to speak pamphlets."[50] Even on the sub-conscious level Temple's mind was active and productive, revealing the intuitive operation of his mind. In the "Preface" of his Gifford Lectures, Temple confesses:

> All my decisive thinking goes on behind the scenes; I seldom know when it takes place – much of it certainly on walks or during sleep – and I never know the processes which it has followed. Often when teaching I have found myself expressing rooted convictions which until that moment I had no notion that I held. Yet they are genuinely rooted convictions – the response, not of my ratiocinative intellect, but of my whole being, to certain theoretical or practical propositions.[51]

Commenting on this passage Matthews writes:

> Temple was an intuitive thinker and his philosophy was built up by the putting together of convictions which had come to him in precisely the way he describes. This does not mean that there is no argument or connected train of reasoning, but it would be true to say that the reasoning is employed to articulate, to communicate and to sustain a vision of Reality which he had enjoyed through a "response of his whole being."[52]

[47] The most complete bibliography of Temple's writing presently available is contained in Fletcher, pp. 349–365.

[48] Quoted by A. E. Baker, "William Temple – The Man" in Matthews, p. 101. In Temple, see *Mens Creatrix*, p. vii.

[49] See Iremonger, pp. 475–476; also Anthony Otter, *William Temple And the Universal Church* (London: SCM Press, Ltd., 1949), p. 19.

[50] W. R. Matthews, "William Temple as Thinker" in Matthews, p. 7.

[51] *Nature, Man and God*, p. ix.

[52] W. R. Matthews, "William Temple as Thinker" in Matthews, p. 11.

Basically Temple was an uncomplicated man who did not seem to be beset by the conscious and semiconscious frustrations and fears which inhibit and intimidate most people. He possessed, in the highest sense, an integrated personality. From this integration flowed the inner assurance, simple trust, and loving devotion to God and fellowman which so characterized all that he did. For Temple the truths of Christianity were not matters of probability about which there was some doubt and, hence, hesitancy to speak; they were assured truths. On the believing quality of Temple's mind, W. R. Matthews writes:

> I should say that by temperament he was the very opposite of a sceptic. He said once that he had never for one moment doubted the divinity of Christ – surely a revealing statement. I believe it to be simply true that he had never had to face as a personal problem the ultimate doubts. His was both a hospitable and believing mind.... On one eminent philosopher he made a sustained attack – on Descartes, ... and he objected, characteristically, to that thinker's famous "method of universal doubt."[53]

Since Temple was certain of what he believed, and consequently was relieved of tension regarding his beliefs, he could devote himself fully both to propounding his views and, at the same time, loving those who disagreed. In this way he never seemed to be on the defensive. The key to Temple's inner security and outward assurance was his "single-minded faith in God."[54] Knowing that God was the source of his strength, he retained his humility and sought God's presence often. It is also significant to realize the importance of his sense of mission. From his early youth he felt the hand of God upon him and the need for integrating all areas of life, showing how they all find their unity and illumination in the Incarnation.[55]

It should be recalled that for a time Temple thought that philosophy would be his profession.[56] Concern with the formulation of fundamental principles regarding any issue remained foremost in his thinking to the end, but the bent of his mind and inclinations were toward the application of philosophical thought to concrete problems of living. As Iremonger states concerning Temple's interests in philosophy: "His concern with philosophy became centered on its practical significance for the conduct of life, and – when he grew conscious that there was a

[53] *Ibid.*, p. 9.

[54] Iremonger, p. 524; see also A. E. Baker, "William Temple – The Man" in Matthews, pp. 109–110.

[55] See Iremonger, pp. 512–513.

[56] See Temple's statement in the "Preface" to *Mens Creatrix*, p. vii.

social problem – for the proper ordering of society."[57] Similarly, Temple's approach to religion was more that of the prophet and teacher, than that of the professional theologian. Ramsey refers to Temple as an example of the amateur theologian *par excellence*.[58] Above all he sought to comfort anyone who would listen with what he considered to be the relevance of the will of God to the perplexing problems life poses.[59] Prayer was for him the heart of the personal religious life, and evangelism was the real job of the church. The latter task he interpreted in the widest sense as witnessing for Christ in all areas of life, and in the twentieth century this meant particularly in the political and economic realms. A passage from the Introduction to his last book provides an admirable summary not only of the message Temple sought to convey through his life and work, but expresses as well a challenge that we have not yet met:

Our need is a new integration of life: Religion, Art, Science, Politics, Education, Industry, Commerce, Finance – all these need to be brought into a unity as agents of a single purpose. That purpose can hardly be found in human aspirations; it must be the divine purpose. That divine purpose is presented to us in the Bible under the name of the Kingdom (Sovereignty) of God, or as the summing-up of all things in Christ, or as the coming-down out of heaven of the holy city, the New Jerusalem.[60]

[57] Iremonger, p. 19. Also see the statements evaluating Temple's lecture notes recorded in Iremonger, pp. 62–63.

[58] See Ramsey, pp. 146–147.

[59] A reference to his own attempt to discern God's will regarding a decision he faced is made in *Christian Faith and Life* (New York: The Macmillan Company, 1931), p. 51.

[60] William Temple, *The Church Looks Forward* (New York: The Macmillan Company, 1944), pp. v–vi.

PART I

THE CONSTRUCTION OF A CHRISTIAN PHILOSOPHY

CHAPTER 2

THE PHILOSOPHIC ENTERPRISE

A. THE PHILOSOPHIC APPROACH

The philosophic task represents for Temple the most serious efforts of man to comprehend the meaning of existence. The philosopher makes "a determined effort to think clearly and comprehensively about the problems of life and existence."[1]

In this attempt to weave all of experience into a clear and meaningful pattern, the philosopher moves beyond the uncriticized impressions which prevail in most areas of life. Most men exercise their critical faculties to some extent in organizing their sense impressions and distinguishing these from dreams. But here the reflective process is often of short duration, and the guiding principle is practicality, not theoretical satisfaction of the will to know or integration of all of one's experience into a coherent system of beliefs. The philosopher does not stop his investigation at what appears to be sufficient for the business of daily living. Far from simply accepting impressions and feelings as they come to man, he strives to organize all of experience and to relate sensory data to other data such as that derived from man's aesthetic moral, and religious experience.[2]

Hence, when its task is conceived in this broad sense, philosophy is identified with metaphysics. In fact, Temple at one point makes this identification explicit by defining philosophy as "the study of reality as such,"[3] and he appeals to Aristotle to support this definition. The

[1] Temple, *Mens Creatrix*, p. 7.

[2] Insofar as each of these areas represent activities of the human mind, they are equally subject to philosophy. However, religious experience suggests an object not only independent in the sense of existing in the world apart from any individual experience of it, but as the source of the world and all experience. Religion in this sense serves as the completion of the other activities of the mind. See *ibid.*, p. 260. This point is developed below; see chapters 5 and 9.

[3] *Christianity in Thought and Practice* (London: Student Christian Movement Press, 1936), p. 13.

various divisions of philosophy supplementing or presupposed by this metaphysical task are relegated to the status of sciences. Accordingly, epistemology, ethics, or physics, as separate disciplines, are considered Scientific Philosophy. The term philosophy is restricted to the comprehensive task of relating all the separate analyses of experience and integrating them into some meaningful explanation of the totality of experience.[4]

Thus the procedure of the philosopher is to collect all the facts of experience that can be gathered and, without giving priority to any one area of experience, to construct a system which accounts for all the areas. As such, philosophy proceeds without any assumptions other than the single one of the efficacy of reason to comprehend the universe; that is, that the universe is rationally intelligible to the mind of man. As Temple states: "Philosophy assumes the competence of reason – not necessarily your reason or mine, but reason when free from all distraction of impulse – to grasp the world as a whole."[5]

However, there is a difficulty which the philosopher encounters from the start in this task because "our observation is, in fact, very largely determined by the general conceptions with which we undertake it."[6] The philosopher does not begin his examination of experience in a vacuum. He is a product of his culture and thus brings to the investigation a mind already overflowing with facts and theories. Furthermore, the process in which he is engaged does not yield to exact measurement. As philosophers, Temple concludes, "we start with a vision of the world coloured by our history, our family, and our temperament; and precise and detached observation in this field is not to be attained."[7] Temple's point seems to be that the philosopher can and must look for an hypothesis to explain all the facts which on the basis of the separate areas of investigation cannot be justified. It is there that religion plays a significant role for Temple.

Though Temple does indicate that the guiding principle of the philosophic quest is the theoretical satisfaction of the will to know and not practical guidance in the daily business of living, another emphasis is evident in his writings. Philosophy is held to be integral to life, on the

[4] See *ibid.* However, elsewhere Temple distinguishes between Scientific Philosophy and Theological Philosophy and restricts his use of the term philosophy to the former. See *Nature, Man and God*, p. 44; especially n. l. See below, chapter 5.

[5] *Mens Creatrix*, p. 2.

[6] Temple, *Christianity in Thought and Practice*, p. 14.

[7] *Ibid.*, pp. 15–16. The implications of this procedural difficulty confronting the philosopher are examined below; see chapter 5.

one hand, and life is held to require the guidance that a philosophical world view alone can provide, on the other hand. Hence, the ultimate aim of philosophy for Temple would seem to be that of providing insight into, and guidance for, the life man lives in the universe.[8] When philosophic world views are examined and evaluated by Temple, that one which provides the individual with inner assurance and practical guidance for living is held to be superior even if it fails to provide a coherent account of the facts. Temple does not adequately reconcile these different interpretations of the philosophic task.

This raises the question of how the philosopher should proceed in his work so as to gain an adequate understanding of the universe and to provide guidance for living? The problem is to discover a philosophic method which can satisfy the demands of the philosophic enterprise.

B. THE PHILOSOPHIC METHOD

An analysis of the methods of philosophic inquiry must begin by acknowledging the fact that much actual thinking occurs on a level below conscious awareness.[9] A person confronted with a problem may find that his mind momentarily goes blank, only to be aware moments later of some comment he wishes to make, after which his mind may go blank again. In a similar way an individual may find himself asserting a strong conviction on a subject in the course of a discussion which up to that moment he was not fully aware he held.

Much of man's thinking thus goes on in the semiconscious regions of the mind. The rightful authority of a number of social conventions resides precisely in the fact that many men over an extended period of time collaborated, though with only partial awareness, in determining certain courses of conduct as preferable to others. This process is praised by Temple, and the conclusions reached are considered to be representative of "truly scientific induction."[10] The possibility of relevant facts being omitted in this process is far less, Temple contends, than when a single individual consciously strives to consider all the relevant data and infers from them a legitimate conclusion.

Temple seems to be indicating his preference for non-directed or

[8] See *Christianity in Thought and Practice*, pp. 33–34; *Mens Creatrix*, pp. 3–4; *Christus Veritas*, p. 88.

[9] See Temple, *Mens Creatrix*, p. 10. In *Mens Creatrix* this type of thinking is held to be true of everyone, but in the Preface to *Nature, Man and God*, pp. viii–ix, Temple refers to two different types of thinking, only one of which is primarily of a semiconscious nature.

[10] Temple, *Mens Creatrix*, p. 11.

spontaneous thinking as opposed to an extensive conscious effort specifically designed to work through to conclusions from acknowledged premises. When this preference is related to Temple's own intuitive type of mind, then a significant insight into Temple's approach to philosophical problems is evident. This is, perhaps, one of the bases, though never so stated by Temple, on which Descartes' method of conscious doubt is rejected.

1. Deductive and inductive methods

However, it is with the conscious processes of thinking and inferring that the philosopher must be concerned. This is the domain of logic, and two chief logical methods have evolved: deductive and inductive. Each one is inadequate, and yet both are necessary and are, in fact, used together.

The difficulty with deduction has become commonplace. Starting as it does from a major premise from which necessary conclusions are inferred, the deductive method fails to establish the certainty of the initial premise. Furthermore, the theory of evolution has destroyed the sharp divisions into distinct kinds of beings once believed to prevail in the natural order. Such absolute divisions can no longer be drawn any more than one can separate absolutely manhood from boyhood in the life of any individual. Knowledge is not of static objects clearly distinguishable from one another and once defined evident and clear-cut in essence. The theory of evolution in discarding Real Kinds also pointed up the fallacy of Aristotelian logic, for in life clear-cut distinctions based on definitions cannot be made, or if made, are irrelevant. In order to know what a thing is, according to evolution, it is necessary to know how it arose since the meaning of certain things is derived from the process by which it came to be. It is for this reason that the historical method has become so significant in modern thought. Hence, deduction is no longer adequate as a philosophic method.

However, induction is not a sufficient method taken alone either. Though it has the advantage of starting with the particular facts of experience and thus avoids the criticism of irrelevancy levied against deduction, it fails to establish with certainty the conclusions to which it leads. The only way to establish the certainty of a conclusion arrived at inductively would be by demonstrating the impossibility of all possible alternatives, which is itself impossible. This poses something of a paradox for the philosopher in search of an adequate method: "If knowledge is of actual experience it lacks cogency: if it has cogency it is not concerned with actual experience."[11] The difficulty with both deduction and induction as separate philosophical methods may be briefly summarized: "The difficulty about Deduction is that we have no certain right to our starting-point. The difficulty about Induction is that we have no certain right to any conclusion."[12]

The criticism Temple makes against induction is on the basis of its failure to give the same logical certainty for its conclusion that deduction does, but what prescribes that logical certainty is the ideal sought? Temple's appeal to logical certainty as the norm seems especially strange since he is critical of Descartes, and of much of modern philosophy, for using mathematics as the ideal discipline.

2. *The dialectical method*

This does not mean that there is no hope for the philosopher or that there is no sound philosophic method. The clue to the discovery of an adequate method is to be found in the evolutionary process by which a thing has its being in the very process of coming to be. Applying this insight on a broader scale leads to the use of the historical antecedents and present prevailing conditions. The thinking process also must be understood in terms of its historical origins and development:

> We now recognise that the understanding of all other existing things is to be reached in part by study of the historical process which has led to their being what they are; is it not probable that in like manner the understanding and consequent evaluation of thought is to be reached by a study of the history of thought?[13]

The conclusion to which Temple is led is that logic should be conceived differently both in terms of the objects with which it deals and the method by which it strives to interpret them. If logic is to be relevant to life, it needs to be concerned with the actual changing world, that is with the World-Process. It can no longer be confined to the eternal unchanging entities of Greek philosophy or of mathematics. Logic is to deal not merely with the formal relations among ideas in separation from the real world, but with the actually existing facts of experience. Therefore, logic must come to be thought of as the discipline which

[11] Temple, *Nature, Man and God*, p. 91.

[12] Temple, *Mens Creatrix*, p. 15. See also *Nature, Man and God*, p. 90.

[13] *Nature, Man and God*, p. 106. The origin of mind in the World-Process is considered in the next chapter.

traces the historical development of thought itself as manifested, for example, in the history of philosophy. Logic defined in this way becomes "the logic of facts" or "the logic of the situation."[14] Following Bosanquet, Temple proposes as the synonym for logic "the spirit of totality."[15] However, exactly what Temple means by logic and how the history of philosophy exemplifies it remains unclear.

But how is the philosopher to proceed in understanding the world which is in process? This can be done by following the manner in which thinking actually functions, including both deduction and induction at one and the same time. In the analysis of any problem one does not start without any clues to an interpretation, but, rather, one begins an analysis of the facts at hand with the assumption that the data constitute some pattern and some hint of the nature of that pattern. When the facts are explored, the theory of their relationship is modified in accordance with the insight gained by the further investigation. Thus the deductive and inductive methods are both employed, each complementing the other. It is a matter of "see-sawing" back and forth between facts and theory so that "knowledge of both grows together."[16]

It is not possible to start either with pure facts or pure generalizations.[17] What the significant facts are can be determined more adequately at the conclusion of the investigation, and apart from some facts thought to be relevant to the problem there would be nothing from which to generalize. Thus Temple states:

> It is at the end, not at the beginning, of our intellectual process that we are in possession of the "facts." Hence our "conclusion" should always modify its own premises; for our goal is not the formation of one judgment whose truth is guaranteed by others, but a whole system whose parts support each other and in which all the "facts" are found.[18]

Such an approach is called by Temple the dialectical method and has similarities with the Hegelian approach but is closer to the critical method of Kant and Plato. By the dialectical method is meant "the attempt to reach truth by the putting of different points of view over against each other and trying to do justice to them all."[19] Such a reasoning process is indeed circular, but it is all right to reason in a circle so long as the circle is large enough.

[14] See *ibid.*, p. 108.
[15] See *ibid.*, p. 108; also Bernard Bosanquet, *The Principle of Individuality and Value* (London: Macmillan and Co., Ltd., 1912), p. 23.
[16] Temple, *Mens Creatrix*, p. 15.
[17] The epistemological basis for this will be indicated in the next chapter.
[18] *Mens Creatrix*, p. 16.
[19] *Christianity in Thought and Practice*, p. 18.

How logic, the history of thought, and the dialectical method are related is never clarified by Temple.[20] What does seem clear is that Temple follows the dialectical method in the *exposition* of his views and perhaps in doing so means to provide, by way of illustration, the meaning of logic when applied to solving philosophical problems.[21]

According to Temple, the correct method by which thought should proceed in the quest for knowledge is to continue to work with the data, manipulating the data into a scheme of thought and altering the scheme to fit the facts until they are so arranged as to constitute an intelligible system. When such a coherent scheme is formulated, one can be assured that truth has been attained, at least for that stage of analysis. The circularity of thought is thus evident in the attempt to understand facts by moving around the facts, building up a system on them, all the while gaining more understanding of the facts and their significance.[22] In this way the philosopher moves from particulars to a generalization based on them, which in turn enables him to understand better the particulars. Such a shuttling back and forth between fact and theory is essential if both particulars and universals evident in all facts are to be adequately understood and interpreted, and dogmatism is to be avoided. In a descriptive passage that calls to mind Whitehead's famous analogy of philosophic method and the flight of an airplane, Temple states the proper relationship between facts and generalizations based on them:

> We need to come back to the world with our generalization in our mind, and see the world again in the light of it; and then to return to the generalisation with the new material obtained by our last vision of the world.[23]

This conception of the philosophic method rules out absolute logical certainty for the philosopher but encourages growth in knowledge. What is known now may have to be modified in light of new knowledge yet to be determined, but what is now held to be true, for example in medicine, represents a closer approximation to truth and certainty than when magic prevailed. The philosophic method, then, consists in "the

20 See Thomas, *William Temple's Philosophy of Religion*, pp. 38–39.

21 See especially the procedure followed in *Mens Creatrix*. Temple does not, as we shall see, employ the dialectical method to arrive at, or to check, his own conclusions.

22 See Temple, *Christianity in Thought and Practice*, pp. 20, 39. See also William Temple, *Studies in the Spirit and Truth of Christianity* (London: Macmillan and Co., 1914), pp. 42–43, and *Mens Creatrix*, p. 17.

23 *Mens Creatrix*, p. 19. Alfred North Whitehead in *Process and Reality* (New York: The Humanities Press, 1955), p. 7, states: "The true method of discovery is like the flight of an aeroplane. It starts from the ground of particular observation; it makes a flight in the thin air of imaginative generalization; and it again lands for renewed observation rendered acute by rational interpretation."

progressive systematisation of our experience as we apprehend it."[24] Temple would seem to have returned to a view of knowledge as probability that is very much like the kind of knowledge induction yields and which he criticized for failing to provide logical certainty. Temple offers here a defense of philosophical probability as opposed to logical certainty. However, he is not content to accept probability as the adequate norm, but also demands that a view provide psychological certitude.

3. *Meaning and task of philosophy*

As a result of this analysis of how philosophers strive to philosophize, Temple proposes a fuller definition of philosophy, its aim and the method by which it should proceed:

> Philosophy attempts to deal with all the facts as related in the one system of the Universe, and with that one system as uniting them. And its method is neither Inductive nor Deductive. It aims at a comprehension covering the multitude of particular facts and penetrating to the principle of unity which holds them together; it does not proceed from first principles or to them, but it allows particulars and universals, differences and unity, parts and whole, to influence one another in the intellectual construction which it forms, until all facts are seen knit together in one system whose principle is the explanation of the world.[25]

It is the responsibility of the intellect to carry out this task and it does so by following the dictates of its own inner demand for coherence. But since it is the facts of experience which must cohere, coherence as an abstract norm of thought can not be the principle of unity that is sought. The principle of unity must be more than intellectual; it must include both the facts of experience and the coherence demanded by the intellect. Hence, the intellect organizes the facts of experience in accordance with its own standard of coherence; the facts, in turn, direct the pattern that results while at the same time the facts become meaningful in terms of the pattern. Following Kant's general analysis in the First Critique, Temple contends that the facts provide the content and the intellect the form, and each modifying the other culminates in a meaningful system of explanation.

A narrow conception of both mind and philosophy is hence rejected, for both encompass more than intellectual activity taken in isolation from other activities of the mind such as imagination and conscience. All of these activities are the function of mind. So too philosophy is

[24] *Mens Creatrix*, p. 20. See also *Nature, Man and God*, p. 108.
[25] *Mens Creatrix*, p. 22.

concerned with the totality of experience and not just a disembodied intellect. Thus, "Philosophy – the attempt to grasp the whole as a whole – requires Imagination as well as Intellect, the artistic as well as the scientific capacity."[26]

The purpose of the philosophic enterprise therefore is to discover a principle which renders the universe meaningful to man. Deprived of logical certainty in such matters, man can still hope for psychological certainty and concrete guidance for living. Indeed, until the latter are provided, the philosophic enterprise remains incomplete, though to complete the task may mean moving beyond what philosophy alone can establish. Before these issues can be pursued further, it is necessary to turn to Temple's analysis of some of the basic problems arising from the knowledge venture itself.

[26] *Ibid.*, p. 23.

CHAPTER 3

THE KNOWLEDGE VENTURE

A. ORIGIN AND IMPETUS

1. Thought as the extension of organic process

As the discussion of the philosophic method revealed, it is Temple's contention that to know anything one must trace its historical origins and the process of development which it has undergone. The mental activity of man must also be understood in terms of the history of its occurrence and development in the World-Process. An analysis of the function of thinking in the development of the human species through the evolutionary process indicates that thinking is itself an extension of the organic process from which it arose, serving as an additional means by which an organism strives to adjust to its environment.

The scientific world view clearly indicates the priority of the physical world to the appearance of mind which apprehends it. Thus, the apprehension of the world by the mind of man is not primary in terms of temporal sequence but derivative: "So far as our experience is concerned, *Apprehension takes place within the world, not the world within apprehension.*"[1]

Furthermore, man's ability to apprehend intellectually the natural order with some accuracy is not surprising when one realizes that the intellect came into being in interaction with the natural order.[2]

[1] Temple, *Nature, Man and God*, p. 111. The significance of this fact for an interpretation of the universe and man's status in it is explored in Chapter 6.

[2] That it is not surprising does not diminish for Temple the metaphysical significance of a kinship between mind and reality as an examination of Temple's theism indicates. See *ibid.*, p. 148, and Chapter 9 below.

2. *Desire as the impetus of thought*

Mental activity, then, is rooted in the organism's total response to its environment as one means of satisfying the needs of the organism. As such, desire constitutes the impetus initiating thought. The object of desire in the lower stages of mental activity is what will satisfy the immediate needs of the organism. Selectivity by the mind among the objects presented to it is thus present from the start but at the lowest levels operates solely to serve the needs of the organism. This is the rudimentary stage for what later becomes ideally, at least, the love of truth for its own sake.[3] It is doubtful if one is ever motivated only and totally by the will to know. Nonetheless, the latter impulse does develop and serves as the motivation for all creative thought.

3. *Practical and speculative interests*

Even on the higher stages of man's development two impulses may be noted which motivate man to pursue knowledge: Practical and Speculative. Thus, knowledge is often sought because the insight gained may be put to use to solve some pressing problem which confronts the individual. In this case the knowledge is not desired merely as a possession or enjoyed for its own sake, but is prized for its practical usefulness. However, one may also seek to know something simply for the sake of knowing it, to satisfy one's own intellectual curiosity on an issue quite apart from the use to which the knowledge gained may be put in the business of living.

In terms of the history of the human race it is evident from the above discussion that the practical interest preceded the speculative interest since mind itself arose precisely for that end. But once the speculative interest developed, then it is irrelevant to ask which one of these impulses exercises priority in any individual's quest for knowledge.[4] At this level the difference between the two lies not in the method employed to learn or the knowledge gained, but rather in the sort of answer which satisfies the quest. The "practical" interest will stop the quest as soon as an answer is attained which seems to meet the immediate demands of the problem at issue; but for the speculative interest understanding the universe as a whole is the terminal point.

[3] See *Nature, Man and God*, pp. 139–140.

[4] This point represents making explicit what is implicit in Temple when the relevant material in *Mens Creatrix*, pp. 27–35, is related to that in *Nature, Man and God*, pp. 109–134.

When a general will to know is the motivation for enquiry, then Reality is sought; and only when it is grasped is the mind content. In this way insight is gained into the nature and status of man as finite, but as also possessing a mind which enables man to understand his finitude against the background of a seemingly infinite universe. To recognize one's finitude is, in part, to transcend it, and thus the will to know for the sake of knowledge itself is one example of self-transcendence. Such an effort on man's part to rise above his limited self and situation is the source of the quest for truth, beauty, goodness, and holiness. The knowledge venture, then, whether it be "practical" or "speculative" arises under the impetus of some interest which the individual seeks to satisfy. But the interest, while posing the question to be answered, does not also supply the answer which will terminate the quest.

A distinction may now be drawn between "logical" and "rational." The former refers to the process by which an answer is sought to a question raised but does not include the raising of the question itself. "Logic is therefore the science of intellectual process so far as this leads to knowledge; choice and preference have nothing whatever to do with it."[5] However, in order for this intellectual process to begin, a non-logical interest must initiate it. The total process in which a question is raised and an attempt made to answer it is designated by the word rational. And in this sense it is a legitimate question to ask whether the desire initiating the quest is, in fact, rational or irrational.

Defense of the practical impulse would seem to be unnecessary since by its very nature the question posed is one demanding immediate resolution growing out of man's present needs. But can the speculative impulse be held to be rational and hence a legitimate quest for knowledge? Some questions would seem to be useless (e.g., How many dollar bills are necessary to reach around the earth?), and under certain circumstances merely satisfying one's impulse of curiosity could be a temptation to be avoided, as with any other impulse. For Temple then, whether a certain desire to know something is rational depends on the effort to be expended and what other values must be neglected in order to achieve it. In general one could state: "To satisfy any desire is good; whether it is to be done depends on the amount of other good so prevented from being realised or the amount of harm incidentally involved."[6]

When such considerations are applied to some of the major philosophical issues (e.g., Is there a God? Is man free? Is there life after

[5] Temple, *Mens Creatrix*, p. 30.
[6] *Ibid.*, p. 31.

death?), it is no idle curiosity which man is tempted to satisfy at the expense of other more significant problems. The meaning of his life and his status in the universe are at stake in such questions; and, whether or not man's nature is altered by the answers he proposes, what he does with the nature which is his is vitally affected. Furthermore, even though "we may not be able to use for our ends any faith we reach with regard to these matters; but it may use us; and it may even be true that in letting it use us we find the fulfilment of our own destiny." [7] Thus, for example, man finds himself in a universe which he did not create and does not control, except in a very limited way. The world as man comes to know it is ordered and the question he finds confronting him is: "What is the nature and character of the Power or Force that orders it?" [8] But even in knowing what the principle governing the world is man does not possess it and "knowledge of it will not add to our skill in weaving or in carpentering, in medicine or in generalship. But without it everything is uncertain, and all resolution becomes infected with ultimate doubt." [9]

4 The knowledge venture itself justified

What, then, of the knowledge venture, is it rational and legitimate whatever avenue it may take? Temple offers the following answer: "So far as the possession of knowledge is the exercise of a natural function and the satisfaction of a real impulse, it is a good thing." [10] However, as has already been noted, knowledge is rarely, if ever, pursued for its own sake so that the intrinsic worth of knowledge and the results produced, even when not directly sought, are both to be valued. Knowledge is intrinsically valuable and is at the same time one of the chief instruments for attaining other values. Furthermore, its own intrinsic worth is enhanced by its interrelation with the other interests and activities of man. Accordingly, though knowledge is and should be pursued for its own sake, it does not follow that this is the sole motivation for knowledge or that it can be isolated from other interests of the self.

This is as it should be. For knowledge to be sought there must be some impulse to know, which in turn must take on the characteristics

[7] *Ibid.*, p. 32.
[8] *Ibid.*, p. 33.
[9] *Ibid.*
[10] *Ibid.*

of something in particular. To learn man must want to know the answer to some particular question, however generalized the curiosity may be, and the particular issue that is raised will be determined by the interests of the individual. The decision to be a scientist, for example, does not carry with it the necessity of being a botanist or a chemist, and which field is chosen is determined by something other than simply the will to know. The decision cannot be avoided since to come to know anything the individual must settle on some one area of investigation, and the field of investigation is determined by one's own interest. This is so because knowledge is knowledge sought and attained by persons and results in your knowledge, his knowledge, and my knowledge. Further, the place where one starts his quest is determined by the personality of the individual making the venture.

Thus knowledge exists in and for persons and is valued by them. What value it has is relative to the individual personality. But for no one can it be the highest good since the latter "is a condition of the whole soul in which knowledge takes its place with other good things."[11] That knowledge cannot be considered an absolute value or unconditionally good is indicated by the realization that it is conceivable that it would be better for someone not to know something or not try to know it. This is not to be viewed as a defect in the knowledge itself but, rather, serves to point out that knowledge is relative to the person who knows. To affirm that knowledge is not the supreme good does not diminish the high value of knowledge, for "it is one of the proper treasures of a complete personality, the first and simplest deliberate work of the creative mind."[12]

B. THE CARTESIAN ERROR

The knowledge venture has been launched and its justification established even for the speculative problems of philosophy. But how is it that man knows, and what are the objects of thought in the knowing situation? To ask these questions is to pose the traditional problems of epistemology. Using Descartes as the pivotal figure, Temple outlines the main solutions proposed in the history of philosophy to the problems of epistemology.

For Temple the emphasis on the self and what the self can know on his own was initiated in the modern era of philosophy by Descartes (in

[11] *Ibid.*, p. 35.
[12] *Ibid.*

the religious realm by Luther and politically by the rise of nationalism). Though the emphasis on the individual was necessary to offset the exclusive reliance on the authority of the church, it has already passed its stage of usefulness and from the beginning represented an exaggerated claim. Thus he begins Lecture III of his Gifford lectures, entitled "The Cartesian Faux Pas," with the words:

If I were asked what was the most disastrous moment in the history of Europe I should be strongly trempted to answer that it was that period of leisure when René Descartes, having no claims to meet, remained for a whole day "shut up alone in a stove".[13]

There seems little doubt that Temple is being somewhat facetious here, but the import of the remainder of the chapter reveals the seriousness of the charge as well.

1. The dialectical movement of thought[14]

The history of thought, Temple claims, is best understood in terms of the Hegelian dialectic. According to this view the thesis is rooted closely in the dictates of "common sense" and thus represents as true what appears to be the truth. But there are always limitations to such an unsophisticated view, and the antithesis stage emerges as a result of the recognition and formulation of these limitations. The result is a new beginning based on the aspects of the problem previously neglected or a challenging of the unquestioned principles of the thesis stage.

Limitations, however, are equally evident with regard to the antithesis since the antithesis tends to neglect that which was affirmed by the thesis. It has the additional disadvantage of being purposely, and hence artificially contrived. Though it may be ingenuous, it is less apt than the thesis to be truly wise.[15] There is, hence, a necessity for a synthesis. The latter does not consist of a mean between thesis and antithesis, but is rather a return to the thesis while correcting it by incorporating the valuable aspects of the antithesis.

In applying this "dialectical movement of thought" to the problems

[13] *Nature, Man and God*, pp. 57.

[14] See *ibid.*, and also *Christianity in Thought and Practice*, pp. 39–45. The latter source represents a summary of the material presented in *Nature, Man and God*, pp. 57–81.

[15] Temple seems to be employing his preference for semiconscious and intuitive thinking noted above as a norm for evaluating other thought processes. Thus, he assumes that what is consciously sought and attained is less valuable and desirable than what is spontaneously achieved. This emphasis on spontaneity does not seem consistent with his high regard for personality defined in terms of purposive will, anticipation, and conscious self-determination; see below, Chapter 7.

of epistemology, Temple views the thesis as comprising most of ancient and medieval philosophy. The basic principle of this stage was "that in experience we are directly aware of real objects."[16] A doubting of the authority of the state apart from the ruler who makes the state's laws (Machiavelli) and of the church apart from the individual's conscience (Luther) gained its intellectual expression in René Descartes. In this way the antithesis was formulated which asserted that the individual must start with himself if he is to attain truth. The self isolated from the external world and from the authority of state and church must proceed alone in quest of truth. Individualism is thus proclaimed in the antithesis against the collectivism of the thesis.

2. *The ultimacy of the subject-object relationship*

Disclaiming any attempt to assess Descartes' principles or procedure from the standpoint of logical validity, Temple does, nonetheless, challenge some of Descartes' conclusions and the premises on which they are based.[17] While Descartes is correct that one cannot doubt himself when doubting, this assurance of the self is merely psychological. Furthermore, can one really doubt at the moment of doubting that not only the self but also the earth, the stars, and other people exist? These entities seem just as evident in the process of doubting as does the self.

The point is, Temple contends, that Descartes has separted quite arbitrarily and falsely the content of thinking from the thinking process. Such a separation is impossible, for when man thinks he does not think in general but must think something. To isolate thought from all objects of thought eliminates thought itself, and it is this isolation of the objects of thought from thinking itself which is the crux of the Cartesian problem. Despite a certain superficial cogency in regard to Descartes' famous dictum *cogito, ergo sum*, it fails to provide certitude precisely because there can be no separation of what is thought from the process of thinking itself.[18]

Temple confesses that what disturbs him is the notion that the assurance of the self is primary and all other beliefs derivative and secondary. Furthermore, Descartes' doubt can just as well be extended to include the self also, thereby making all of one's experience a possible

[16] *Nature, Man and God*, p. 60.
[17] Descartes' procedure *is* held to be invalid by Temple, but a formal refutation is not being offered.
[18] See *Nature, Man and God*, p. 64.

dream state. Descartes' doubt is forced; it is doubting for doubting's sake and as such is artificial. As Temple puts it: "What Descartes indulged in his stove was purely academic doubt; he was really as sure of the stove as of himself."[19] Such academic doubt is but the "extension of nursery make-believe" to the problem of doubt itself, and the real point of Descartes' doubting must reside in his effort to find a basis for his beliefs other than medieval tradition. Temple's analysis of Descartes' position though quite astute also partially misses Descartes' point. The question certainly is not whether Descartes in fact believed the stove to be real. Assuredly he did! But the question which puzzled Descartes, and which Temple neglects, is on what basis can such a belief be affirmed in light of the fact that man does dream and that error also exists.[20]

According to Temple, even if Descartes' approach is taken seriously what one arrives at in doubting is not a self isolated from all else but a self in relationship to all else. Thus, referring to the termination of Descartes' procedural doubt, Temple states: "What he [Descartes] ought to have reached as the irreducible basis of all thought, including doubt, was the subject-object relationship."[21] Instead Descartes arrived at the self alone with all the difficulties for gaining knowledge of anything beyond the self which this entails. Descartes justified belief in the external world through recourse to God who guarantees the veracity of one's clear and distinct ideas but whose existence is dependent on these very same ideas. Such difficulties are due entirely to the unnecessary and hypothetical doubt and by the unjustified conclusion Descartes drew from his untenable method. If Descartes' method and conclusions are accepted and the self, as such, is taken to be the starting point of knowledge, then the only knowledge one can get must also be of the self. But such a conclusion is plainly absurd even as the method on which it is founded is unnecessary. The fault, then, lies in Descartes' method and the abstract formula of his conclusion, which is inherent in the procedure itself. Thus, for Temple, there is an inherent error in assuming *"that in knowledge the mind begins with itself and proceeds to the apprehension of the external world by way of construction and inference."*[22]

[19] *Ibid.*, p. 66.

[20] A critical evaluation of Temple's analysis of Descartes is offered in Chapter 16 below.

[21] *Nature, Man and God*, p. 66. On this point Temple quotes approvingly from Baron Von Hügel who holds that experience involves simultaneously experience of the subject, the object, and thought which connects them both. See *ibid.*, pp. 78–79.

[22] *Ibid.*, p. 73.

3. The failure of Hume and Kant

The problem which Descartes bequeathed to the history of thought is a false one and the dead end to which Hume ultimately pushed the issue shows the inherent absurdity of the approach initiated by Descartes. If all man has to build knowledge upon are his own impressions of which there is no impression of continuity or of causality, then the universe itself, Hume reasoned, must be built up by principles of association as applied to the impressions. Kant sought to solve this untenable view of the world, as composed of discrete and disconnected impressions which even Hume had to repudiate in practical living, by showing that the mind itself contains the organizing principles by which impressions are related. But remaining true to Hume's analytic method, Kant held that the mind only knows the sensations it receives but not the source of these sensations which Kant called things-in-themselves. Knowledge for Kant is the process of organizing these sensations by the mind's understanding in the very act of perceiving them.

There is truth in the familiar expression that "what Hume gave to Kant as a problem Kant handed back unchanged as the solution."[23] However, Kant did open the way for a more adequate solution by means of the critical method which he employed. According to this method one does not proceed either deductively or inductively in regard to the facts of experience, rather, one "interrogates the conditions of experience in general to ascertain the principles presupposed in its possibility."[24] It is Kant's critical method of seeking the conditions implicit in experience itself as principles of explanation which supplies "the true substitute for that scholastic Logic which had both guided and cramped thought for centuries, and which the Cartesian philosophers had discarded without providing any substitute."[25]

4. Merits of antithesis and thesis

The chief merit of the antithesis consists in the principle of individual judgment, and "what this great principle affirms is the obligation upon every rational intelligence to master his own experience as fully as he

[23] *Ibid.*, p. 74.
[24] *Ibid.*
[25] *Ibid.*, p. 75.

can."[26] The ideals of individuality and of self-reliance fostered by this principle are excellent. However, the results of carrying out the implications of this principle historically have been negative since it produced the departmentalization of fields of study and of work (e.g., politics, art, philosophy, science). Each area became independent of the others, and devotees of art proclaimed "art for art's sake" and of business, "business is business." For philosophy the result was equally disastrous since it became preoccupied with how it is possible for one to know. But neither science nor mankind in general could wait while philosophy solved this issue, and they proceeded to get on with their business without philosophy.

The strength of the antithesis in placing rightful emphasis upon the integrity and autonomy of the individual in knowing and in doing must be supplemented by, indeed be encompassed in, the more basic contribution of the thesis as represented particularly by the medieval thinkers. Their contribution consists of the insight that knowing must be viewed in the perspective of the whole of experience of which knowing itself is but a segment.[27] Applying this principle to the issue of how man comes to know and what it is he knows, Temple claims that there is the need to "return to the concrete richness and bewildering variety and still more bewildering interconnexion of actual experience" as the necessary "mode of deliverance from that false scent on which Descartes set the modern mind in its search for truth."[28] Temple's own attempt to resolve the epistemological issues must next be propounded.

[26] *Ibid.*, p. 76.
[27] See Temple, *Christianity in Thought and Practice*, p. 44.
[28] *Nature, Man and God*, p. 80.

CHAPTER 4

THE UNDERSTANDING OF REALITY

Before the presentation of Temple's suggested synthesis to the epistemological problem, it may be well to review briefly the problem as he has developed it. Descartes' emphasis on the self isolated from everything else and, thus, necessarily dependent on its own ideas for knowledge of the world has been shown to be fallacious. But it is not desirable nor possible to return to the naïve realism prevalent in the medieval period which claimed that the mind is directly aware of real objects in experience and gains direct knowledge of the world. The latter represents the thesis in the triadic attempt to solve the problems of epistemology revealed in the history of thought, of which Descartes' proposal is the antithesis.

A synthesis of these two positions is needed if epistemology is to be set on its proper task; but this synthesis will not be a mere relating of the two alternatives. Rather, it will consist of a return to the organic wholeness of thought with its objects indicated by the thesis while incorporating the significant claims of individual integrity maintained by the antithesis. There must be a return to the unity and variety which constitute actual experience in the act of knowing and from which the thesis and antithesis have both abstracted their respective positions with varying degrees of accuracy.

The analysis of philosophic method has shown that Descartes' quest for logical certainty, such as mathematics provides, and based as it is on deductive reasoning, is inadequate and misleading in dealing with the real world. Nor does the inductive method supply the need since its conclusions lack certainty. A combination of induction and deduction is necessary for the philosophic method so as to enable one to grasp a thing in its total context. This ultimately means the universe as a whole, of which its own historical development constitutes a significant facet.

Hence, the clue to the solution of the epistemological problem is to be found in tracing the origin of man's thinking as an episode in the process of the world's history and in an examination of one's own concrete experience. As was pointed out in the discussion of the origin of knowledge, thinking arose as a function of the organism in its effort to adjust to its environment. But if thought arose as a result of the organism's interaction with its environment and for the sake of facilitating adjustment, then thought is in interaction with the external world from its very inception and there is no question of being disassociated from the world. Thinking is not a peculiar operation of a unique organism unrelated to the physical world and operating distinct from a physiological organism. Thinking is, in fact, an extension of the total organic process by which an organism strives to adjust to its environment.[1]

It is a significant fact that the physical order existed long before anyone perceived its existence. As Whitehead rightly asserts: "Consciousness presupposes experience and not experience consciousness."[2] Whether or not the principle of continuity of all levels of reality from inorganic through organic to the personal is fully accurate, there can be no doubt of the historical priority of the inorganic and hence the need for understanding what develops later in the perspective of what came before.

A. KNOWLEDGE AS THE APPREHENSION OF REALITY

1. Rudimentary consciousness as organic reaction to environment

It is essential to examine the operation of mind at the lower levels of life. As a matter of fact, a rudimentary consciousness is evident in the organism's response to its environment so as to adjust to it. Cognition is a later development growing out of the mind's conative activities and aiding the mind to pursue its ends more effectively. In its most elementary form thought is rooted in desire. It arises in the effort of the organism to satisfy its needs. The interaction of the organism with the

[1] See Temple, *Nature, Man and God*, p. 107. The position developed by Temple in the Gifford Lectures (see Lectures V, VI, VIII) would seem to represent a further explication of the views on knowledge expressed in *Mens Creatrix*, pp. 27–90, 153–161. On some issues the latter source is the more complete one.

[2] Whitehead, *Process and Reality*, p. 83. Quoted by Temple in *Nature, Man and God*, pp. 112, 121, 217, 490, 497. Temple acknowledges his debt to Whitehead for much of the material he presents on this issue, though it is debatable whether Whitehead always means what Temple seems to think he means.

world is the fundamental fact; and if the organism is mental, then one type of interaction is apprehension. All higher intellectual development rests and must be based on the interaction that transpires between an organism and its environment. An organism can exist only within an environment and only by reacting to it. The conscious process itself arises as a result of the effect of the environment on the organism and, in turn, the organism's response to its environment, including not only the natural order but other organisms.[3]

Desire provides both the motivation for and the direction of thought about the world; but it is not mere random desire, for satisfaction of the needs of the organism is at stake. Thought even at this stage is selective in what it takes note of in its environment; however, desire is itself unspecified except in the most general way. Some *kind* of object is wanted, namely, what will satisfy the needs of the organism; but no one particular object of that kind is sought. An example at a higher level would be when someone is very hungry. At such a time it is food that is desired and not specifically steak or ice cream. Thought is not first concerned with particulars as distinct objects from which more generalized concepts are later developed, but is in the first instance directed toward particular objects as representative of a general object which is sought.

Desire, as the effort of the organism to satisfy its needs, produces and is produced by a condition of tension within the organism due to the fact that its needs are not being met, and once these needs are met, desire ceases temporarily. Another response of the organism to its environment grows not out of the tension created when a need is felt which is not being satisfied, but out of a feeling of intimate relationship with objects in the environment. This is the response of affection and is, perhaps, the more basic form of consciousness since it is not dependent on tension due to a felt need to be satisfied. Affection as the experience of trust in the presence of certain objects can lead to desire when the objects are absent; but affection remains when the need has been fulfilled. When desire and affection as the two fundamental forms of consciousness are developed in man's intellect, they result in science and art respectively. Though the latter disciplines become ends sought for themselves, they never become totally free of the conditions which originally produced them. Thus, science seeks laws and treats the individual in terms of the universal; art deals with the universal through what is individual.

[3] See *ibid.*, pp. 221, 138–139. Temple notes approvingly Bergson's insight that one of man's distinctive traits is his ability to use the environment for his ends; see *ibid.*, p. 122.

2. *The real world as given in experience*

It is evident that the human mind far surpasses in complexity of response its rudimentary counterpart consisting of mere reaction to the environment for the sake of furthering survival, but it is never independent of its origin in organic reaction to environment. Therefore, the mind from its crude beginning to the highest level of philosophic speculation does not merely know itself or its own subjective states, but always knows the world and itself as *in* the world. What the mind apprehends is in process, but this poses no problem for the mind since it too is in process; and "so long as mind and occasion move together all is straightforward."[4] That mind can grasp what is in process offers no difficulties, for mind itself appears in the flux of the World-Process precisely as the capacity for apprehending the process.

The conclusion to be drawn from this analysis is that the mind always apprehends reality. This follows from what has been shown to be the fundamental fact, namely, the interaction of the organism with the world; and that one type of interaction is apprehension. But then this apprehension is of the world and not of ideas as mere mental states. In fact, "reality is the presupposition of thinking ... and the distinction between mind and its objects is drawn within the given *totum* of experience."[5] This does not mean that naive realism is correct in its claim that an object is the same whether known or not, but the issue is meaningless and quite irrelevant. The point is that "in cognition the subject-object relation is ultimate, and neither term is in any degree reducible to the other. Apprehension is of the object."[6] For mind when it thinks, thinks objects of the real world, even as on a lower level the activity of mind consists of the organism's response to objects of desire to satisfy a need. There is thus no gap to be bridged from thinking subject to an external world; for the two are always joined, and mind *is* the consciousness of them.

Thus the embryo exists first in relationship to the mother, so that for the child the "habit of organic self-adjustment, and of using the environment for self-maintenance, is already well established" before the child is born.[7] The child's first awareness is of the mutual relationship shared with the mother which elicits the response of affection. Hence,

[4] *Ibid.*, p. 120.
[5] *Mens Creatrix*, p. 51.
[6] Temple, *Nature, Man and God*, p. 126. See also *ibid.*, pp. 151–152.
[7] *Nature, Man and God*, p. 122.

the individual is never isolated within himself but rather begins a corporate existence. The child's "rudimentary consciousness is not of objects as such, but of this actual process of responsive adjustment."[8] Although the mind possesses "at all stages of its growth a numerical unity as subject of its experiences," it only attains a full unity through its contacts with other minds.[9] It is false to suppose that the mind's unity from the start is such that by organizing discrete impressions which it receives it can infer from them that some originate from other minds like itself. The distinction of itself from other selves is a gradual process made possible by the locus of sensation which the body provides and through intercourse with other minds. The earliest distinction which the child makes is that between self and not-self and not between subject and object.

Furthermore, the union of subject and object in the act of thinking is confirmed when one's own concrete experience is examined. The varied distinctions which are elaborated by the mind are in the first instance given in conscious experience. They are part of the undifferentiated continuum and are distinguished from the unity by analysis. To consider some object beautiful, for example, does not mean that its extension in space was perceived separately from the quality beauty. Rather, the mind in perceiving discovers them both "and it discovers them because they are there."[10]

The fact is that everything is contained in the initial experience, and knowledge is not built up by inference from one's subjective states to supposed objects in an external world. Rather, it is discovered by analyzing the contents of the experience as one's interests direct and by building it up piece by piece into a meaningful pattern. From the child's gradual understanding of himself and his world to scientific and artistic knowledge, all is part of the initial undifferentiated datum.[11]

3. Knowledge as built up gradually

Ideas are the mind's apprehension of reality and not some intermediary between a mind and something external to it; but though the ideas apprehend reality, they are not always an adequate apprehension. What is an internal organic disturbance may be apprehended as existing ex-

[8] *Ibid.*

[9] *Ibid.*, p. 126. The problem of the unity and identity of the self is raised explicitly, and Temple's solution proposed, in Chap. 7.

[10] *Nature, Man and God*, p. 125.

[11] See *ibid.*, p. 128. See also *Mens Creatrix*, pp. 51, 74, 76.

ternally, which is what occurs in a hallucination, but this is no basis for doubting all of one's apprehensions. Nonetheless it must be acknowledged that the "first apprehension is always precarious, usually defective, and sometimes erroneous."[12] The mind is not a mere receptacle for the facts of experience upon which theories may later be constructed, both always occur together; without a frame of reference in which to fit them, the facts cannot be understood. At the lowest levels the mind selects among the objects of its environment based on organic needs; at higher levels practical and theoretical interests merge to constitute a principle of selectivity, so that interpretation and apprehension occur together as one activity of the mind in its grasp of objects. Mere particulars in abstraction from any generalization are not grasped, for no sensation is pure. There is always the selection and interpretation of it by mind. This point is clearly illustrated by reference to the organism's response to its environment in terms of some object either of desire or of affection. If the response is desire, then some kind of object is sought which will satisfy a need; and any particular object is perceived in terms of its capacity to satisfy this general character. If the response is affection, then the object sought is not only individual but also universal; it is not a mere particular. In the former case the object perceived is first universal and then a particular, and in the latter instance it is distinctively individual, combining both universality and particularity.

Mind, therefore, from its inception as a response of the organism to its environment to the higher stages of speculative thought operates within the world which it apprehends. What it apprehends is always the real world and never merely its own subjective states. However, at times the mind misinterprets the real world, so that reality is fully apprehended only at the end and not at the beginning of mental process; it must be built up.[13] The problem error poses is considered by Temple as one aspect of the problem of evil.[14] This would seem to be significant in that Temple does not take error to be of sufficient importance to deal with it extensively as an epistemological problem. The form that error takes for him is that of falsely equating different objects which occurs only in the act of synthesis. "It is a mistaking one thing for another."[15] One aspect of the epistemological problem is by-

[12] *Nature, Man and God*, p. 147.

[13] This contention is directly related to Temple's view that the facts are known only after intellectual inquiry and not at the beginning. See *Mens Creatrix*, p. 16.

[14] See below, Chapter 10.

[15] Temple, *Mens Creatrix*, p. 274.

passed since no mistake is possible when analyzing one's own experience. Temple never questions how one knows that at any moment what one is apprehending is, in fact, the real world. He assumes that one always apprehends the real world, and the only question is whether it has been fully apprehended.

The error of naive realism is evident at this point since it claims that the real world is not only grasped in the act of thought but also adequately understood in one's apprehension of it.[16] Thus, knowledge of reality is equated with man's apprehensions of the world so that the mind is held to have direct knowledge of reality. This is too extravagant; but it is more correct than false, for it states unequivocally the relation of mind with the real world. The qualification which must be made is not a rejection of this affirmation but acknowledging in addition the necessity for the mind to build up its knowledge of the world, based on its apprehensions but not fully evident or understood in any one apprehension.

Descartes may also be viewed in his proper perspective now. The problem which Descartes posed of how a mind confined to its own ideas can be assured that its ideas refer to a world beyond is a false one. To start from mind and ask how one can get to matter is itself the blunder; for mind is one of the elements given within the totality of experience. Accordingly, Temple concludes: "We do not have to ask how Mind effects a transition from its own ideas to an objective world, because we see Mind first appearing as the consciousness of processes which had been going on in the physical world before that appearance."[17] Descartes' error is more serious than that of the medieval thinkers since he separated the mind from the world. However, he was correct in acknowledging the need for the mind to build up its knowledge of the world. The difference between the synthesis and the antithesis at this point is that granting that knowledge must be built up, it is not constructed with ideas distinct from external objects but with ideas which themselves are the apprehension of real objects.

The synthesis Temple proposes is thus based upon the joining of two propositions which taken separately constitute the thesis and antithesis respectively: "Those propositions are: first, that what the mind ap-

[16] Temple does not explicitly refer to the error of naive realism in this way, but it would seem to follow from his analysis. The same is true of the analysis which follows to the end of the section. Though Temple does not explicitly bring together his discussion of the epistemological problem in the way suggested, it seems implicit in what he does state. See *Nature, Man and God*, p. 126.

[17] *Ibid.*, p. 217.

prehends, even when it apprehends mistakenly, is reality; secondly, that the true apprehension of reality is attained not at the beginning but at the end of the mental process."[18]

B. KNOWLEDGE, TRUTH, AND REALITY

1. *Knowledge as distinguished from truth*

Mental activity has its origin in the course of the World-Process in the interaction of the organism with its environment. When mind emerges, it does so as the organism's apprehension of the world of which it is a part. In mental activity the world itself is what is apprehended. Knowledge is built up by relating and integrating these apprehensions of the real world into a system of explanation which will satisfy the practical and theoretical interests of man. When this is achieved, one is said to "know the truth." This expression, though meaningful and even appropriate at times, is not fully accurate; one should say, "I have a true apprehension of reality," or "he apprehends reality truly."[19] These are more accurate expressions, for what the mind apprehends is reality and not some mental entity or idea standing between mind and the world.

Common usage refers to the mind's quest for truth rather than the quest for knowledge. This is well-founded because the former expression correctly conveys the impression that what the mind enjoys in knowing is what it discovers and not merely the act of discovery, as significant as the act is. It is in this sense of providing the mind with an understanding of reality that truth makes a claim on one and is conceived as independent of the knower. Truth is, therefore, a discovery of reality, of something which is there to be discovered and not merely the activity of mind constructing a world out of its own mental activity. When truth is discovered, the discoverer, rather than possessing it, feels possessed by it.[20]

The distinction between knowledge and truth implicit in the above exposition needs to be made explicit. Knowledge and truth may, of course, be used interchangeably without loss of clarity, and no absolute distinction between them can be made. But knowledge may properly be designated as the mind's activity in knowing and consists in the

[18] *Ibid.*, pp. 147–148.

[19] See *Nature, Man and God*, p. 150.

[20] See *Nature, Man and God*, p. 153. Value arises for Temple when the mind in apprehending the world recognizes a kinship with itself; see *ibid.*, pp. 135, 149, 153. This is considered in Chapter 11 of the present study.

meaning which objects have for the mind. Truth also is an act of the mind in so far as it is represented in propositional form. Individual minds formulate propositions held to be true; but in so far as truth is a quality of propositions, it exists equally for all minds and thereby gains independence from any one mind. Knowledge and truth can be distinguished in still another sense.[21] Knowledge is the broader term, and it encompasses the total apprehension of reality by all the activities of the mind. Truth is the goal of intellect, one of the primary activities of the mind but not the only activity.

The theoretical aim of the intellect in knowing is to formulate a system of propositions which renders fully intelligible all of experience. When this is achieved, the ideal of scientific truth would be fulfilled. The truth or falsity of particular propositions could then be determined on the basis of their fitting into the system of propositions. The cogency of this system, however, depends on precision of definition; and this is procured at the expense of relevancy to the real world where process and continuity reign and absolute distinctions cannot be made.

2. *A twofold criterion of truth*

Temple's criterion of truth becomes evident at this point and involves two facets. In regard to any particular object the mind apprehends, its truth is grasped when the mind discovers in the object the same principles operative within itself. As a number of interpreters of Temple have pointed out, Temple does not make clear how this emphasis on the mind's finding itself in its object is related to his contention that what the mind knows are objects and not its own ideas.[22]

In order to discern these principles in the object the mind must discipline itself so as to concentrate on the object and what can be observed regarding it, as well as refrain from too hasty a formulation of the principles which explain it. The philosophic method as a combination of induction and deduction is thus necessary in which observations of the object are fitted into a scheme of interpretation suggested by the knower who in turn modifies his scheme in light of the demands of the object. Only by continually reformulating one's sys-

[21] Temple does not explicitly refer to such a distinction, but it would seem to follow from his discussion of the limitations of intellect and the need for the intellect to unite with imagination to gain a complete grasp of reality. See *Mens Creatrix*, p. 51.

[22] See, for example, John P. McGarvey, "Modernism in Archbishop Temple's Metaphysics and Value Theory," Eugene Skelton, "The problem of Evil in the Works of William Temple"; Owen Thomas, *William Temple's Philosophy of Religion*, pp. 70–72, 79–80, 120–121.

tematization based on one's observations of the object can the truth of the object be obtained. This is so because there is no *a priori* scheme of truth in the form of a system of propositions to which one can appeal and from which deductions can be made regarding the validity of particular propositions. Such a scheme of truth is the ideal of mathematics and provides absolute certainty but does so at the expense of relevancy to the actual world characterized by time and change. Thus any system of truth relevant to the real world must be built up gradually on the basis of objects of this world and even when fully formulated can only command a high degree of probability. One of the illusions of the Cartesian method was its false promise of logical certainty in regard to matters of fact, but no such certainty is possible with respect to a world in process.

How, then, can one determine the truth of propositions about the real world as a whole? The second aspect of Temple's criterion of truth operates at this point. The mind does not merely submit to the object to determine its characteristics; it also brings to its observations a standard of its own, and that standard is the unity of all the data in a coherent system. In this way the mind resists attributing greater significance to one aspect than is warranted when the totality of experience is considered. The mind thus possesses its own standard of judgment. "Its standard is that of totality – the embrace of all relevant reality in a comprehensive unity – and by this it must guard itself from prejudice, from inaccuracy, and from acquiescence in partial apprehension."[23] The mind's own appeal, then, is to coherence. But this cannot be merely logical consistency or a necessary system of ideas; for what is to cohere are the objects of the real world apprehended by the mind. That hypothesis interpreting the real world is held to be true, in the sense of a high degree of probability, which best embraces all the relevant facts.

It is at this point that the distinction is most evident between the quest for truth motivated by theoretical as opposed to practical interests. Whereas the practical man is apt to stop his reflection and search for evidence as soon as he comes upon facts which tend to support a dogma he already believes, "the philosopher is engaged in testing that very dogma, not only by the intellectual criterion of self-consistency, but also by the practical and empirical criterion of applicability to the facts."[24]

[23] Temple, *Nature, Man and God*, p. 166.
[24] Temple, *Mens Creatrix*, p. 9.

The truth which coheres is not some logical harmony which may be equated with the absence of contradiction, but whatever harmony the actual facts warrant. Hence Temple states: "We begin to give content to our principle of coherence; it passes from the mere absence of contradiction into the concrete harmony of different elements."[25] The ideal of knowledge which governs mathematics, in which one starts with self-evident premises and every proposition is related to every other in the system by logical necessity, must be replaced by the recognition that the areas of knowledge where logical certainty is possible are few. Thus what must be sought is a system which enables one to distinguish between degrees of probability.

Temple presents a cogent argument for accepting as probably true that hypothesis which relates most coherently the relevant facts. However, in his own evaluation of the adequacy of a philosophy he tends to demand inner assurance and practical guidance for living, more than a coherent account of the facts.

3. The inability of intellect to comprehend reality

The limitation of the intellect taken as one activity of the mind is now apparent. This is not to diminish the significance of intellect, for it operates at all levels and realms of experience and cannot be excluded from any one: "So soon as any part of experience becomes matter of reflection it enters the sphere of intellect, and must be handled by the principles of intellect."[26] The same universality applies to reason. No area of experience, including religious experience, can arbitrarily be labelled "out of bounds" to reason.[27] Nonetheless, though the intellect pervades all of experience, it does not in itself encompass all experience. This is illustrated by the procedures and goal of science. Every act of apprehension is a unity of mental activity, concentrating on the content and neglecting the mental counterpart, thereby failing to deal with the full particularity of the facts of experience. "Scientific truth ... is a system of contents – or, as we may express it, a nexus of relations; but we cannot suppose that Reality is a nexus of relations, for a relation at least implies related terms."[28] Truth exhibits the same

[25] *Ibid.*, p. 22. Temple would seem to be purposely distinguishing his view of coherence from the abstract harmony of F. H. Bradley to whom Temple refers in *Mens Creatrix*, pp. 66, 68.

[26] *Ibid.*, p. 68.

[27] See Temple, *Nature, Man and God*, p. 17.

[28] *Mens Creatrix*, p. 68.

relation with Reality. It is one element in reality, representing as it does apprehension of reality and not some intermediary between mind and reality called idea, but Reality includes something besides truth. Thus knowledge of Reality must encompass more than intellectual activity with its goal of truth.[29] The result is that truth cannot provide the complete system which it seeks and which would correlate all of experience into one necessary system.[30]

The will to know operates as an impulse to transcend the particularity of the individual's place and time in the world so as to grasp the world as a whole and thereby discover one's place and status in it. But on the basis of intellect alone the whole arrived at is the physical world on the one hand and a society of intellects on the other, complementing and correcting one another as each strives to comprehend the world. This is so because each mind apprehends the world from its own perspective, and even a mind which encompasses the whole universe could do so only by focussing the world in terms of its particular historical and geographical location and its individual conditioning. An individual can only secure relative independence of his environment. Even at the highest levels of life in the mind of man, the factors operating within and without that gave rise to a particular individual help to determine him and his outlook.[31]

4. Beyond intellect in quest of an explanatory concept

Still a further difficulty must be noted in man's quest for an adequate understanding of the universe. Though the philosopher is obliged to seek the most coherent explanation based on all the relevant facts, he should not be misled into believing that this task is ever completed or even entirely possible. The attempt to gather all the relevant facts is itself an impossible task, and to think that one has done so is deceiving. The philosopher is, therefore, thrown back to his own resources, interests, background, training, and personal experience in order to discover what appears to him to be an adequate principle of explanation. Though his choice of an explanatory concept need not, and indeed should not, be arbitrary, neither is it purely rational nor empirical. In regard to such ultimate concepts everyone is and can only be an

[29] Truth is conceived as scientific truth here; see *ibid.*, p. 50.

[30] See *ibid.*, p. 71.

[31] This is consistent with Temple's emphasis on the historical method and the necessity for viewing mind in terms of its origin and development in the World-Process.

intuitionist. That is, when confronted with something held to be of ultimate value, one either responds sympathetically to it or one does not; argument on the issue is of no avail. Thus, Temple states:

> The highest good can never be justified. To justify is to approve as righteous by reference to some external standard; righteousness itself, therefore, which constitutes the standard, cannot be justified; we can only describe it and ask – Do you like it or not?[32]

Having decided on some ultimate concept, then, the philosopher proceeds to explain all the facts in accordance with that principle and, in turn, to justify the particular principle he has chosen on the basis of the facts. Though it seems inconsistent with the inductive-deductive method Temple has advocated, he does not suggest that the principle employed should itself be subjected to critical analysis or the possibility of its being modified in the process of relating it to the facts.

Hence, whereas the intellect culminates in a physical world and a society of intellects seeking to comprehend the world, it could accept as explanatory of both world and intellect another principle if suggested and supported by other activities of the mind, though not itself demanding it. The intellect merges with the imaginative activities of the mind in this way to arrive at a complete comprehension of reality. Herein reside the significance of art, morality, and religion, for they may suggest an explanatory concept which encompasses all the activities of the mind which the intellect alone could not discover but which it can accept and submit to.[33] Particularly pertinent in this connection, for Temple, is the relevance of the Christian faith to the solution of the problems of philosophy.

[32] *Plato and Christianity*, pp. 71–72; also see *ibid.*, pp. 38–39, and *Nature, Man and God*, p. 250.

[33] Thus for Temple the intellect working alone does not lead to a theistic God who is transcendent as well as immanent. But if these other activities of the mind lead to the belief that the universe is the result of the purpose of a Transcendent Will for the sake of realizing value, then the intellect could acknowledge and accept it as completing its own demands. See *Mens Creatrix*, pp. 86–89. This approach is developed below as one of Temple's arguments for God; see Chapter 9.

CHAPTER 5

THE RELEVANCE OF CHRISTIAN PHILOSOPHY

A. THE RELATION OF PHILOSOPHY AND RELIGION

1. Tensions between philosophy and religion

Philosophy, as the effort of the mind of man to comprehend all of experience, probes of necessity into the articles of faith held by religious people. The primary difference between philosophy and religion is apparent at this point; for starting from experience as philosophy does, it seeks to formulate a coherent explanation of experience without assuming beforehand what the nature of this explanatory concept must be. Its only assumption is in regard to reason's validity to make the quest and, thus, that the world is sufficiently rational to be capable of rational explanation.

The existence of God is for philosophy one of the questions at issue; and if belief is affirmed, it is as the conclusion of an argument. The nature of God in such a case is determined by the demands of the argument to explain what can only be explained by reference to him.[1] Temple's own position is not philosophical in this sense which he calls Scientific Philosophy; rather, he starts with a conception of God and seeks to explain the world by reference to it, which is the method of Theological Philosophy. What philosophy may reach as a conclusion of a long process of reasoning, namely God, becomes for the religious man the basic affirmation of his faith and hence the starting point of all his endeavors, theoretical and practical. God is held to exist for such a man, not because philosophical discourse has shown the need to infer his existence to explain the universe, but because in his own personal experience he has felt grasped by the being of God.

Thus, whereas philosophy starts with a problem to be explained

[1] See Temple, *Mens Creatrix*, p. 2.

and strives on the basis of the most coherent interpretation of the facts to find a solution, religion begins with the belief that God is adequate to solve any problems that may arise. This methodological difference between philosophy and religion Temple summarizes in the following statement:

> *The primary assurances of Religion are the ultimate questions of Philosophy.* Religion finds its fullest expression in absolute surrender to the Object of its worship. But the very existence of that Object is a main theme of philosophical disputation.[2]

The difference in method used by religion as opposed to that employed by philosophy arises from a still more basic difference between the two fields, namely, the different attitude or mood which each fosters in its devotees. The aim of philosophy is to enable people to understand the world; the knowledge it seeks is for the purpose of increasing one's understanding. The aim of religion is to promote a more intimate fellowship between man and God; the knowledge it seeks is for the purpose of improving and assisting man in his worship of God. Hence, philosophy and religion are separated by two contrasting attitudes, one of understanding (philosophy) and one of devotion (religion).

Thus, though in terms of the conclusions which philosophy and religion might separately reach there is no conflict in principle since truth is one and they must ultimately coincide, it does not follow that at any stage in man's apprehension of truth they will, in fact, coincide. Present evidence would suggest quite the opposite. In any case the difference in the method by which the ultimate principles of explanation are reached remains different. Philosophy tends to work from the part to the whole, or from the outside (the world) toward the center (God); whereas religion works from the whole to the part, or from the center outwards.[3] Furthermore, the mood and attitude of the philosopher as opposed to the religious believer remain disparate. Though both live by faith, their faiths are quite different; for the philosopher lives by faith in reason with knowledge of the world as his goal. The religious believer lives by faith in God with intimate fellowship with God as his goal. For Temple the security man seeks is ultimately rooted in faith, not knowledge, whatever path is chosen, and it is won by personal loyalty not by rational discourse; the test of such security resides in the experience of life, not in logic. Hence,

[2] Temple, *Nature, Man and God*, p. 35. See also *Christianity in Thought and Practice*, p. 28.

[3] Temple has employed both methods (up to a point) in separate works on philosophy and theology respectively; viz., *Mens Creatrix* and *Christus Veritas*.

though Temple has given up logical certainty as a legitimate goal, he replaces it with a demand for psychological certitude.

2. *Values and disvalues of the tensions*

There are, therefore, tensions between philosophy and religion which cannot easily be dismissed. Such tensions can be fruitful for the development of each discipline but may also be detrimental to each. Religion provides philosophy with some relevant data that should be given careful scrutiny, while offering hope of rendering the service of explaining the nature of the universe. At the same time philosophy serves religion by purging it of fallacious dogmas too readily accepted on scanty evidence and too hastily given universal application.

However, religion renders philosophy a disservice when it tries to dictate to philosophy the interpretation it must give to the religious data it offers. In the same way philosophy renders religion a disservice if it seeks to shift the nature of an acceptable solution from that which increases fellowship with God to what is most reasonable, independent of God and a relation with Him. The significant difference involved here can be illustrated by reference to the Book of Job and the nature of the solution proposed by the author to the problem of human suffering. The answer provided is not a philosophical explanation of evil in the world but is rather experiental; the solution lies in Job's own relation to God. For "in his fellowship with God he has found that nothing matters in comparison with that fellowship."[4] The real solution, then, is not an answer at all in the sense of an intellectual explanation, which is, in fact, left unsolved. The real solution in Job is "the attainment of a state of mind in which there is no desire to ask it."[5] One might ask Temple whether or not reasons are sought for the truth (or falsity) of the state of mind attained; otherwise, how does one know one has not been deceived?

3. *Scientific philosophy versus theological philosophy*

Such tension, Temple contends, necessarily exists between religion and philosophy. What is involved can perhaps be clarified by distinguishing between two types of philosophy, namely, Scientific Philosophy and Theological Philosophy. Religion always proceeds to explain the facts

[4] Temple, *Nature, Man and God*, p. 43. See also *Christianity in Thought and Practice*, p. 33.
[5] *Nature, Man and God*, p. 43.

of experience by reference to its assurance of God and the fellowship shared with God; whereas philosophy proceeds by inquiring into the data of experience, seeking to derive an explanation on the basis of them. The latter procedure tends to foster the scientific explanation in which the higher is always explained by reference to the lower. This approach Temple calls Scientific Philosophy and signifies "any philosophy which takes its start from the departmental sciences, ranging from Physics to Epistemology or Ethics, as distinct from a philosophy which takes its start from the deliverances of religious experience as formulated by Theology."[6] To seek to account for the facts of experience by reference to the nature of a Supreme Spirit held to exist, upon whom the inquirer recognizes his dependence and with whom he maintains fellowship, is to pursue what Temple calls Theological Philosophy. He acknowledges that it is for him the only approach that can hope to be adequate.[7]

Some reconciliation, however, between the two approaches can be suggested at least in principle. The effort must be made to separate the chaff from the wheat in regard to the doctrines of religion. What is truly central to religious belief needs to be distinguished from what is merely incidental. Most important, those doctrines which are held because of personal sentiment, but which have negligible spiritual value and have scientific evidence against them, must be discarded. Scientific Philosophy must also make some concessions in behalf of reconciliation with religion. Primary here is the recognition that while it has the right to use the lower categories of experience to explain the higher, it does not have the right to deny the application of the higher by other disciplines. A corollary to this would be that science recognize that there are areas of experience where its own method is inapplicable and that one of these, namely the realm of personal relations, is that which best exemplifies the type of experience with which religion deals. Is not the conception of a philosophic method already noted adequate to this task? The problem may be due to Temple's narrow conception of Scientific Philosophy for which the only alternative is Theological Philosophy.

To understand another person one must become related to that

[6] *Ibid.*, p. 44, n. 1. For Temple tension between religion and philosophy would remain even if all the departments of philosophy were combined, including philosophy of religion, in an effort to comprehend reality. This is the case with metaphysics since it is still not the standpoint of a religious believer who *starts* with God.

[7] See *ibid.*, p. 44, and *Christianity in Thought and Practice*, pp. 32–34.

person and, indeed, assume an attitude of sympathetic understanding.[8] In these relations between human beings bound together by intimate ties of friendship and love are to be found the closest analogies to what the religious believer experiences in his relation to God. Thus, to understand religion and what its devotees experience one should not look to astronomy or mathematics, for "the heart of religion is not an opinion about God such as Philosophy might reach as the conclusion of its argument; it is a personal relationship with God."[9]

Tensions between philosophy and religion do exist and should continue to exist, for they are inseparable from the tasks each has to fulfill and the attitude and method each employs. The tensions could be overcome only by a capitulation by one to the demands of the other, resulting in the assimilation of philosophy by religion, or religion by philosophy.

B. A CHRISTIAN PHILOSOPHY

1. The need of philosophy for religion

Throughout the discussion of Temple's conception of philosophy it has become apparent that the aim of philosophy to render a coherent account of all of experience cannot be fulfilled. Particular philosophic disciplines (e.g., ethics and philosophy of religion) promise a unity and fulfillment which cannot be satisfied. Even all of the departments of philosophy joined together by the metaphysician in an attempt to comprehend reality falls short of complete intellectual satisfaction. The knowledge venture, thus, when pursued under the impetus of the theoretical will to know, leads only to a society of intellects united together to correct and supplement each other's apprehension of reality. But no assurance is given that the knowledge gained is fully accurate; nor is a principle of unity produced such as each demands. A sceptic can still contend that this supposedly coherent account provided by a combining of all the minds and fields of endeavor is a delusion since it falls short of certainty. The very necessity for philosophy to weigh all the evidence, balancing one area of experience with another renders impossible the attaining of theoretical certainty with regard to ex-

[8] Such a relationship has been made famous by Martin Buber in his *I and Thou*, trans. Ronald Gregor Smith (Edinburgh: T. & T. Clark, 1937). See Fletcher, 48–49, also the Analysis by William Hordern, *Speaking of God: The Nature and Purpose of Theological Language* New York: The Macmillan Company, 1964), Chaps. 8 & 9.

[9] *Nature, Man and God*, p. 54.

perience as a whole.[10] Thus, as with all inductive methods, the conclusions reached remain tentative and subject to revision.

Frustrated at every turn to discover a fully adequate principle of explanation to account for an ordered universe and sufficient to satisfy the mind's demand for coherence, the philosopher finds both the need and justification to turn to religion. For in man's religious consciousness of a Supreme Spirit whose will controls the universe for the sake of good an hypothesis is offered which meets the requirements.[11] The God of religion supplies the lack philosophy exhibits. But for the philosopher to accept belief in God as an hypothesis which best explains the facts is to develop a philosophy of theism in which God is and can only be an hypothesis subject to the abundance (or its lack) of evidence in favor of the hypothesis. In such a case the philosopher may decide on the basis of the evidence as well as on practical grounds that though the existence of God cannot be proved philosophically, he will nevertheless accept God and act on that basis. With theoretical certainty lacking, such a conclusion is quite rational and justified. But what needs to be emphasized is that as a philosopher one is committed to accept only what is established as being probably true by the greatest amount of evidence in its favor. Philosophy must, therefore, be unrelenting and even ruthless in criticizing all beliefs which assert more than the evidence warrants.

Is philosophical theism adequate? Does it provide the principle of unity and practical guidance that a satisfactory explanation of the world and man's place in the world require? It certainly is more philosophically sound than when the attempt is made to explain the universe apart from any reference to something beyond man. But religion rooted in and tested by human experience and a philosophy taking its cue from religion are still incomplete.[12] Human religion, conceived as one activity of the mind, aspires after a fulfillment in an object worthy of love and devotion and upon whom the entire world is held to depend. But an hypothesis that God sustains the unity of the world, though intelligible, remains inconclusive on the basis of philosophical speculation alone. Taken by itself religious experience may be doubted as lacking authenticity. God is subject to the uncertainties

[10] See Temple, *The Universality of Christ* (London: Student Christian Movement, 1921), pp. 44–45.

[11] See Temple, *Mens Creatrix*, p. 259. This is not intended to represent Temple's argument for God which is presented in Chap. 9 of the present study. At this point the concern is to indicate how and why the philosopher can make use of the concept of God.

[12] See *ibid.*, p. 259. By religion is meant, in this context, to convey what is usually referred to as philosophy of religion; see *ibid.*, pp. 352–354.

of inference and thus cannot provide the assurance and guidance life commands. God too can be doubted; chance may rule the world. Indeed, when one considers the evil evident in a world supposed to be operated by a Supreme Will for the sake of good, it is difficult to avoid scepticism; and the entire intellectual structure of a philosophy of theism crumbles under the weight of this contrary fact. Something more is needed; something personal and particular so as to be capable of providing individual assurance and specific guidance, but at the same time universal so as to illuminate the entire World-Process.

Thus, Temple forsakes the philosophical ideal of discovering an adequate principle of explanation of the universe on the basis of an empirical investigation of experience. The demand for a coherent account of the facts is replaced by the demand for practical guidance in living; likewise, the demand for logical certainty has been relinquished only to be replaced by the demand for inward religious certitude. In this way Temple makes a shift from the approach of philosophy to the deliverances of religion, from the conclusions of a philosophical theism to the commitments of the Christian faith without justifying adequately the transition and, apparently, without being aware of the ambiguities involved.

2. *The Christian faith as supplying the need*

Where, then, is the philosopher to turn for a clue to the completeness life demands and for which philosophy yearns but cannot provide? The alternative is not a partial turning to religious data interpreted by the philosopher, but a complete surrender. The philosopher must place his tools at the disposal of religion, and for Temple this means to the service of the Christian Faith. A philosophy founded on general religious principles though formally correct fails to supply sufficient content to deal with the particularity of actual living involving both good and evil. To procure such guidance philosophic theism must become Christian philosophy.

> A vague theism is futile. The cutting edge of faith is due to its definiteness. The kind of deity established (if any is at all) by the various "proofs" – ontological, cosmological and the like – is completely insufficient; it is usually little else than the rationality of the world presupposed in all argument about the world. The Christian has made a decision for God who has spoken – in nature, in history, in prophets, in Christ.[13]

[13] William Temple, "What Christians Stand for in the Secular World," reprinted in *Religious Experience*, p. 245.

How can the Christian philosopher hope to succeed where so many others have failed? The answer lies in the intimate relation with life itself, in the practical guidance and historical specificity of the Christian faith. No mere formal solution is provided for the perplexities of life, but a concrete faith rooted in specific events of an historical figure. The intimacy with life that philosophy lacks and which thereby hinders it from providing the guidance and assurance needed for daily life is dramatically demonstrated in the life of love Christ lived and for which he died. When these events are viewed as revealing God's loving purpose for man and the world, a metaphysics is evident. For if the universe represents the purpose or expression of goodness of a Supreme Spirit whose essence is sacrificial love, then man who understands and sympathizes with such a purpose is satisfied.[14] Thus what man by reason could not achieve is discovered by faith to be revealed in the person of Christ:

> Though from the point of view of human science the dogma of the Incarnation is mere hypothesis, yet it is an hypothesis which explains all the facts, and there is no other such forthcoming. Reason cannot prove it; we live by faith and not by demonstrative knowledge; but Reason welcomes it as the needed completion of its own work.[15]

When such a stance toward the world and its explanation is taken, then scientific philosophy, or even philosophy conceived in its broadest sense as metaphysics is replaced by theological philosophy, indeed by Christian philosophy. The presence of evil in the world is resolved when one sees in the life, death, and resurrection of Christ the sacrificial love of God, taking the evil of the world on Himself so as to serve as the dramatic and actualized event which can elicit from man the love he needs to win him to goodness.[16] The tentativeness of a philosophical explanation of evil in the world is replaced by the certainty of God's love as experienced in fellowship with Him.[17] Herein lies one of the significant differences between philosophical theism and a Christian philosophy.

3. *The justification of Christian philosophy*

Hence, Temple's conception of philosophy is put at the disposal of his own mission as a Christian so as to make him a Christian philosopher.

[14] See Temple, *Nature, Man and God*, p. 219; also see *Christianity in Thought and Practice*, pp. 62–64.

[15] Temple, *Mens Creatrix*, p. 253.

[16] See *Mens Creatrix*, pp. 290–292.

[17] See *Temple, Nature, Man and God*, p. 43.

The justification for this approach has in part already been noted by the failure of philosophy to provide the completely coherent system which the intellect seeks, and by the fact that an individual, even a philosopher, cannot transcend his particular culture and heritage to survey all time and existence. A totally impartial evaluation of all the facts is not possible even if all the facts could be gathered. Indeed, the facts can only be understood in light of a theory which provides a frame of reference for interpreting them. The mind itself, rooted as it is in the evolution of the species in the organism's response to its environment, and though at the highest levels able to transcend partially its limited vision, can never fully escape from the factors which condition it. Nor is sufficient emancipation provided if God is accepted as the legitimate conclusion of a philosophical argument. But the situation is significantly altered if one starts with the assurance of God as the Supreme Spirit and strives to explain everything from the vantage point of fellowship with Him. Thus, the tensions between the philosophy and religion noted in the previous section are temporarily resolved by the capitulation of philosophy to religion. Temple acknowledges that there are dangers involved in this approach and notes that if fantasies are to be avoided, then Theological Philosophy must be "constantly checked by a purely critical Philosophy which makes its approach from the other end."[18] This is a noteworthy aim, but one which is not actually carried out by Temple. At no crucial point (e.g., the problem of evil) does he, in fact, check the deliverances of Theological Philosophy against the conclusions of critical Philosophy.

Thus, the Christian philosopher begins his quest for a comprehension of reality from the perspective of the Christian faith. He strives to apply the principles of Christianity to the problems of life and to see if insight into them and guidance for living in reference to them are provided. If insight and guidance follow from the application, then the principles are vindicated. Though the principles of the Christian faith are not completely vindicated, all problems yield to its insights; and this justifies employing the Christian faith and following it wherever it leads. When the philosopher starts with the Christian faith, he is able to offer a more comprehensive system of explanation for the universe. To this extent, then, the Christian faith is philosophically superior to all other alternatives which proceed without giving priority to it. Hence, though the granting of priority to the Christian faith and

[18] *Ibid.*

thereby the assumption of its authenticity from the start is less sound than the minimal assumptions of philosophy in beginning its quest, the greater comprehensiveness of the solution which the Christian faith provides justifies the initial assumption. Therefore, Temple concludes, as tempting as theoretical certainty would be when based on a completely comprehensive philosophic world view, it must be relinguished as impossible of achievement and replaced by the more modest but fully adequate practical assurance which a Christian philosophy affords.[19]

Temple seems unduly concerned about the priority he grants to the Christian faith, but insufficiently concerned about how he makes use of the priority when it is granted. That is, the philosopher need have no qualm about granting such priority so long as it is vindicated by offering an intelligible account of experience, and so long as the original assumptions are modified in accordance with the facts as both emerge in the process. Such a procedure would be in accord with Temple's dialectical method. But when a body of doctrine is assumed to constitute the Christian faith which does not itself undergo critical evaluation and modification, then this is not philosophically justified and is inconsistent with the philosophical method Temple advocates. Hence, insofar as Temple's method is to accept certain doctrines of the Christian faith as final without subjecting them to modification even when the facts of experience require modification, then he departs from the role of philosopher (including that of the Christian philosopher) and takes up the cudgels on behalf of Christian apologetics.

C. SUMMARY AND CONCLUSIONS

The argument presented in the previous section served as a review of many of the ideas raised throughout Part I. However, not all of the major issues covered in the first five chapters were explored. It may be well, therefore, to offer at this point a brief summary statement of the arguments proposed and the conclusions reached at this stage in the exposition of Temple's position.

1. The theoretical inadequacy of scientific philosophy

Temple conceives the philosophic task to be the discovery of a principle which will render the universe intelligible to man. The best method

[19] See Temple, *Christianity in Thought and Practice*, p. 34.

for achieving philosophic understanding of the world is the dialectical method in which fact and theory emerge jointly in the process of interpreting the data of experience and in which conclusions are constantly checked by the facts.

The epistemological position advocated by Temple may be described as critical realism. He seeks to synthesize the naive realist's emphasis on the object in knowing and the certainty of one's knowledge with Descartes' emphasis on the subject as isolated in knowing and the uncertainty of any object known. The clue to the solution of the epistemological problem is found in the origin of knowledge in which thinking is held to have arisen as a function of the organism in an effort to adjust to its environment. From the very start, therefore, mental activity is in interaction with an external world. Each apprehension by man is of reality, but not each one is equally significant. Furthermore, momentary apprehensions of reality must be checked with other apprehensions; knowledge is built up gradually. Error occurs only in an act of synthesis when different objects are falsely identified, therefby serving as a stimulus to knowledge. Truth, then, means not logical coherence, but the degreee of unity warranted by the relation of the facts. Probability replaces certainty as the legitimate ideal. One can accept as probably true that hypothesis which most adequately integrates the relevant facts. Such a task, however, is never completed; and it is deceptive to think that one actually proceeds in this way.

The aim of Scientific Philosophy to derive an explanatory principle capable of unifying all of experience by the process of inquiring into the data of experience cannot be realized. The conclusion that is sought cannot be reached apart from some prior understanding of the principle itself. The complete objectivity and the theoretical certainty of a logically coherent system is not possible. However, man can expect and demand of philosophy inner certitude and outward guidance. Indeed, the philosophic enterprise is held to be incomplete if psychological certainty and practical guidance are not provided. A legitimate basis for moving beyond philosophy is thereby established.

2. *The practical adequacy of Christian philosophy*

As we have seen, the choice of an explanatory principle such as philosophy seeks is not purely rational or entirely empirical, though it need not be arbitrary. Ultimately one is thrown back to one's heritage and personal encounter with reality for a clue to the nature of reality. Temple's heritage of western Christianity and his own personal experience of God in Christ supply the needed principle. The philosophic goal of formulating an intelligible world view, Temple concludes, is not possible apart from the assurance of personal fellowship with God and apart from the perspective of the Christian faith. Theological philosophy is Temple's name for this approach, though it should more accurately be labeled Christian philosophy.

The philosophic quest is not initiated by Temple in the mood of doubt or uncertainty; he knows from religious experience that there is a God and he is certain that in Christ the nature of God – and therefore the nature of ultimate reality – is revealed. Turning to the Christian faith to supply the unifying principle that philosophy lacks but needs is justified by the result attained: intellectual illumination of the problems of life and specific guidance for living. Thus Christian philosophy succeeds where Scientific Philosophy fails; though theoretical certainty resulting from a fully coherent metaphysical system must be forsaken, insight and concrete guidance are provided.

The philosophic enterprise has been launched. Temple's stance toward the problems of philosophy is evident. He will bring to bear on all of the issues of life and thought the Christian faith as he understands it in order to see what illumination and inner strength it provides. One issue of prime importance for any philosopher is the nature of man. Temple's conception of personality – both human and divine – is especially significant since personality is the key concept in his philosophy. It is imperative, therefore, that a careful exposition be offered of the ideal of personality operative in his thought.

PART II

A CHRISTIAN PHILOSOPHY OF PERSONALITY: HUMAN AND DIVINE

CHAPTER 6

PROCESS AND PERSONALITY

The structure of reality exhibits various levels or grades, of which personality is, for Temple, the highest. These levels need to be examined as they have emerged in the World-Process; at the same time, it is germane to discover how Temple employs personality as a metaphysical principle of explanation.

A. PROCESS, MIND, AND VALUE

1. The historical priority of matter

Any attempt to understand the universe must recognize the significance of two facts: first is the fact that man is capable of apprehending the world; second, man himself arose within the World-Process and, hence, the physical order existed prior to anyone's apprehension of it.[1] These two facts must constantly be kept in mind. The danger of any interpretation of the universe is to emphasize one of them to the exclusion of the other, resulting in either Idealism or Materialism.

The problem is further complicated by the fact that when man strives to understand the process of which he is a part, he begins with both facts already accomplished and thus he is not able to observe the process by which the one led to the other. Furthermore, as potential knower, man is inclined to choose as a starting place himself isolated from the rest of the world and to build up his knowledge of everything else on the basis of his ideas as if they were separated from the world. This was the error of Descartes and leads nowhere. A clue to the procedure to be followed is to be found in the view which science

[1] See Temple, *Nature, Man and God*, pp. 111, 217.

presents of a material order existing and changing long before man came on the scene. Here the proper perspective for understanding all that the processes of physical change have produced and the logical place to initiate an inquiry into the World-Process are both provided.[2]

The historical priority of the physical world, or of matter, must be acknowledged. In this sense every philosophy is materialistic. Furthermore, this fact of the priority of matter in time is significant for an understanding of all that follows. It means that matter is the necessary condition for everything else, though it does not follow that it is the sufficient cause. Further, what emerges is related to that from which it arose; and since matter is temporally first, this means matter is basic to everything else. Matter is, therefore, real whatever else may be discovered about its ultimate status. Finally, it signifies that there is continuity in the world, and the differences which are evident stand in causal connection to one another.

2. *The axiological priority of mind*

Matter is the necessary condition of everything in the universe, even as it is temporally prior to all that appears. But matter is not all that has appeared. Other levels of reality are also evident which are not reducible to matter, though not conceivable in human experience apart from matter.

Four such levels may be noted: Matter, Life, Mind, and Spirit. All of these strata occur within the World-Process; each is, in fact, one episode in that process. As such, to refer to four levels is misleading in that it suggests discontinuity in what appears as a continuous process. Nonetheless, distinctions can and must be made even though they should not be taken as precise lines of demarcation in the process itself but as abstractions within the process as a whole.[3] But if the distinctions which do occur are not to be blurred, then it is necessary to note each level and the characteristics each exhibits.

Matter, representing the so-called inorganic realm, is characterized by action and reaction of chemical and physical elements with one another. This is the realm of the material universe and operates under the impetus of efficient causation. Little if any initiative other than

[2] See *Ibid.*, p. 198.

[3] See Temple, *Christus Veritas*, p. 5. A. E. Baker in *William Temple's Teaching* (Philadelphia: The Westminster Press, 1951), p. 52, attributes this conception of the universe to the influence of Samuel Alexander.

the resistance offered due to inertia is evident at this level. What occurs can be accounted for on the basis of stimulus-response in light of the components of each chemical compound or physical entity.

It should be noted at this point that Temple is neither explicit nor consistent in his interpretation of matter. He does refer to the changed view of the atom. The older view held that the atom consisted of tiny, irreducible particles; whereas according to the newer view it consists "of revolving centres of electrical force – a kind of minute solar system."[4] At times – particularly in *Nature, Man and God* – the term process is employed in a way which almost replaces matter. Process signifies the more dynamic view of the material world exhibiting continuous change and giving rise to new entities related, but not reducible, to previously existing entities. However, Temple continues to refer to matter at other times as inert, unconscious "stuff," or even as "dead matter."[5] It is this latter view of matter which seems to be employed at this point since it is the inertia of matter as contrasted with life that is emphasized.

At the level of life a different principle reigns, for the organism acts as a whole and, though analyzable into physical components and chemical elements, these parts must be understood in terms of their relation to the whole organism. Further, with life self-movement is evident that is more than mere inertia. Though the power of self-motion is only explicit at the animal level, the beginnings of motion are evident in the vegetable world:

> As we pass from the purely physical and chemical world to the vegetable world, we find the beginnings of self-motion in the phenomenon of growth. There is in the Vegetable a principle which determines its reaction to environment, so that from the same soil and the same water two plants draw the nourishment of quite different forms of foliage and the like.[6]

What has occurred up to this point in the world was due to an external stimulus producing a corresponding reaction in another object. Movement in this sense can be described as a push from behind. But with life there is direction from within the organism toward something outside. There is movement which can best be described as pull from in front, or attraction towards. With life occurs determination by attraction, then, and not simply efficient causation.[7]

[4] *Nature of Personality*, p. xv.

[5] Temple, "Some Implications of Theism" in J. H. Muirhead (ed.), *Contemporary British Philosophy* (New York: The Macmillan Company, 1924), I, 426.

[6] Temple, *Christus Veritas*, p. 51.

[7] See *Nature, Man and God*, p. 478.

The principle of self-direction based on needs of the organism as a whole takes on an additional quality when Mind appears in the development of organic life. The responsiveness of the organism to its environment for the sake of fostering adjustment to it is the occasion for the appearance of Mind. Mind is the extension of this process. But, Mind enhances self-direction by enabling the organism to envisage various means toward the end of adjustment and to select among the alternatives those means most appropriate to the desired end.

Mind was, when it first emerged, restricted to the demands of the organism to survive. It was limited in its apprehension to what was directly available in the environment which corresponded to the organism's needs, and the power of selection was confined to the actual alternatives it directly encountered. Gradually, however, as life developed, Mind was freed from seeking means to the end of survival only and developed a life of its own by which it considered alternatives and courses of action not immediately concerned with adjustment. In this way Mind produced ideas which do not directly refer to any object in the environment but to a possible end that might be attained. To percepts are added concepts, or "free ideas."[8]

When the direction of the organism is in terms of some object in the future which it conceives to be good, then the level of Spirit has been reached. The distinctive characteristic of Spirit is in the direction it provides for the sake of a felt obligation which at its highest finds fulfillment in the fellowship of shared love. The unique element in personality is likewise evident in this transition from mind to spirit: "The main point is that Mind may be chiefly, or indeed wholly, concerned with the finding of means to fixed ends, whereas Spirit (the distinctive element of Personality) appears in the choice between ends, which is made possible by the capacity of Mind for 'free ideas.'"[9]

3. *The supremacy of spirit*

An analysis of the structure of the world thus reveals that Matter is prior in point of time to everything else but that other levels do appear. Furthermore, when these levels do emerge, each one exercises some control over the one before it. The living organism makes use of the chemical and physical elements composing it for the sake of its own

[8] See *ibid.*, pp. 202, 212, 492.
[9] *Ibid.*, p. 190, n. 1.

total adjustment and then develops a life of its own. Finally, with the emergence of Spirit the initiative of the organism becomes most complete, and the direction it seeks is for the sake of a good it envisages.

The conclusion to be drawn from this twofold relation between the lower and the higher is that while the lower is the necessary instrument for the realization of the higher, the lower finds its fulfillments in the higher. Thus, Spirit, though last in temporal sequence, is first in terms of significance; and Matter, though temporally prior, is of least significance. Matter is the necessary means to the end which is Spirit, but is only a means. Spirit, dependent on Matter, is nevertheless supreme over it.[10]

The full significance of Mind as an occurrence in the process is now apparent. When once it appears, it alters the entire course of the process, for something has been produced which does not merely respond to other parts of the process as determined by its component parts, outside stimulus, or mere adjustment to the environment. Instead, Mind initiates activity, making use of what is available for the sake of its own ends and even of ends which are not yet evident but which are ideals it has posited. It is this fact of control over the organism and environment which entitles Mind, when it attains the level of Spirit, to its supremacy. The response to stimuli by an object to which the object contributes only inertia and the response of an organism which itself initiates the action taken for the sake of a desired good reveals the essential difference between Matter and Mind (or Spirit).[11]

Thus, though the starting place is the Materialism science conveys the conclusion is a rejection of materialism as inadequate to account for Mind and Spirit in their supremacy over Matter and Life. But Idealism is equally false since the apprehension of a mind cannot be separated from the process it apprehends and from which it arose. The alternative to both Materialism and Idealism is to join Matter and Mind without blurring the distinctive characteristics of each. Matter is real but secondary; it is the means for the realization of Spirit which is supreme.

The stage is now set for a solution to be proposed to the problem posed by the emergence of the various levels of reality within the World-Process.

10 See Temple, *Nature, Man and God*, pp. 474–475, and *Christus Veritas*, pp. 5–6.
11 See Temple, *Nature, Man and God*, p. 488.

B. THE QUEST FOR AN EXPLANATORY PRINCIPLE

The philosopher's task is essentially identical with that of the metaphysician: to understand systematically the nature of reality.[12] It is the philosopher's responsibility to relate all areas of experience with a view to comprehending the universe. It is he who asks and seeks to answer the question: Is there any meaning to the world as a whole? The philosophic task, then, becomes the quest for an explanatory principle adequate to account for what experience reveals to exist.

Some basic questions arise at this point: Are things to be conceived as having an existence independent of value so that the value of a thing is incidental to its reality? Or is value to be taken as what is real, in which case things constitute the forms through which value is expressed? Also, is the appearance of mind (or spirit) in the World-Process explicable if everything is reduced ultimately to matter. Or is the occurrence of both matter and mind in the World-Process made more intelligible if the process is itself grounded in mind? The issue raised by these questions is whether the universe can be more satisfactorily explained by the lower or by the higher stages which the process exhibits. The philosopher is confronted here by a fundamental choice.

Philosophies inspired by natural science take as their maxim that the higher can best be accounted for in terms of the lower. Whatever scientific analysis reveals to be ultimate (e.g., atoms, or electrons, protons, neutrons, or space-time) is claimed as the starting point for the world. Everything that the universe eventually exhibits is considered to be a further development of, or emergent from, these primitive realities. In this way an empirical scheme is devised which remains in close contact with observed facts.

The problem which such a scheme poses is the place of the higher levels in the process. How, indeed, can mind or value occur in a process devoid of both? Mind and value stand out as a breach in the continuity of the process.[13]

Thus, mind on such a view is sometimes held to be an epiphenomenon, an effect produced by the complex combination of physical entities but not itself capable of producing any effects. Or mind may be seen as an addition inserted into the process by a Creator external to

[12] See above, Chapter 2.

[13] Temple argues for the theistic hypothesis in this way in *Nature, Man and God*, and the case he presents is developed in the next chapter.

it. Neither account is satisfactory. Mind is experienced as initiating activities in the World-Process. Hence, to reduce it to the status of epiphenomenon is to flout one's experience of mind. The other alternative is equally fallacious. To admit the necessity of another principle external to the process itself in order to account for the occurrence of mind in the process is to abandon the theory that the lower can explain the higher.

The existence of value is likewise precarious if a purely physical account of the world is proposed. Value has no ground in the structure of reality itself. Its status is confined to the subjective mental states of persons who respond appreciatively to their world. There is truth in this position regarding value, but it is a half-truth at best. The subjective factor in value-experience is acknowledged, but the objective basis of value in the world is neglected. When one responds appreciatively to some object, one does so believing that the reason for the response is the nature of the object and not the feeling alone.

> The Value only fulfills its essential nature, only achieves its essential excellence, in the moment when it is appreciated. It exists as value for Mind; Mind finds it and appreciates it; but Mind does not invent or create it in the act of appreciation.[14]

To believe that man is deceived in relation to value-experience so that what he considers a judgment about an object is really only his own emotional response is to wreck the entire philosophic and scientific enterprise.[15] Extreme scepticism regarding the knowledge venture itself would seem to be the logical conclusion of such an approach.

The fact of the matter is that a physical account of reality based on the analysis of physical science concentrates so intensively on the object of knowledge that it fails to take adequately into account, and thereby to account for, the knowing mind. Knowledge is itself a fact of the World-Process which cannot be ignored; but it is ignored by the scientific method. The latter "concentrates all attention upon the object under investigation, and gives none to the attention so concentrated."[16]

It is perfectly legitimate for science to ignore certain aspects of

[14] Temple, *Nature, Man and God*, p. 215.

[15] See *Ibid.* Though Temple did not have the emotive theory of ethics in mind, his criticism is relevant to it. Cf. the criticism made by Brand Blanshard in "The Impasse in Ethics – and a Way Out," *University of California Publications* in Philosophy, XXVIII (1955), No. 2, 92–112, and in *Reason and Goodness* (New York: The Macmillan Company, 1961), pp. 92–94, 199–213.

[16] Temple, *Nature, Man and God*, p. 215.

reality in fulfilling its task, but quite illegitimate for scientists (or philosophers following the scientific approach) to deny the existence of what is ignored. Temple concludes that starting with what is lower in the structure of reality, one cannot account for the occurrence or significance of the higher:

> If we begin with mindless and valueless fact we cannot give any place in our scheme to Mind or Value without breaking up the unity of the scheme itself. The very activity which makes science possible remains unaccounted for in the theory of the world which men have constructed in the activity of science.[17]

If this is the case, then can the other alternative fare any better, that is, can the lower be explained by the higher? What, in fact, would constitute a satisfactory explanation, if one can be found?

C. PERSONALITY AS A METAPHYSICAL PRINCIPLE OF EXPLANATION

1. *Purposive will as the only adequate explanatory principle*

The fundamental issue to be faced before a satisfactory explanation of the World-Process can be found is what sort of explanation of the universe would really explain it. The inadequacy of attempting to trace what occurs later in the process by reference to what is temporally prior has already been noted. Such a procedure is fine for scientific investigation, concerned as it is to point out causal sequences and causal connections. But when an account of the process as a whole is sought, such a method fails; for the issue is not how one event follows from another, but why there are any events at all and why these events in particular. Thus, the issue is not just how mind and spirit are related to life and to matter, but why any of these levels should appear and why these in particular did appear.

When the question is posed in this way, then it is clear that what is sought is a self-explanatory principle. Some principle is required which itself requires no further explanation. The only principle offered in human experience that can satisfy these demands is purpose. Recourse to physical causation to answer the question why something occurs is to embark on an endless quest; but when one shows the purpose of something occurring, then the issue is resolved and understood.

> When we find that the position of a given set of material objects is due to their having been arranged with a view to facilitating the accomplishment of some intelligible purpose, our minds are satisfied. That a plank should lie across a

[17] *Ibid.*, p. 216.

stream may call for much explanation if no human beings have ever placed it there; but if men laid it across to form a bridge, so that they could cross over dry-shod, no further explanation is needed.[18]

Intelligent choice provides the clue for solving the problem of an explanatory principle. One may be confused by an action which another has taken, but that is a case of not being able to imagine anyone doing such a thing and not a failure to explain the act as the actual choice of another. Furthermore, the confusion is also removed when an act is traced to a purpose with which one can sympathize. To understand means, in regard to human questions, to sympathize. The mind is satisfied when an action is explained as the activity of a purposive will with which one is in sympathy. Applying this reason to an explanation of the universe one can, at least, be clear as to the type of explanation that would satisfy man:

The only explanation of the Universe that would really explain it, in the sense of providing to the question why it exists an answer that raises no further question, would be the demonstration that it is the creation of a Will which in the creative act seeks an intelligible good.[19]

However, the possibility exists that there is no explanation of the universe's existence. That is, perhaps the best that can be attained is an account of the world in which each part is seen supporting every other part so as to be internally coherent. The whole as such would not then be accounted for, but that this may be the case cannot be considered eliminated.

There is the possibility that another explanation exists different from either of the two proposed. Personal existence is the highest level yet attained in the evolutionary process, and it is natural and legitimate to take the activity of personal beings as providing the best clue to understanding the process as a whole; but there is no reason for ruling out the possibility of a still higher level emerging, not now knowable to man. The explanation of the process might reside in this higher form, but man could not at present know this.

Nonetheless, what is clear is that at the present stage of the process if an explanation of the world as it is now known is to be found, purpose rooted in will offers the only available hypothesis. One must choose between theism and scepticism.

18 Temple, *Nature, Man and God*, pp. 131–132. See also *The Faith and Modern Thought*, pp. 16–19; *Nature of Personality*, pp. 85–88; *Mens Creatrix*, pp. 88–89; *Christus Veritas*, pp. 7–10; *Christianity in Thought and Practice*, pp. 61–66.

19 Temple, *Christus Veritas*, p. 7.

Although there is some cogency in this formulation of the issues at stake, it is largely sacrificed when Temple goes on to state that the real alternatives are scepticism or *Christian* theism.[20] It is this tendency – sometimes explicit, more often implicit – to identify philosophical theism with a particular interpretation of the Christian faith without justifying the identification that renders Temple's metaphysics suspect. This point will become more apparent in the next chapter when the arguments for a personal God are examined.

Thus, for Temple, if the universe is to be intelligible, it must be the creation of a living God. The levels of reality which the process exhibits can, therefore, best be explained by reference to a will acting for a purpose which is conceived as good. A value-centered metaphysics is the conclusion to which the argument leads. The consequences of a value-centered metaphysics as applied to an understanding of the structure of reality must now be made explicit.

2. *A value-centered metaphysics*

The place to begin an interpretation of the World-Process is with the totality of that process as it appears to man. Matter, life, mind, and spirit all occur within the process. Thus, the totality of experience includes both matter and mind. There is no need either to start with matter alone and strive to find how mind is derived from it, or to start with mind and strive to find how matter occurs. The former is the Materialistic blunder and the latter is the Cartesian blunder.

Matter is not to be conceived as a mental state of some kind; nor is mind a complex combination of matter. Both matter and mind must be accepted as they are and neither one reduced to the other.

> What is presented to us is a given articulated continuum in the form of a process, wherein, at a certain stage of development, Mind is found to be active. We take this Mind as what it appears to be, in its initial dependence on the data of experience, in its subsequent independence of particular circumstances, in its comprehension of succession and extension, in its purposiveness, in its freedom.[21]

Since mind arises within the process as the organism's response to its environment, there is no necessity for asking how a transition is effected from the ideas of the mind to the objective world. Matter and material processes existed prior to mind; and when the latter emerged,

[20] See Temple, *Nature of Personality*, p. 95.
[21] Temple, *Nature, Man and God*, p. 217.

it did so as consciousness of an environment which is partly material.[22]

From its very inception, then, mind exists as apprehension of matter. Likewise, from the start mind aspires toward value. Desire serves as the impetus of thought. The organism has need to be satisfied and the process of selecting suitable objects to satisfy these needs is what initiates thought. Similarly, the organism's feeling of intimacy with certain objects in its environment elicits a response of affection that persists even after needs are satisfied. Hence mind is both passive and active in its response to the environment. The awareness of certain objects in the environment as conducive to the organism's survival is the passive character of the mind; but when the mind selects certain objects among those presented to satisfy its needs, it is active. In both cases the mind is apprehending value, either negative or positive. Value is actualized when the mind finds satisfaction in certain objects in its environment; and disvalue occurs when objects are apprehended as not being satisfying.[23]

Thus, fact and value occur together in the World-Process just as matter and mind do; any explanation of the process must account for both combinations. If a mindless and valueless universe cannot adequately account for mind and value, then the question arises whether a universe held to be grounded in mind which is directed by good can account for matter and mind, fact and value.

Such would seem to be the case. At some point in the development of the World-Process an organism arises which is conscious of the process itself. At that moment value also is actualized. This means that mind in apprehending the World-Process finds something of like character with itself. Value occurs when the mind recognizes itself in its object. The significance of this fact cannot be underestimated:

Mind, then, though it appears within the Process at a late stage, discovers throughout that Process the activity of Mind – universally in the form of Truth, commonly in the form of Beauty, sometimes in the form of Goodness. That Mind is pervasive of Reality is a necessary inference from this method of apprehending the world. If that method is justified ... the conclusion is inevitable. Mind is the principle of unity in Reality, or at least the fullest expression of that principle known to us.[24]

Process is subject to mind. The activity of mind in expressing itself through process is what is meant by purpose. Further, mind as purposive is guided by what it considers to be good. This means that value is logically prior to existence.

[22] See above, Chapter 3.
[23] See Temple, *Nature, Man and God*, p. 218; also below, Chapter 11.
[24] Temple, *Nature, Man and God*, p. 219.

The relation of this conception of value to the traditional philosophical concept of substance can now be stated. The term substance must be redefined in terms of value. If substance is taken to refer to a real thing, then substance equals value plus existence. However, if the substance of a thing is distinguished from its accidents, then substance equals value. Following Plato's notion of the Good in *The Republic,* Temple offers a metaphysical conception of value:

> Value is the element in real things which both causes them to be, and makes them what they are, and is thus fitly called Substance in so far as this is other or less than their totality.[25]

Substance and actuality are distinguished in this definition. Though values are in one sense always realized in the purposive mind which is the source of everything, not all values are actual in the World-Process at any one time. Indeed, value becomes actualized in particular objects when apprehended as valuable by a conscious being. Thus, the good cannot be separated from the object which is good except in abstraction. To do so is to succumb to the same error committed by Hedonism in ethical theory.

There is a subjective factor in the actualization of value in the World-Process since a conscious being must respond to the world in order for value to become actual. But this subjective response is elicited by a valuable object, and hence the subjective factor cannot be separated from the objective element in value actualization. The subject and object distinction which first appears in the conscious experience of man is bridged in the very act of its appearance. Similarly man, whose conscious awareness of the world poses the problem of why there is a universe, also suggests a solution by responding appreciatively to objects in the world and thereby experiencing the world as good.

> For, if our whole theory is sound, value determines existence, but value is only actual when it is appreciated; therefore, Man's appreciation of the world is the first installment, so to speak, within the Time process, of the realisation of that for which the world was made, though in the eternal Mind which comprehends all Time this is actual eternally.[26]

The universe itself, then, is grounded in Mind determined by good. The purpose of the universe is to serve as a medium for the expression of value and to produce beings capable of consciously sharing in this value. "Symbolism is thus the supreme philosophic principle. The universe

[25] Temple, *Christus Veritas*, p. 15.
[26] *Ibid.*, p. 19.

exists to reveal the goodness of God so far as it evolves intelligences capable of receiving the revelation."[27]

The World-Process which starts with physical things and gradually gives rise to life, mind and spirit is seen to be best understood in terms of the level of personal being. The transition has been completed within the World-Process from a physical world constantly in flux through the interaction of one part with another to the world of personal beings able to bring some permanence out of the change and to act themselves upon the world from which they arose; it is the movement from process to personality. Personality as the highest level of reality revealed in the process also offers the best principle for explaining the process.

[27] Temple, *Christus Veritas*, p. 19. Cf. also "Symbolism as a Metaphysical Principle" reprinted in *Religious Experience ...*, pp. 77–86.

CHAPTER 7

HUMAN PERSONALITY

Temple's use of the concept of personality as a metaphysical principle of explanation is already evident. In the sections that follow we shall examine the use which he makes of the concept of personality to solve some traditional philosophical problems in the areas of moral and social philosophy, and the philosophy of history. It is important at this point, therefore, to expound Temple's understanding of the meaning of human and divine personality, and to clarify the ideal of personality that is operative in his thought.

A. THE UNION OF MATTER AND MIND IN MAN

1. Man as a psycho-physical organism

The unity-in-diversity of Matter, Life, Mind, and Spirit provides the clue for an adequate understanding of man. In man all the levels of reality are present as a unity in one composite being. It is for this reason that man is taken to be the fullest expression of reality yet attained in the evolutionary process.

> In our bodies we belong to the physical, chemical, vegetable, and animal worlds; these bodies are largely directed by our minds or intelligences; our minds are capable of being directed by spirit, or, in other words, of exerting themselves in the fulfillment of obligation.[1]

Man is thus a psycho-physical organism; he is combination of matter and mind united in a living organism. Man too is continuous with the entire World-Process from which he emerged. Consciousness in man, though far removed from its rudimentary counterpart as mere response to the environment, is nonetheless one with man's total nature.

[1] Temple, *Christus Veritas*, p. 49.

My consciousness is not something else within the entire organism which is myself, taking note of the relations of that organism to its environment; my consciousness is itself that organism, being not only physical but psycho-physical, as related to its environment, namely to the universe of which it is a part, though as the spiritual elements in the organism become predominant, the concomitant physical relations become relatively less important and may finally drop away.[2]

In this way is resolved the perplexing mind-body problem which has plagued philosophy for so long. Mind and body are not two separate entities which interact with one another; nor are they two separate but parallel series in which simultaneous events occur. The mind and body are one, for man is a psycho-physical organism. The direction the organism takes is provided by non-physical activity but operates through a physical organism. Mind is thus the principle of control, and the body is the medium through which it executes its plans: "Where mind is found, it is found as potentially, and always in some degree actually, the principle of unity of that through which it is active."[3]

Body and mind are not, however, to be viewed as two distinct entities, one physical and the other mental; they are organically one. Further, no transition of a plan of action envisaged by the mind and communicated to the body for execution is discernible. The will to move some part of the body is to act in a way that results in the movement. The mind, then, provides the unity and direction for the organism as a whole; for mind and body are one and to the extent that mind is active it is dominant.

It is questionable whether Temple has done any more than rephrase the mind-body problem. The fundamental issue which is not answered is the relation of the non-physical activity of the mind to the physical activity of the body. Furthermore, he refers to mind and body as organically one, though the mind is dominant. But, can a single organism be "present with" or "dominant" over itself?

The problem of the unity and identity of the self may also be solved along these same lines. Man's unity is at first formal only, rooted as it is in the numerical identity of the individual as distinct from everything else; but also from the start the self is a conscious flowing stream of diverse activities and contents. The soul-substance view is rejected in which an underlying ego is posited as the ground for the unity and diversity experienced on the conscious level. The identity of the self persists in and through change, and there is no other self:

[2] Temple, *Nature, Man and God*, p. 487.
[3] *Ibid.*, p. 201.

> The self is the self-conscious system of experience. ... A change in my experience is a change in me; but this does not destroy my personal identity, because this consists in continuity of growth and not immutability.[4]

Hence the unity which is the self consists in the total psychic life of the individual. Three distinct ways in which this unity is revealed may be noted. First is the unity provided by the physical organism itself. The bodily organism, though a part of the physical order, is also distinct from it and serves as the particular medium through which the self is expressed. As an organism it operates as a whole; and though bodily parts change, there is continuity and identity of the body as a physiological organism.

A second unity is evident in conscious experience which constitutes a unity of activities so that certain objects are selected and attention fixed on them to the exclusion of others. This unity of the self is incomplete, for many impulses from within and stimuli from without seek to dominate the activities of the conscious self.

A potential third unity, however, is evident at this point when the self achieves a harmony of interests as a result of integrating its activities and impulses in the service of a purpose which it seeks to fulfill. The personal unity of the self which is only potential at the start is then realized. Temple summarizes the threefold unity which constitutes the person:

> So a man is one person partly because his body is one, partly because his "soul" is a distinguishable group of psychic forces which can only be all active so far as they combine, but most of all because there is possible for him a unity which it is his life's business to achieve. In achieving it he reveals the full nature, not only of his psychic endowment, but also of the bodily organism which is its physical basis.[5]

2. *Man as a personal being*

When man attains the full unity of which he is capable, the distinctive traits of a personal being or personality become evident. Matter, life, mind, and spirit have been united together so as to act as one entity under the supervision of spirit but by means of the activities of mind and through the physical elements composing the body (matter and life). The function of mind is no longer merely that of responding to the

[4] Temple, *Christus Veritas*, pp. 65–66. There is an affinity here with the Personalistic position referred to as self-psychology. See Brightman, *Introduction to Philosophy*, pp. 202–211. However, Temple includes bodily activity within the unity and identity of the self, and Brightman does not. The distinction involved is explored more fully below; see Chapter 17.

[5] Temple, *Christus Veritas*, p. 68.

environment for the sake of adjustment only. The mind itself initiates activities of its own and even uses the environment for its own ends such as a goal it envisages in the future toward which it directs the organism.

The significance of this capacity of the mind to escape partially from the bondage of its particular location in space and time needs to be noted further. The entire knowledge venture is made possible in this way, but also, an insight into the process itself is gained in the capacity of the mind to form "free ideas." The mind is enabled, by projecting itself beyond the fleeting moment, to detach itself from the successiveness of the temporal process. The present moment which the mind experiences is not some hypothetical midpoint between the past and the future; it is itself a time-span. Arising as the mind does out of the flux which constitutes the World-Process, the mind is a consciousness of that process. And at any particular time-span this means a consciousness of a portion of that process: "The present is so much of the empirical process as is immediately apprehended." [6]

The mind's experience as covering a span of time and its ability to detach itself from the flux through memory of the past and anticipation of the future enables the mind to attain some permanence in and through the changing world. It can by observing the order of the change which occurs postulate unchanging principles which describe the change. This is the foundation and procedure of science. Another permanence is attained in the mind's capacity to hold before it in conscious awareness a period of time extending through a number of successive events in time. This is the basis and method of art.

The most significant characteristic of mind does not, however, reside in its ability to apprehend the existing world and to formulate principles to describe it or even to hold before itself a succession of events, as important as these are. What is more amazing still is the purposive character of the mind by means of which an anticipated goal in the future is envisaged, and the past and present are directed toward making the world conform to that goal. This tendency of the mind to be lured on by the future constitutes, as was noted in the last chapter, the primary and distinctive trait of the mind of man and represents the unique element in personality.

A shift in Temple's view of mind and its relation to the physical organism seems to have taken place. His analysis of mind now suggests

[6] Temple, *Nature, Man and God*, p. 203.

that mind has a more independent status within the human organism than was allowed for in the previous discussion of the organic union of mind and body. A separate or even an entitative state for mind seems to be implied here.

B. DIFFERENCE BETWEEN PERSONAL AND SUB-PERSONAL

One of the ways in which Temple clarifies the meaning of personality is by distinguishing between a Thing, a Brute, and a person.[7] These distinctions correspond in a general way to the levels of reality noted in the previous chapter, namely, matter (Thing), life (Brute) and mind and spirit (Person).

None of these categories, of course, may be completely applicable to an existing entity. The category Brute, for example, may not in fact apply fully to one particular animal. Temple's point, however, is not dependent on such an empirical identity of definition and existing object. He means these terms to apply to any existing object which can be so defined, and any object may be labeled a Thing, a Brute, or a Person to the extent that one of the definitions is applicable to it. These terms are, then, generalizations for the sake of classification, and their merit is clarity of meaning; so that when the terms are used, the meaning is evident.

The procedure will be to suggest two types of experiences and to examine each as it applies to the Thing, to the Brute, and to the Person. The first is the level of conscious awareness, and the second is the degree of self-determination as opposed to external determination.

1. A Thing

By a Thing, Temple means an object devoid of conscious experience and almost completely determined in its action by outside forces. A Thing simply is; it exists as an object only, never as a subject. Since a Thing does not feel or think, it is neutral in terms of value and disvalue.

How a Thing is treated is neither good nor bad in itself. When one kicks a football, for example, there is no need to view the effect of this action on the football or from the perspective of the football.

Because a Thing is externally determined, what individuality it

[7] See Temple, *Nature of Personality*, Sect. I; also *Christus Veritas*, pp. 50–52.

possesses may be almost completely ignored and certainly is irrelevant for most purposes. This is what is meant by matter, the chief property of which is inertia. Though even here Temple cautions that such a description refers to an ideal limit and not to any actual entity. But the point is, "at the purely mechanical stage, whether it is real or not, individuality counts for nothing, and the motion of a body – the only activity open to it – can be calculated from a knowledge of its mass and the force acting on it."[8]

2. *A Brute*

Conscious experience and a limited degree of self-determination are evident at the level of a Brute. A Brute has feelings and, therefore, what happens to it does make a difference; it is aware of itself as a distinct entity and, hence, is a subject and not just an object. Animals for example, experience pleasure and pain and to that extent are involved in good and evil. However, the experience of pleasure and pain does not extend beyond the present and the sensations of the present. Consciousness, therefore, for the Brute is limited to the events of the present moment.

The Brute is capable of some degree of self-determination by virtue of its powers of self-motion and its ability to select among the means of survival provided by the environment.

But it is a determination based on present needs and what is at the moment available in the environment to satisfy those needs. The Brute lives by adjusting inborn needs to momentary sensations.

3. *A Person*

When the category of personality is reached both existence as an object merely and consciousness confined to the present are superseded. Furthermore, whereas the ideal limit for a thing is complete external determination, the ideal limit for a Person is complete self-determination. Thus, self-determination is most fully evident at the level of the Person. The Brute has the ability to select means to a given end, but at the level of the Person alone is the choice of the ends themselves possible. As was shown in the last chapter, this distinction indicates the transition in the levels of reality from mind to spirit.

[8] *Nature of Personality*, p. 16.

A living creature is personal when he is aware of his existence in the present moment, but also remembers his past existence and anticipates his existence in the future. What has happened and what will (or could) happen have value as well as what now is happening.

It is because of this awareness of one's continued identity, of a self who *has* a past (even though in the present) and who *looks forward* to a future (also in the present), that a Person is morally responsible for what he has done and has certain rights. A person is legally defined in terms of his rights, but the fact that a Person has rights clarifies the meaning of Personality and distinguishes it from Thing and Brute. To have rights it is necessary to be a subject and not an object merely, and so a Thing has no rights, per se.

Even a Brute who does feel and hence has a perspective of its own can make no moral claim on us; nor can it be held morally responsible for its actions since its subjectivity is restricted to the sensations of the passing moment. As such the Brute does not, indeed cannot, organize its sensations and direct its action toward a goal it shares in common with Persons. A Brute cannot be a member of society. But a Person can be a member of society precisely because he is aware in the present of his past and possible future action and can direct his actions toward a goal he is consciously seeking and which he shares with other persons. In a word, a Person is purposeful. He is therefore responsible for the purpose chosen and the execution of it.

The distinctions between the three levels of existence may be summarized as follows: the Thing possesses no conscious awareness and is set in motion by forces outside itself; the Brute is conscious and likewise is capable of determining its reactions but only in the modified sense of the present moment; the consciousness of the Person spans past, present, and future, and he can determine his actions at least as much as anything else which acts on him.

C. DIMENSIONS OF HUMAN PERSONALITY

Temple rejects the analysis of man into the three separate faculties of will, emotion, and reason. Man cannot be compartmentalized in this way, for he is a conscious unity of diverse and competing activities. The concrete person is thus redefined as a self-organizing system. However, as we have already noted, the unity of self is only partially complete at any stage of development and is a lifelong endeavor. As noted above, the bases of the self's unity were seen to reside in the identity of the physiological organism, in the unity of consciousness, and in the integrative effect of purposive activity. How this unity may be achieved and the dimensions of the self that compose it need to be carefully examined.

1. Individuality and self-determination

Complete determinism is held to be complete nonsense.[9] To reduce an individual's behavior in the present to behavior in the past or to his present environment is to fail to account for the particular individual himself whose behavior is in question. What was it that determined him – his past behavior or his environment? Furthermore, where is the end of such regression? It would seem to result in an undifferentiated substance which itself cannot account for the differentiated being that is the issue. But to admit differentiation is to reject complete external determination. The extent to which anything can be explained by reference to other things or resists such reductionism indicates its degree of individuality.

Individuality counts for little, we have seen, at the sub-personal level of a Thing or even a Brute. However, individuality gains in importance as organisms become more complex until in civilized man individuality is equal in significance to universal and generic qualities.

There is, therefore, a sense in which freedom may be attributed to anything that deserves the name individual: "We may say that Freedom – underived essence – is a factor in every individual object; but it is a negligible factor in the case of mechanical objects, and by no means so in the case of human beings."[10] Exactly how much any individual contributes, on the basis of his individuality, to the course of things in the universe can never be calculated, though the efficacy of such action cannot be denied.

For Temple, "every individual has in him some underived element which assists in the determination of his conduct; if it were different, he and his conduct would be different. To whatever degree this element affects his conduct, he is morally responsible."[11] Temple calls this formal freedom and views it as a mixed blessing. Freedom in the fullest sense is still to be presented.

Combining formal freedom with the individual's interest in past,

[9] See *Nature, Man and God*, p. 227.

[10] *Nature of Personality*, pp. 18–19. See also *Christus Veritas*, p. 56, and *Nature, Man and God*, p. 230.

[11] *Nature of Personality*, p. 20. See also *Christus Veritas*, p. 57.

present, and future results in the conditions that make possible the distinguishing marks of any person, namely, character and purpose.

The development of personality requires an awareness of one's identity through time. Though all that has happened to anyone cannot at any time be remembered by him, it is essential that some of these past events be remembered as constituting *his* life.

In this remembrance of past events as part of one's life is to be seen the difference between organic growth (e.g., a tree) and personal growth. A man does not merely go through a number of stages; he is always relating the present stage to those previous and to those anticipated in the future. Actual events in the past are related to an ideal future, and conduct in the present is shaped by this comparison. Though Temple does not state explicitly what is meant by character, it would seem to mean the personality as a whole organized in the present in terms of past influences and future aspirations.[12] As such character is constantly in the process of formation throughout one's life.

How is character formed and what role is played by the will in its formation? At the lowest levels of life initiative is based primarily on appetition. Thus in man there are the basic drives for food and drink. Not pleasure is sought, but objects that will satisfy this hunger and thirst. Further, individuality is revealed in one's tastes. What is chosen and liked depends on the individual. Temple affirms unequivocally that though one's taste may be developed, there is no disputing that what is desired at any time is for that person a fact. Initiative, then, is rooted for man in his desires. Hence, the desires constitute the material on which intellect and imagination operate to mold the resulting purpose. Purpose, therefore, consists of desires, imagination, and intellect.

Will as a separate faculty of the self is rejected.[13] However, volition is significant since one's character is expressed in the activity of the will, and when fully developed volition becomes purpose.

The question is not whether man has a will which is free, but as Locke rightly stated: "Is man free?" Furthermore, the issue concerns specific instances of choice.

Choice for Temple is best explained by reference to Aristotle's conception of choice as a uniting of intellectual and appetitive functions. Plato has best expressed the ideal toward which man aspires, namely,

[12] See *Nature, Man and God*, p. 237, and *Christus Veritas*, p. 61.

[13] See *Nature of Personality*, p. 25; also *Mens Creatrix*, p. 167; *Christus Veritas*, pp. 60–61; *Nature, Man and God*, pp. 231–237. It should be noted at this point that most of the material in Lectures III, IV, and V of *Nature of Personality* are incorporated verbatim into *Mens Creatrix*, Chaps. XIII and XIV. See *Mens Creatrix*, p. 167, n. 1.

that the many functions become unified into one. However, the function of reason is not limited to discovering the means to some end that desire has already established, for reason may itself *evaluate* possible ends proposed by both appetite and aspiration and decide which ones relate most harmoniously to those already chosen or anticipated.

To choose in this manner does not necessarily mean that it was a purposive act. Purpose entails more than reflective choice. It means a deliberate act has been performed after consideration of the consequences to which the person gives full consent. A choice might be made to which one does not fully give consent. In fact choice and purpose are sufficiently distinct so that one often chooses what runs counter to his purpose. Such inconsistency in conduct – emphasized by Aristotle – and helplessness in character expression – stressed by St. Paul – warrant further elaboration.

For Temple the mass of chaotic impulses that constitute the natural and "original" state of man cannot be termed either good or bad in themselves.[14] Rather, these interests and impulses are the raw material, so to speak, out of which one forms his virtues or vices. Thus, just as these natural impulses are not to be condemned or denied, neither are they to be accepted as they are. It is only by dint of discipline that they can be molded into anything resembling an ideal human life.[15] Building such a life is further complicated by the fact that left alone no man can bring the chaotic impulses into a meaningful unity.

The first task of character formation is that of unifying these natural impulses. The discipline necessary to integrate the chaotic impulses into a coherent moral life cannot be managed by the individual alone, "for he *is* just the chaos of impulses."[16] Society must educate and discipline the individual. Only when the self is thus trained and his activity unified so that he operates as a single self is he truly free.

A distinction must now be made between what was previously called formal freedom and what is here designated true freedom. Formal freedom signifies that the self contributes something distinctive (i.e., its individuality) to an act of choice. True freedom, however, means that the whole man is acting as one. All the various facets of his self are unified into one coherent totality which as a whole directs the choices

[14] Original sin in this meaning of the term is rejected.

[15] Original sin defined in this way is affirmed, though how man's natural impulses can legitimately be called sin is not clear. See Temple, *Nature of Personality*, p. 29.

[16] *Ibid.*, p. 30.

made by the self. Such freedom is based upon formal freedom but surpasses it. Freedom in this sense means liberation from internal compulsion as well as from external control. Simply to be able to (or have to) say, "I did it and not another" is not necessarily true freedom. This may be bondage to something within the self from which one seeks release.[17] Only when one can say, "I did it and I am glad, and I would gladly do it again," is he truly free?

The key to true freedom, then, is found in an overall purpose which unifies and guides one's interests, passions, and aspirations. Without such a guiding purpose the self finds itself in continual inner conflict with first one part and then another commanding the whole. Such a disintegrated self is exemplified in the most extreme form in Plato's description of the despot in the *Republic*.

Discipline and even external restraint are not, therefore, antithetical to freedom but are necessary for the operation of freedom. To posit as truly free the man whose whole being controls and directs the diverse functions that make up a self is to suggest another ideal limit of personality.[18]

In the perfect personality reason rules, guiding all the diverse impulses and uniting them into one self. Temple exalts the ethically free man whose acts are always in accord with a supreme purpose that motivates his entire life. Such a man alone is truly free.

> When regarded from within, the freedom not to sin is formal only; the self-centred will must choose selfishly.... Freedom of choice is a necessary precondition of morality; but it falls short of true spiritual freedom.
>
> True spiritual freedom would be the state of a man who, knowing an ideal which completely satisfied all aspects of his nature, always in fact conformed to it and could perfectly trust himself so to do.[19]

However, the completely unified person does not exist. Most people find themselves dependent on the environment that surrounds them, discovering that they do not, and cannot, always control the forces within them that vie for supremacy. Hence, the most apparent exercise of will is in restraining certain passions, and one's purpose is too often expressed in such inhibitions rather than in positive acts which concretely embody the ideal.

[17] Temple has in mind here an evil act committed by the person for which he is sorry but from which he sees no escape in the future. In this way he interprets St. Paul's confession: Rom. 7:24 (R. S. V.) See *Nature of Personality*, p. 31; *Mens Creatrix*, p. 170; *Nature, Man and God*, p. 240.

[18] See Temple, *Nature of Personality*, p. 32.

[19] Temple, *Nature, Man and God*, p. 242. The relevance of Temple's conception of freedom for the moral dilemma of man is stated below; see Chapter 12.

Now it is clear that freedom when conceived as good must be equated with self-control. This freedom is not gained except by struggle and even then not by the individual alone. An external power must operate on and with him if he is to become fully free. In this way can be seen the significance and necessity of social groups (e.g., family, school, state) for the development of human personality, and indeed, the social dimension of personality itself.

2. *Society and the need for fellowship*

In order to grasp the role which society necessarily plays in the development of human personality we must be aware of the predicament in which man finds himself when he relies solely on his own powers. It is in this context that the doctrine of original sin can be profitably examined for what light it sheds on the nature of man.

The formulation of the doctrine which makes all mankind *guilty* because Adam's sin has corrupted man's nature is dismissed as nonsense. Even if man's nature is corrupted, all that this proves is that he is evil by nature. By this very fact, then he cannot also be guilty of the evil. More important, however, the doctrine suggests that one is not morally good by nature. Further, if he is to become morally good, he must work at molding the diverse impulses that have been inherited into something distinctly human. In place of Adam's fall may be put man's long evolutionary descent originating in non-human ancestors, and the evil of society into which each generation is born. To assert these modern versions is not, however, to remove the insight contained in the doctrine of original sin that man needs to recognize how far from being good he is by natural inclination, and that alone he cannot achieve a new nature.

It is necessary to point out that Temple has failed to define carefully his terms. However, in the context what seems to be meant is that man does not begin with a unity of purpose, but is composed of conflicting impulses from within and is confronted by, at least partial, social disintegration from without. Hence, man cannot hope to achieve *any* goal without first being organized into some unity, and he cannot will his own unity.

The self cannot attain a unity of impulse alone any more than the self can survive alone. Persons need the fellowship of other persons if each is to attain the full stature of personal existence. External restraint is not antithetical to the achievement of self-unity any more than it is antithetical to true freedom. The order and restraint provided by society are integral to the development of human personality.

This is not to suggest that man's desires are naturally social; many are to the detriment of society. Nonetheless, man does possess a social instinct exemplified in his strong desire for social approval. To satisfy the desire to be approved by one's fellows necessitates acting in accord with the welfare of society.

The essentially social nature of personality is thereby revealed. To be cut off from society means to that extent man cannot become human. "Personality is inherently social; only in social groupings can it mature, or indeed fully exist."[20] Both the ideals and temptations that man possesses, as well as the worth attributed to human personality, are derived from the relation a man has to the society of which he is a member and to the human race itself. There is no doubt that other human beings play the most significant part in the development of one's personality.

> From his parents he derives the body, which is the physical basis of his being; from his family – its traditions, outlook, circumstances, hopes, fears – he derives the main direction of the impetus which carries him out into life; from his country ... he receives the influences which either modify or stereotype that direction. His whole being is a condensation of society. He *is* his fellow-men's experience focussed in a new centre.[21]

It is not clear whether Temple means that personality in the sense of a self with some degree of unity and purpose cannot exist apart from society, or that a certain type of personal unity can only mature in society. The distinction involved here is blurred by Temple. It is one thing to affirm that a certain type of personality (e.g., as found in a civilized society) can only develop in human social groups; it is quite another thing to claim that an individual could never attain any self-unity apart from human society. An ideal conception of personality is operating in Temple's thinking as a standard of judgment without being made explicit.

3. *Fulfillment and the need for service*

In order to understand the final dimension of personality as expressed by Temple it is necessary to combine Temple's emphasis on personal

[20] "What Christians Stand for in the Secular World," reprinted in *Religious Experience* ..., p. 246. See also *Christianity in Thought and Practice*, pp. 59–60. The significance of this view of man for Temple's theory of the origin of society is expounded in Chapter 13.

[21] Temple, *Christus Veritas*, p. 71.

consciousness with his emphasis on the social dimension of personality. The Person, we have seen, moves beyond both the Thing and the Brute by his awareness of past and future as well as the present. However, the distinctive feature of personality in terms of its relation to time is that the future holds the greatest significance. The more fully developed personality becomes, the greater is the role played by the future, and the less important are past and present.

The reason for this priority of the future over past and present for personality is that the primary characteristic of personality is purpose. Though the past serves as the basis for the purposes envisaged and provides the initiative to realize them, it is not to the past that one looks for their realization but to the future. What is good in the past acts as inspiration and guide for the future (e.g., heritage of a nation). The value of the past in the present is precisely in terms of what it enables one to achieve in the future.

Even past evil finds its meaning and value (as well as its resolution) in the future. What has occurred is finished and in this sense cannot be altered. But what can happen is that the value attached to a particular event in the past may be significantly altered in the future.[22] The future offers hope at least. The more complete one's personality is, the more fully purposive he is; hence the more significant is the future and the less interesting is the past.

Recognizing that purpose is the distinguishing characteristic of personality and that in order to fulfill this purpose the individual is directed beyond himself to the good of society, it is necessary to examine how he goes about discovering this good. The clue is to be found in Temple's understanding of man as by nature social. Furthermore, since man can only develop his humanity by means of the society of which he is a member, each person will make his own contribution to the whole group as he strives to realize his place in society. In a passage reminiscent of both Bradley and Royce, Temple affirms:

> Each man is a unique and irreplaceable member of the system with his own bit of the value of things to realise; and in developing his moral faculties, his devotion to the public good, he will reach the right value-judgments.[23]

Thus, though a man cannot be criticized for failing to adopt or to realize a set of values affirmed by another, he can be judged by whether

[22] The significance of this issue for an interpretation of the historical process is developed in Chapter 14.

[23] *Nature of Personality*, pp. 72–73. See F. H. Bradley, *Ethical Studies* (New York: The Liberal Arts Press, Inc., 1951), p. 113, and Josiah Royce, *The World and the Individual* (New York: The Macmillan Company, 1899–1901), II, 286.

or not he achieves the values peculiar to him and to his membership in society.[24]

Employing his own ideal conception of the moral man, Temple affirms that man is moral when he has developed character which in all its expressions seeks the good of others. The spirit of service to others is the spirit of life itself:

> Biology, Ethics, Politics, all teach the same lesson; a species has significance through its assistance in the evolutionary process; moral advance means widening the boundaries of the sphere of our service till all humanity is included; political progress is the growth of insistence on the duty of each to serve all.[25]

To serve others is to seek their welfare, but what is their welfare? What is good for others and for society? It is now clear that the highest good for an individual is to love others and help them realize their good, but to do this he must know what their good is. Kant's view that each person should seek his own perfection and the happiness of others is a tempting answer.[26] However, if one is commanded to love and, hence, is to make the expression of love to others the aim of life, then in loving the goal is to enable others also to love and be loving. In this sense the will that wills itself is the good will, for it wills its universalization. For Temple, then:

> Love is the supreme goal of personality; at that we aim for ourselves; and having acquired it we seek to pass it on to others. If we want to find the right thing to do, we must ask what will do most to increase the volume of love. Love alone has absolute moral value.[27]

Human personality is confronted with a dilemma at this point. It is by loving that personality is fully realized; but since love means forgetting one's self, it is impossible for anyone to acquire it by his own effort. To seek self-forgetfulness as a good for the self is a contradiction and thus cannot be reached. To attain it would mean to destroy the self in the very attainment.

It should be asked at this point whether Temple has forgotten that one can love another only by being the best self he can and by knowing

[24] See Temple, *Kingdom of God*, pp. 46–47.

[25] Temple, "The Divinity of Christ," in *Foundations* ..., p. 256. A complete analysis of Temple's ethical theory is presented in Chapters 11 and 12.

[26] See Temple, *Nature of Personality*, p. 75. It should be noted, however, that Kant distinguishes between the supreme good (deserving happiness by virtuous living) and the complete good (enjoying happiness). The highest good for any individual would include both; see Immanuel Kant, *Critique of Practical Reason and Other Writings in Moral Philosophy*, trans. and ed. with introduction by Lewis White Beck (Chicago: The University of Chicago Press, 1949), pp. 214–215.

[27] Temple, *Nature of Personality*, p. 76.

the good of another? Otherwise, he would have nothing of value to contribute. Temple's own stress on character seems to be violated.[28] Furthermore, only an abstract conception of the self makes it impossible for one to forget oneself in an act of loving.

However, Temple insists that love cannot be attained merely by seeking it; it must be stimulated by the love of another whose acts of love elicit the response of love. "Love can only be produced in us by the love or need of another calling out our love ... Still the ideal of life is universal love."[29] To attain a state of universal love would require a community in which individuality is transformed into the common consciousness of a universal being. It is not enough, therefore, to claim that the self is realized through self-sacrifice for "self-sacrifice is self-realisation."[30] Temple seems to have forgotten his own emphasis on the uniqueness and primacy of individuality.[31]

D. THE IDEAL OF PERSONALITY

The analysis of Temple's conception of human personality developed thus far has ranged over a wide variety of subjects, some of which will be developed more fully in the succeeding chapters. However, it will facilitate a more adequate analysis of the role personality plays in Temple's Christian philosophy if the chief characteristics of human personality noted throughout the present chapter and the previous chapter, are summarized at this point. Also, it is important to present the conclusions Temple reaches regarding the limitations of human personality when compared with what he takes to be the ideal personality.

1. Chief characteristics of human personality: Purpose, fellowship and love[32]

The primary characteristic of human personality is purpose. This fact has been made evident at several places in the preceding discussion.

[28] See Bradley, *Appearance and Reality* (Oxford: The Clarendon Press, 1930) pp. 368–369, 375.

[29] Temple, *Nature of Personality*, p. 76. Such a response toward the world and persons is the *I-Thou* attitude of which Martin Buber speaks. For Buber no one enters into a relation merely by seeking it. It is a meeting but one into which each person must step by choice. One is chosen and yet he chooses. See Buber, *I and Thou.*

[30] Temple, *Nature of Personality*, p. 77.

[31] See *Ibid.*, p. 58.

[32] Professor Joseph Fletcher is to be credited with suggesting these three characteristics as summing up Temple's view of personality. See *William Temple*, p. 53.

In the emergence of the various levels of existence, the stage of Mind is reached when the organism itself initiates action by choosing among alternative means to a desired end. When Spirit arises, however, a new initiative is possible in the choice that is made among available ends to be sought. Herein resides the distinctive element in personality. Furthermore, the person is not restricted to ends presently available in experience. As one who is aware of his continued existence in a way not possible to the Thing or the Brute, the person can, through memory of the past and anticipation of the future, identify himself with ideal goals. Thus, the future takes on greater significance for the person than for other living creatures. What has occurred in the past can be utilized in the present for the sake of an end envisaged in the future.

The same is true in regard to the unity and identity of the self. As a physical organism man's body persists through temporal sequences, and by means of memory one is linked in the consciousness of the present with his experiences in the past. However, full psychical unity is attained only when the competing impulses of conscious experience are integrated and directed toward the realisation of an end to which the total self is committed. True freedom also is revealed in the purposive action of the person whose every choice reflects the goal toward which he is striving. The meaning of person is to be viewed in this context: "A 'Person' ... is a self-conscious and self-determining system of experience, and human persons are in process of achieving the complete unification of the experience which constitutes them."[33] Personal action, therefore, is purposeful action in which the total conscious life of the self is organized so as to achieve some end. In such a case the body is the medium through which one's purpose is expressed in the physical world. The personal level of existence is attained, then, to the extent that one's total being, mind and body, is unified around some end apprehended as good.

However, this unity cannot be attained by the self alone, just as the self cannot exist by himself. Persons need the fellowship of other persons if each is to attain the full stature of personal existence.

The second characteristic of human personality is fellowship. To be a person is to be a unified self always choosing in accord with one's purpose. However, the self begins life disorganized and dependent on others for survival. What regularity his life exhibits is largely due to the order imposed by others. Such external restraint is absolutely es-

[33] Temple, *Christus Veritas*, p. 68.

sential if the individual is to achieve some measure of self-unity and relative independence. The social aspect of personality must not be minimized. "Personality only comes to itself, only becomes what it is capable of being, through its development in the reciprocal relationships of society ... Personality is always a social product."[34]

The individual needs society for still another reason. The purpose which each one requires to unify his various tendencies must be able to encompass his total nature. One aspect of that nature is the desire for the approval of others and the need to be joined in fellowship with them. Hence, only a purpose common to the interests and welfare of all mankind is adequate to satisfy the individual person and to unite persons together in a bond of universal fellowship.

Fulfillment of the self is possible only in and through service to others. To discover one's own good he must also discern the good of others and devote himself to realizing it. But what is the good that one should seek to realize both for himself and for others? What is the good of society? In attempting to answer these questions the third dimension of personality becomes evident.

The third characteristic of human personality is love. According to Temple, love for another always takes two forms: "Concern for his welfare with desire to serve it, and insight into his needs so that I may judge wherein his welfare truly consists."[35]

The unity which the self seeks and the purpose which supplies the impetus and goal by which integration of the impulses is attained are now seen to reside in a community of persons bound together by love. In the expression of love for others the highest manifestation of personality is attained. To realize oneself means to sacrifice self in service to others.

Purpose, fellowship, and love constitute the chief characteristics of human personality for Temple. A person is one whose unity resides in the purpose he has to promote universal love. However, in the course of the analysis of human personality certain deficiences have become evident. It is worthwhile to take stock of them at this point, making explicit the limitations involved, and noting what type of being would be required to satisfy the ideal of personality.

[34] Temple, *Christianity in Thought and Practice*, pp. 59–60.
[35] *Ibid.*, p. 59.

2. *Divine Personality as the completion of human aspiration*

A Thing, it has already been noted, is not conscious and a Brute is only conscious of the present; whereas a Person is a conscious unity encompassing past, present, and future. Nonetheless, the Person is plagued by a limited vision intellectually and emotionally. The ideal of a Person whose concerns are those of all mankind is never attained. The interests of an individual arbitrarily stop short of this ideal.

The same is the case in regard to human freedom. The completely external determination (for practical purposes, at least) of a Thing is replaced by the determination of a person rooted in his individuality coupled with external forces. But this too falls short of the ideal of full self-determination. What Temple fails to consider, however, is whether it is the *ideal* that is faulty. Could any person be uninfluenced by other persons and hence completely self-determined?

It was noted that insofar as a person is guided by a purpose he operates as a unified self, but all impulses are never totally integrated. The ideal of a self directed entirely by a single dominating purpose remains unrealized.

Furthermore, Temple argues, personality entails subjecting one's will to the good of the human race without ever knowing for certain what the good is or being able fully to submit to it. Finally, the goal of personality has been found to be love. But to love another necessitates forgetting one's self and this the self cannot do alone. To fulfill itself demands moving beyond the self in a way which is not possible on the human level.

Temple concludes that only in Divine Personality are all of these requirements of personality fully manifested. Human personality is, and must always be, imperfect and incomplete. The ideal noted in each instance if ever fulfilled would extend beyond the human domain to a Supreme Being, namely God. Only in God is the fully developed personality to be found. Concerning such a Being, Temple states:

> At the end of the scale most remote from the Thing we have the conception of a spiritual Being to whom all time has a value, and to whom therefore, in some sense, all time is present, but for whom the future is always the governing element in time; a Being determined by Himself alone and in His action always guided by His whole Purpose, never by any single impulse or caprice; a Being moreover whose Purpose is absolutely self-less – a Being who realises Himself in spending Himself for others. But this Being is the God of Christian Theology. If, then, there is such a Being, He is the true norm and type of Personality.[36]

[36] *Nature of Personality*, pp. 78–79.

Temple's conception of Divine Personality is expanded in the next chapter. However, some comments are in order at this stage of the investigation in regard to Temple's conception of the ideal Personality. It is important to inquire whether the ideal which Temple has proposed is properly conceived in each instance. That is, do the empirical facts of personality justify the ideal conception suggested? How does one get from what is experienced about personality to the ideal conception of what a person ought to be, from human personality with its limitations to Divine Personality minus such limitations? Rather than starting with the most ideal conception of personality conceivable (the ontological approach), should not one ask what further extension of personality is necessary to account for what is experienced? Or, if one begins with an ideal conception of personality, then one should be willing to modify the ideal as the facts of experience demand.

Temple's conception of the emergence of human personality in the World-Process and the distinguishing characteristics of personality, especially in comparison with sub-personal levels of existence, have now been presented. But human personality has been shown to be incomplete apart from the Divine Personality. What, then, is the character of Divine Personality?

CHAPTER 8

DIVINE PERSONALITY

An attempt to find a self-explanatory principle capable of accounting for the universe and man as a part of it led to the hypothesis of a personal God whose will for good provides the ground and goal of all that is. But what is the relation of the living God to the World-Process? Furthermore, since the explanatory principle of the universe is based upon the analogy of human personality as the highest level of reality known to man, it is essential that the distinctive characteristics of Divine Personality be made as clear as is humanly possible.

A. GOD'S RELATION TO THE WORLD

1. God as creator

According to Temple the world owes its existence, both its origin and continuance, to the Divine Will, and the world is the expression of His will. This is the meaning of the doctrine of creation. It does not mean that God existed alone and then at some time initiated the creation of the world. There seems no reason to suppose that the world had a beginning, and certainly the view that God at some time had no relations at all to anything other than Himself is meaningless for man.[1]

What is denied by the doctrine of creation is a conception of the world as the necessary emanation from the Divine Being. Also rejected is the view that simply correlates God and the world, each depending on the other for existence. What is claimed instead is that the world is sustained by the will of God, which means that the world is dependent upon God, but God is not dependent in the same way upon the world.

[1] See Temple, *Nature, Man and God*, p. 301, and *Nature of Personality*, p. 87.

If the world is destroyed, God will remain and be capable of creating another world. To be a person means to express oneself, but what is expressed is not equal to the expressor; therefore the world remains effect, and God the cause. However, since God is personal, He desires other persons for fellowship. Hence, in full expression of the character of God in this sense, He needs the world and persons in the world since the World-Process is the medium for God's personal actions.[2] The creator is related to His creation by being both immanent in the process and also transcending it. Such a conception of God is traditional Christian doctrine, but the content Temple gives to these terms introduces some novel elements.

2. *God as an immanent principle of variability*

When God is referred to as immanent, what is commonly meant is that He sustains the world according to certain prescribed principles or laws; whereas God as transcendent is held to possess a reserve of energy which can be utilized on special occasions to intervene in the orderly process. Accordingly, it is often stated that what is immanent in the process is a principle, both a constant principle of action and a principle of constant action. One speaks of a principle as being immanent in a certain action when that action conforms to the principle. Temple employs the following illustration:

> So Nationalism is a principle to which certain policies and politicians conform; it explains their particular methods and actions. It is other than these, but it has no existence apart from these. In other words it is distinguishable, but not separable, from them.[3]

The principle is not identical with the actions; but apart from them it has no objective reality.

If God is personal, then such a view of immanence is inadequate, Temple contends, because personality cannot be confined to this rigorous mechanistic conception. The true immanence of a person discloses itself only in his present conduct. Thus, a man's personality cannot be truly seen in a record of his past conduct; it can be inferred, but it is in the adjustment that the personality makes to present circumstances that most correctly reveals the immanence of the person. So too with God; as an immanent principle His will determines

[2] However, Temple is neither entirely clear nor consistent at this point as is evident in the discussion of the relation of the Eternal to the temporal; see below, Chapters 15 and 20.
[3] Temple, *Nature, Man and God*, p. 283.

at every moment the various modes of activity of each part of the World-Process. Therefore, personality (both human and divine) when immanent exists as a principle of variability, that is, a principle capable of adjustment to the circumstances of the environment. It is this capacity for making adjustments according to circumstances that the older view of immanence inadequately accounted for by positing unutilized energy. The difficulty is in employing mechanistic categories when only personal ones are appropriate. Temple concludes: "*What a true doctrine of divine transcendence will assert is not a reservoir of normally unutilised energy, but a volitional as contrasted with a mechanical direction of the energy utilised.*"[4] God is immanent in the world in that the entire universe is determined by Him according to His purpose, and the constancy of the process exists because it serves His purpose so to order the world. This means that any particular event might be altered, from the standpoint of human expectancy based on past events, if to do so would be more in accord with the purpose of God.

An intelligible basis for so-called miracles is provided on this theory. Miracles are no more the activity of God than any other events, since all events are directly the result of His will. However, while all events are equally the result of God's activity in the world, not all events equally reveal God's nature. Just as the character of a human person is best known in moments of crisis when courageous or cowardly acts may be elicited, so too the personality of God may be more adequately revealed in certain events than others. God may even choose, when conditions are appropriate, to submit Himself to finite limitations so as to reveal concretely and definitively His character.

> In other words, if the immanent principle is personal, we must not only see the whole universe as the expression and utterance of His activity, but must expect to find in its course special characteristic and revealing acts, which are no more truly His than the rest, but do more fully express Him than the rest.[5]

However, there is nothing capricious or chaotic about the ordering of the universe. Events can be depended on to occur in causal sequence, but the point is, the regularity is not due to the fact that the universe is mechanically determined; it is due to the fact that it is the expression of a personal Being. The uniformity of nature is rooted in the constancy of purpose that characterizes personality, which is not rigid conformity but a constancy of intent, varying its expression when circumstances

[4] *Ibid.*, p. 284.
[5] *Ibid.*, pp. 296–297.

warrant it. Still more fundamental for Temple in assuring activity which is constant with variations according to "sufficient reason," is that God is transcendent and not only immanent in the process.

3. *God as the transcendent self-identical person*

Behind the immanent principle of variability in the World-Process exists the personality of God Himself. Thus, as a personal being God not only is immanent in the world but also transcendent to the world, just as a man is expressed in his conduct but is always more than his conduct. Furthermore, though a person may vary his specific acts depending on the circumstances in a way which will best fulfill his purpose while the purpose itself remains unchanged, so too with God; as an immanent principle God is variable, but as a transcendent Deity He is changeless. Such a view of the transcendent God would seem to contradict Temple's view of creation. Also, it should be noted that human purposes often are modified as a result of circumstances and not merely the means to the ends sought. To be consistent a more radical distinction between God as immanent and God as transcendent would seem to be required. Instead, Temple contends that it is the transcendent God who is immanent in the world, and it is the immanent person who also transcends the world.

God, then, is at work in the natural order as a living person. He expresses a constancy of action by means of variations appropriate to the specific occasion; these variations do not result in an incoherent universe because they are grounded in the identity of the person who transcends particular actions. Temple is not clear as to whether this identity itself endures through time and hence is dynamic or whether it is static. What does become increasingly evident is the emergence of a soul-substance view of unity and identity of the personality of God, though Temple has explicitly rejected such a view on the human level.[6]

According to Temple the immanent person does not operate apart from the transcendent God, so that everything expresses the purpose of the transcendent God. But what also needs to be clarified is whether the transcendent God can operate independent of the immanent person. Man's knowledge of the transcendent God is held to depend on the activity of the immanent person, for God is known only as He reveals

[6] See above, Chapter 7.

Himself. The converse is also true: God is what He is revealed to be; that is, God is only known by His actions, but by knowing God's actions man knows God directly, not inferentially. The meaning of, and justification for, revelation as interpreted by Temple demands fuller examination.

4. God's revelation of Himself

To explain the universe by recourse to the power and love of a personal Being means that the entire universe is the expression of Him. But, if God is personal, it is not only possible but probable that certain acts will reveal His character more fully than others. Special revelatory acts can, then, be expected; and if any acts can substantiate their claim to be the purposive self-revelation of God, then they would provide evidence of the character of God that no evidence to the contrary could refute. At the same time, special revelatory acts are possible only if all events reveal God. If any events are an intrusion into orderly process that is not itself the expression of God, then such intrusion renders the world incoherent. "*But if all existence is a revelation of God, as it must be if He is the ground of its existence, and if the God thus revealed is personal, then there is more ground in reason for expecting particular revelations than for denying them.*"[7]

The forms that special revelations of God have supposedly taken are varied. Confining himself to the Christian tradition, Temple still encounters significant differences. The Bible is held to be the revelation of God, but how is God revealed in the Bible? Temple rejects the traditional interpretation, which holds that the Bible has been divinely recorded and is infallible, because it contradicts man's freedom and destroys the possibility of spiritual development. The natural faculties of man can be enlightened but not superseded. Therefore, the Bible is not itself the revelation of God; the Bible is the record of events which are a unique revelation of God.

It is necessary to reconceive the meaning of revelation. Insofar as God is the source and sustainer of all that is, then the process is guided by God. Man as occurring within the process and as interacting with it becomes aware of himself and the world. Furthermore, as a created Being, man is also under the guidance of God. When the process guided by God and man also guided by God interact, revelation occurs.

[7] Temple, *Nature, Man and God*, p. 307.

Revelation requires, then, the occurrence of special events in the world (objective factor) and the appreciation of these events in the world (subjective factor). The essence of revelation is the intercourse of mind with event and not some propositional formulation of the experience itself; there are no revealed truths, but rather there are truths of revelation. The locus of revelation is in the historical event and is hence objective, but this event needs to be apprehended by one able to appreciate it if the revelation is to be effective. Like all value experience, revelation is an objective occurrence, subjectively conditioned. One's religious traditions influence the interpretation rendered any event, but the impact of the experience may lead to a revision or rejection of the tradition.

Revelation occurs primarily through events and to minds able to apprehend it, though direct revelation by God to an individual also takes place. Thus, Temple holds an inspirational and not an intellectualistic view of revelation. But in terms of his epistemology man directly interacts with his environment; and when this environment is God, then man knows God Himself. The content of revelation, therefore, is not doctrines about God, but is God Himself. What man encounters in a specific revelation *"is not truth concerning God but the Living God Himself."*[8] The meaning of religious faith for Temple is now apparent; it is not believing that certain doctrines are true, but it consists in one's own intimate fellowship with God.

Such is Temple's formulation of his position. However, to refer to truths of revelation rather than revealed truths is misleading in light of what is affirmed about the experience of revelation. Thus, to claim that one encounters God Himself in revelation is itself an interpretative statement of the experience held to be revelatory. Hence, though the distinction Temple makes would seem to be a significant one by ruling out revealed truths, its effectiveness is greatly reduced at this very crucial point. So long as one knows that he has met "the living God" in an experience he has had, then at least that truth has been revealed. This raises the important question of how revelation is authenticated?

Since Temple rejects miracle as traditionally conceived, he cannot appeal to a supposed miraculous event to authenticate God's activity. Vindication of a special revelation is rather to be found through an inner assurance arising from a felt power of activity (especially a power of self-forgetfulness) not previously available. When one sees

[8] *Ibid.*, p. 322.

mercy combined with power, there is God; also, all of life is illumined by what is revealed. The marks of revelation may now be summarized:

> A union of holiness and power, before which our spirits bow in awe, and which authenticates itself by continuous developments to some focal point in which all preparatory revelation finds fulfilment, and from which illumination radiates into every department of life and being.[9]

Finally, the revelation of a personal God to persons could be complete only if God Himself chose to take on the limitations of human personality. Such a personal self-disclosure lies beyond the purview of philosophy to discover or to justify. Nonetheless, that God should become man has been shown to be what morality, society, and, indeed, all of history require to make human life and history truly meaningful and truly worthy. That Christ is God is the faith of Christians. At the same time the revelation of God in Christ satisfies man's desire for meaning and his need for guidance; but such faith is justified only by making the experiment itself.

For Temple, therefore, Christ provides a dramatic and concrete demonstration of Divine Personality toward which the World-Process points. It is necessary that an examination of Divine Personality be made, and for Temple this is best accomplished in terms of the Christian doctrine of the trinity.

B. DIVINE PERSONALITY: A TRIUNE GOD

The discussion of human personality in the previous chapter concludes with an analysis of the limitations of human personality and an affirmation that only in God is personality fully developed. Also, in noting the distinctions among thing, brute, and person an ideal of personality was developed whose consciousness encompasses all of time; who is concerned with all of mankind; who is completely self-determined; who is totally unified under the guidance of a universal purpose; finally, whose will is directed to the expression of love and the development of a fellowship of love among men. Human personality falls short of such an ideal in each instance. A conception of Divine Personality which satisfies the ideal in each case is essential to meet the requirements. However, the conception of the Ideal Personality poses problems which need to be examined before a full exposition of the nature of Divine Personality can be presented.

[9] *Ibid.*, pp. 324–325.

1. Problems posed by the Ideal Personality

The first problem posed by a conception of the Ideal Personality is how such a Personality can both know everything that occurs in the world and also sacrifice Himself for the world through acts of love. It would seem that He must both know the victory of good over evil in the world and experience the suffering necessary to achieve this victory. Temple states the problem in his own words as follows:

> If God is to hold the world together in His Purpose, its whole history must proceed from Him, and be known to Him. But if He is to be the explanation and unifying principle not only of some world but of the world we know, with men and women in it, He must be perfectly loving and must reveal His love in real sacrifice that He may win the hearts and possess the wills of those men and women, so drawing them into the unity of His Purpose. Only so moreover can He fulfil the ideal of Personality.[10]

That is, a conception of God must be formulated which makes possible both actual knowledge of victory over the good and at the same time the experience of sacrifice and suffering in gaining this victory. But these two types of experience are incompatible in human experience.

Historically, it was this problem that led to the formulation of the trinitarian conception of Divine Personality. However, the doctrine of the trinity is not to be viewed merely as the solution to a problem; for primarily it represents a summary of man's experience in the varied relationships shared with God. Some of the difficulty of this problem can be removed by clarifying the meaning of trinity. Temple rejects the view of the trinity which interprets it as three individuals and hence three centers of consciousness. He does not employ the term "personality" in the same way that "person" is used in the trinitarian formula, "three persons in one God."[11] The differences among the persons of the trinity are not the same as those which separate individual minds in human experience, but rather the differences reside in the distinctive qualities of each. However, even this sort of unity-in-diversity is not combined in one consciousness in human experience. Thus, the problem of God's knowledge and experience of suffering is not removed; and from the standpoint of the trinity this is the problem of the relation of the Father to the Son. Another difficulty arises in the relation of the Father to the Holy Spirit. Philosophically conceived, it is the problem of how God can know

[10] Temple, *Nature of Personality*, pp. 99–100.
[11] See *ibid.*, pp. 101–102.

everything and yet the process of the world be real. It would seem that either everything is predetermined, in which case there is no real novelty; or else if there is novelty, then God is not omniscient.

Temple finds the clue to the resolution of this difficulty in the analogy of the artist who realizes his vision in the very process of creating it. Present experience is at once affected by both the past and the future. In this sense novelty is part of the creative experience itself. In regard to history this means that it can be understood only in relation to eternity, but that likewise eternity requires history for its content.[12] Temple affirms both that there is novelty in the world and that God is omniscient. Hence, again two types of experiences are combined within the Divine Personality which on the human level are incompatible. What this seems to prove to Temple is that analogies of human personality are not wholly adequate to understand Divine Personality; what is not considered is whether his ideal of personality is adequate and warrants reexamination as a result of such incompatible experiences.

The relation of the Son to the Spirit still needs to be conceived, and for Temple the distinction here is between the method for saving the world (Son) and the power by which the method is effected (Holy Spirit). In the attempt to solve these issues a positive interpretation of the trinitarian view of God becomes evident.

2. *The trinity as the simultaneous activity of God*

In terms of the logical order of the trinity God as Father, the ground of all that is, has priority; dependent upon Him is God as Son, expressed as the wisdom (logos) creating and governing the universe; finally, dependent upon both Father and Son is God as Holy Spirit, expressed as activity by means of which the purpose of God (as Father) is realized according to His wisdom (as Son). In man's experience, however, this order is reversed. It is the activity of God's power in the world which is discovered first and which leads to an understanding of the purpose guiding and sustaining the activity of God in the world.

The clue to understanding the nature of the power and activity of God operating in the world is provided, as already noted, by the Incarnation. Inasmuch as creation is the expression of God's love

[12] See *Christus Veritas*, pp. 89–90, 282; also below, Chapter 15.

toward the end of establishing a fellowship of loving persons, then God's activity in the world is such as to win men's love and thus in its supreme manifestation is an act of sacrificial love. In this way the meaning which the trinitarian view of God seeks to convey is made explicit:

We have these three moments: God creating the world; God appearing in the form of the thing created that He may manifest to the created beings that Method of Sacrifice which is the Divine Wisdom; God thereby winning from the created spirits that love for the sake of which they were created. Creation, Redemption, Sanctification, constitute the experience from which the doctrine of the Trinity arises.[13]

God Himself is encountered in each of these experiences. It is God who creates, God who redeems, and God who sanctifies. There are not, then, three centers of consciousness of God but a "triplex consciousness."[14] The distinction in each case is inferred by man from the different experiences he has with the one God. Temple turns to the theater for an analogy in human experience of this triplicity of consciousness. When watching a familiar play, one shares in the emotions of the actors as the play proceeds but also knows the import of their actions in light of the whole plot which as characters the actors do not know.

Applying Occam's razor to the interpretation of the trinity as a society of beings united in love, Temple concludes that it multiplies entities needlessly. Furthermore, the Son cannot be separated from the Father and the world as if He were a conscious being distinct from them since to do so is to assert tritheism, not trinitarianism. The crux of the matter for Temple is that the complexity of God's personality, uniting as it does activities and relations far exceeding what is possible for human personality, finds its unity, even as is the case with man, in the purpose which controls, unifies, and directs the personality as a whole. Such a view of God would seem to be a variation of the modal theory of the trinity, the distinctive element being that God Himself is met in each of the three expressions. However, distinguishing his view from the modalism of Sabellius which affirms that the trinity refers not to distinct persons but to the three modes by which God manifests Himself, Temple conceived of God as operative at once in all three activities. The trinity is not three successive modes by which God operates; rather it represents the simultaneous activity of God. All of God acts in each instance.[15]

[13] Temple, *Nature of Personality*, p. 111.
[14] See *ibid.*, p. 112.
[15] See *ibid.*, pp. 115–116. This point is also made explicit in Temple's analysis of revelation; see *Nature, Man and God*, p. 322, and above.

This raises again the problem of how the eternal God can operate in the temporal order as Incarnate Son and Holy Spirit without either reducing history to an illusion or making eternity temporal. In regard to the Incarnation Temple does not accept the two-nature theory of Jesus in which human and divine exist together as two centers of consciousness. Also discarded is the view which proposes that Jesus' conscious self is human and his subconscious is divine. The formula Temple proposes is as follows: "The Form of His consciousness is Human, the content is Divine."[16] Jesus Christ is truly human, but it is as God living a human life. This relation of Christ to God may be expressed in terms of a unity of will so long as by will, in this case, is meant the total personality organized for action. Perhaps the best way of expressing the relation is to state "that in Christ God and Man are personally one; the Person of the Man Christ Jesus is God the Son."[17] Hence, in Jesus Christ is expressed the fulfillment of the levels of reality which the process has disclosed, revealing both what God is like and what man should be like. In Christ real humanity is focussed so that "all the significance and destiny of the human race is summed up in Him."[18]

There is also the question of what difference Jesus' earthly life had upon the Eternal God? God was always what Jesus revealed Him to be from the standpoint of eternity; but, temporally viewed, God's nature is enriched by the concrete experience of sacrificial love. Thus, Temple claims that the Incarnation "does not make Him different but it does not leave Him unaffected."[19] What Temple seems to be suggesting is that what was actual for God as Eternal Being became in Christ temporally actual for both God and man. The difficulty of comprehending such a view for man is readily admitted by Temple, but it is his contention that the difficulty occurs where it is to be expected for human minds striving to apprehend the Divine Personality. That man will always have difficulty trying to comprehend the ultimate principle of explanation is granted; but when contradictions arise, then a revision of the interpretation rendered would seem in order. For example, if God Himself is in Christ as Temple contends, then God Himself is affected by what happened historically to Jesus or else language becomes meaningless. Temple wants God to be self-sufficient and yet

[16] Temple, *Nature of Personality*, p. 116, n. 1. Temple presents a brief summary of the history of the controversy in *Foundations*, pp. 223–242, and *Christus Veritas*, pp. 125–138.

[17] *Christus Veritas*, p. 149.

[18] *Ibid.*, p. 153.

[19] *Ibid.*, p. 279.

directly active in a real process in which novel elements occur. How both can be maintained is far from clear.[20]

It is the trinity, then, which provides the answer to the perplexing problem of permanence and change which the universe exhibits. Change is observed everywhere, and in this process time is significant. But what explains this process cannot itself change and must, therefore, be timeless. The world as change involving temporal sequence is real, but what accounts for this must itself be an unchanging principle distinct from change and time though explaining them as experienced and not as illusory. The activity of God in creating the world and providing the means for saving it, and thereby fulfilling His purpose, occurs in the time process, but the trinitarian formula which renders this process meaningful is changeless.[21] Here Temple, apparently unwittingly, falls back upon a soul-substance view of Divine Personality though he has rejected such a view of the unity and identity of human personality.

The philosophy of the Incarnation offers the only adequate metaphysics just as the doctrine of the trinity offers the only adequate formula for interpreting the history of the universe. Personality, then, finds its fullest meaning and expression in the power which guides the universe according to loving purpose. Such a being supplies the meaning of Divine Personality. Because of the complexity and perfection of God, He is best conceived as personal, though not as a person.[22] If the term person be employed, then such a Being can be understood only in the analogy of a unity which for man would be the activities of three persons; and it is toward an understanding of these activities that the doctrine of the trinity is directed. God is a threefold personality.[23]

Personality arising in the World-Process suggests an ideal of personality not bound by the limitations of human personality. The God revealed by Christ is, for Temple, the embodiment of that ideal; hence the God of the Christian faith is the perfect Person. But does such a being exist? What empirical justification can be offered for believing in a Divine Personality whose purposive will creates and sustains the World-Process? In a word, what kind of a case can the philosopher make for theism?

20 The difficulties involved in this issue are developed more fully in Chapter 20.

21 See Temple, *Nature of Personality*, pp. 118–120; *Christus Veritas*, pp. 279–285; *Nature, Man and God*, pp. 295–300.

22 See Temple, *Christus Veritas*, p. 277.

23 See Temple, *Nature of Personality*, p. 120.

CHAPTER 9

JUSTIFICATION FOR THEISM

A. THE CONVERGENCE OF INDEPENDENT LINES OF ARGUMENT

Belief in God is for Temple justified not by any single strand of evidence or by one argument alone. The approach is rather to gather evidence together from various areas of experience, incorporating the methods of several disciplines. It is the cumulative effect which the convergence of these independent arguments affords that gives both intellectual weight and psychological force to the belief in God.

Two main divisions may be noted in the approach Temple makes to the problem. He always strives to indicate the case for theism which philosophy offers independent of revealed religion. Then, turning to man's religious experience in general and the Christian tradition in particular, he finds that the experience of a personal relationship with God reinforces the philosophical argument. The two approaches converge so as to support one another.

> For the philosophic argument points to creation by a personal spirit capable of personal relationship with persons; and religious experience appears, at least, to be the apprehension from our side of such relations with the infinite reality.[1]

However, to state Temple's approach to belief in God in this way is partially misleading, even though it is the customary manner in which he presents it. It is relevant, at this point, to recall that Temple's approach is that of theological philosophy; that is, he starts with an assurance of the reality of a Supreme Spirit and from the perspective of fellowship shared with God seeks to explain the facts of experience.[2] Thus, though Temple does strive to argue on the basis of empirical evidence that God exists, he does not strive to argue in a strictly inferential manner from empirical facts to belief in God. Direct ex-

[1] Temple, "My Point of View" reprinted in *Religious Experience* ..., p. 104.
[2] See Temple, *Nature, Man and God*, p. 44; also above, Chapter 5.

perience of God combined with faith in His existence becomes a part of the evidence.

Indeed, Temple does state that one can arrive at the Absolute, or a Society of Intellects, or even the Divine by the inferential approach, but following that method does not lead to belief in, or to intercourse with, the living God.[3] The latter rests more on religious experience. It is quite understandable why this is the case. To proceed, as philosophy does, by making inferences based on empirical evidence leading to a conclusion is fine for some things; however "intercourse with God or with men is not the conclusion of an argument, but a mode of experience."[4] In understanding individuals (things or persons) there is no substitute for direct experience, just as a description about a picture is not a substitute for the picture itself. Hence, knowledge of a living God is based upon one's own experience of Him.

For Temple, then, religious experience does not merely confirm psychologically what philosophy has already established. Religious experience contributes something distinctive to the conception of God; it has specific cognitive significance as well as general psychological significance. Nonetheless, religious experience does not stand alone; it needs the independent support philosophy provides so as not to degenerate into self-hypnotism. Thus, the intellectual and psychological resources of philosophical discourse and religious experience are pooled so as to justify belief in a personal God. Thus Temple states:

> If the general argument of philosophy seemed to me to incline towards atheism, I could not confidently reject the theory of some psychologists that all religious experience is illusion. If there were no experience which seemed to be a personal relationship with God, I should have to admit that the balance of probability in the general philosophic argument is not decisive. But the two converge and support each other; it is in the mutual support of general argument and religious experience that we find the main strength of the case of theism.[5]

Temple's candor in this statement is quite commendable; and when he argues in this way, his position is philosophically defensible. However, what is not clear in Temple's presentation of the evidence for God is the precise relation of the evidence of religious experience and the philosophical evidence in their support of God. While Temple affirms that they do not lead to the same conception of God, he does

[3] See the following works of Temple respectively: *Nature of Personality*, pp. 83–84; *Mens Creatrix*, pp. 82–86; *Faith and Modern Thought*, pp. 30–32; "Religious Experience" reprinted in *Religious Experience* ..., p. 61; *Christus Veritas*, pp. 174–175.

[4] Temple, *Christus Veritas*, p. 175.

[5] "My Point of View" reprinted in *Religious Experience* ..., pp. 103–104; also cf. *Mens Creatrix*, pp. 259–260.

not show this to be the case; indeed the impression one receives from the conclusions he draws is that he is proceeding on the assumption that they do support the same conception of God. Thus, for example, no attempt is made to correlate the conception of God Temple believes Christianity affirms with the conception of God supported by philosophical evidence, though the conceptions are held to be different. The ambiguity here is a basic one and warrants careful scrutiny.

B. THE PHILOSOPHICAL EVIDENCE FOR THEISM

Temple's philosophical arguments for the theistic hypothesis seem to fall into four groups: (1) the demand for a principle of unity such as would provide rational justification for the procedures and conclusions of science; (2) belief in God providing the unifying principle man seeks through the activities of science, art, morality, and religion; (3) a personal God offering the only legitimate basis for the reverence man feels when confronted by the authoritative claims of truth, beauty, and moral goodness; (4) the need for grounding the World-Process in Mind in order to account for the occurrence and significance of mind in the process.

To some extent these arguments overlap. But there is merit in taking up each of the types of argument separately, and the fact that each one is based upon a selection from Temple's writings at different periods would seem to justify this approach.

1. The demand of theoretical and practical reason for a principle of unity[6]

The inadequacy of explaining the world by appealing to the methods and conclusions of physical science alone has already been noted. The effort of some philosophers and theologians to prove God on the basis of the necessity for a First Cause to initiate the process is also rejected. God cannot be found by tracing the world back to its starting point, for science admits no such starting point.

However, it is legitimate to ask science to make explicit its assumptions regarding the physical world which it investigates and to examine the implications of them for an understanding of the universe

[6] The earliest writings of Temple comprise the primary source of this argument. See especially, *Faith and Modern Thought; Nature of Personality*; "The Divinity of Christ" in *Foundations*, pp. 213–263.

as a whole. Science assumes that the physical world can be rationally understood by the investigator if he disciplines himself so as to examine his experience and carefully traces out the implications of that experience. The results obtained by such an approach science claims to be facts. This means that the world is held to be rational and that it can be understood by man's reason.

At this point, science stops since it is concerned with physical facts and the unity of the physical order, but not with non-sensory data or with experience as a whole. It is, however, appropriate to take the further step involved in recognizing that the mind which knows is, at least, as significant as the object known. Thus, the knowledge man possesses is itself a fact which must be fitted into the coherent scheme assumed by science. When the mind of man is fitted into the rational unity which the physical world comprises, a further important conclusion can be drawn: all of experience, including the natural order and the mind of man, is of one piece. What is now assumed is that reality is rational and that it is governed by the same principle of reason which operates in man. There is, then, a kinship between man's mind and the universe so that man can understand the world.[7] Furthermore, man will be satisfied only by the facts.

Such assumptions constitute the basis for science, though science does not seek to justify the assumptions or to examine the implications of them for an interpretation of experience as a whole. The scientist is content to explain each event by preceding events, never asking why the series as a whole or why that particular series. These are nonetheless important questions. It is in attempting to answer them that the notion of a First Cause was correctly proposed, though incorrectly formulated. It is not a question of postulating a First Cause of any series of events, but rather of discovering the source of the series as a whole and why this particular series occurred as it did.[8]

When the question is posed in this way and then is applied to the assumptions of science, the issue which arises may be stated as follows: There is a demand to discover a principle of unity that can account for the rational coherence of the universe presupposed and vindicated by the scientific enterprise. Such a principle must not itself raise further questions as to why things are as they are. As already noted

[7] This emphasis on the significance of mind occurring in the universe is expanded and argued in a different form in *Nature, Man and God;* it is presented as the fourth philosophical argument.

[8] See Temple, *Faith and Modern Thought*, pp. 14–16, 25–27.

the only principle which human experience offers that meets the demands of being self-explanatory is the principle of purpose.

To attribute the explanation of the universe to purpose is not to invent something unempirical, for purpose is the common experience of personal beings. One is, therefore, scientifically justified to take purpose as the hypothesis which offers the best hope for explaining the world science reveals. This purpose must be granted complete power since everything in the world depends on it. Thus, the scientific impulse if carried far enough demands a Divine Will, that is, purpose rooted in will.

This interpretation gains further confirmation when joined with the experience individuals have of a power not their own supporting and knowing them. Such an experience corroborates the hypothesis of Divine Will sustaining the world:

> This experience of a Power in whose hands we are, seems precisely to correspond with such a Will, for its leading characteristics were, that we are altogether in the hands of this Power, and that this power is intimate with us and with our own most inmost thoughts as no other human being can be, as only the Maker of souls could be.[9]

Turning to the history of man, Temple finds still another fact must be fitted into the scheme. That is, the principle that explains the world must be adequate to account for the fact of Jesus Christ, his life, death, the resurrection faith, and the church founded on these facts. The power which produces the world cannot be conceived as being inferior to that which arises in the world: "If Christ is a fact, then, ... the governing Power of the world must be something capable of expressing itself in that fact; it must be adequate to its own greatest achievement."[10]

Hence, the clue to the nature of the Supreme Power of the universe is provided in the character of Christ. Christ reveals the nature of this Being to be love expressed through sacrifice which renders suffering meaningful as a necessary condition for self-sacrifice and which conquers sin.

Thus Temple, starting with the assumption of science that the world is a rational whole, attempts to show that this demands that the world be a unity governed by the principle of reason. But this leaves open the question of the character of the principle of reason. His hypothesis is that Christ provides the clue to the nature of the

[9] *Ibid.*, p. 27.
[10] *Ibid.*, p. 158. See also *ibid.*, p. 61, and *Nature of Personality*, p. 96.

principle governing the world and at the same time points the way to a resolution of the problem of evil which is a stumbling block to those who call this principle good. This is another way of stating that man's theoretical reason – of which science is the supreme example – demands that the universe be conceived as a coherent whole and that man's practical reason – of which morality is the example – will settle for nothing less than Purposive Will. Combining these two demands, it is credible to affirm, though not proved, that "the Principle of Reason which governs the world is the eternal victory of love over selfishness at the cost of sacrifice."[11]

That the necessity for appealing to the hypothesis Temple has proposed has not been logically demonstrated, he quite readily admits. In fact, such demonstration is not possible on such an issue. If man is to understand, he must first believe; that is, he must first be willing to accept the hypothesis, and trusting in its adequacy – though this has not yet been fully established – put it to the test by experimenting with it in his life as he seeks to align his will with the Divine Will.

Here is an explicit illustration of Temple's appeal to practical guidance and inner certitude as the ultimate test of the adequacy of a world-view.[12] Also to be noted are the subtle shifts made in the argument from the assumption of science that the world is a rational unity to the assumption that a Divine Will is required to provide the unity, to the further assumption that faith in the God revealed in Christ provides the only adequate interpretation of the character of Divine Will and, hence, is the necessary starting point for understanding the world.

2. *The need for God to complete man's search for unity through science, art, morality, and religion*[13]

Not only do the assumptions and conclusions of science, when the implications of its approach are made explicit, suggest the existence of God conceived as Purposive Will; so too do art, morality, and religion. In each case the effort is to bring unity out of the multiplicity which confronts the individual as he explores the world in which he finds himself; the individual seeks a cosmos out of the chaos of his conflicting experiences of the world. The transitoriness of human life

[11] Temple, *Foundations*, pp. 221–222.
[12] See above, Chapter 5.
[13] This represents Temple's basic argument for theism in *Mens Creatrix*.

threatens to reduce thought and action to futility unless some principle of permanence can be found operative in all of man's activities, which by unifying them gives them ultimate meaning.

Intellectual activity, typified by the procedure of science, assumes that the universe is a rational whole and, operating on the basis of this assumption, provides man with an understanding of the world enabling him to control it to an extent which justifies the assumption. But the principle of unity that makes the universe intelligible to man's mind required by such a procedure is not discovered by the scientific approach or the intellect alone. Laws operating within the natural order rendering it comprehensible to man are discovered.

However, that which makes the whole system of laws a unity remains beyond the apprehension of the intellect alone. Also, the knowledge of the world as a unity resides in the finite intelligence of each knower who grasps the whole from his perspective. Such a unity is incomplete and precarious; to become complete and certain would demand a mind separate from human intelligence whose purpose orders the rationality of experience. To accept such a principle of unity is to move beyond intellect in order to provide the full satisfaction and completion of the intellect.

Art through the imaginative activity of the mind is able to provide an apprehension of the world's unity which science postulated as necessary but only partially glimpsed. The mind is freed from time and even conquers it temporarily in aesthetic experience. The mind, by grasping as a unity in the present a sequence of events encompassing both past and future, overcomes the transitoriness of the world. Also, the value of the whole series is symbolized in such a way that when the mind responds appreciatively to the symbol, the meaning of the whole is grasped. This means that the mind could apprehend the meaning of the whole world if the principle expressing it were symbolized in an event (or series of events) in time. Further, the contemplation of such an ideal experience to appeal aesthetically must incorporate the tragic struggle of good subduing evil, though partially succumbing to it in the process.

However, that which symbolizes the meaning of life could not be simply a work of art, but would have to be the actual embodiment of the ideal in a living person whose life revealed the meaning of the entire drama of life. Art aspires after the actualization of such an ideal but never fully attains it, and the contemplating mind must remain to that extent dissatisfied.

When one turns to morality, the embodiment of the ideal in the lives of great men is partially attained. The purpose which governs the individual's life transcends the transitoriness of the events in the world, giving meaning and direction to his life as a whole. When such a purpose is directed toward the actualization of the moral good of man found to consist in a life of love and in a fellowship of men bound together by love, then a principle of unity for all mankind, individually and collectively, has been discovered. The attainment on earth of such a fellowship is the ideal or morality.

However, the attainment of the ideal lies beyond the powers of human will to produce. Indeed, it is precisely the individual's self-will which is the chief obstacle to the life of love and universal fellowship that constitute the ethical aspirations of man. Some power is needed beyond man to break in upon both the individual and his society, which is capable of effecting a renovation of both. Only the power of sacrificial love embodied in the life of one whose attitude and act reflect a love that is entirely self-forgetful to the point of self-sacrifice can produce such results. It is such sacrificial love each man needs but cannot by himself attain.

Thus, the mental activities of intellect, imagination, and will which find expression through science, art, and morality respectively, all have been shown to point to an ideal which if actualized would perfectly satisfy the demands of each, but the ideal is not attained.

> The goal of science is not reached; Science only exists in departmental fragments; physics, chemistry, biology and the rest. The goal of Art is not reached; there is not experience obtainable through the aesthetic faculties in which the soul can find satisfaction forever. The goal of Ethics is not reached; it would be realized in the pursuit of a purpose, lofty enough to claim the allegiance of all our faculties and rich enough to exercise them all, conducted in a fellowship bound together by ties of mutual love; but man cannot evolve out of himself that purpose, nor can he of himself create that fellowship.[14]

When one turns to the religious experience of man, the purposive will unifying and directing the universe, which science, art, and morality seek but do not find, is claimed to be directly encountered. The religious experience of men of all ages testifies to what is believed to be communion with the ruling power of the universe. Such an experience carries with it absolute certitude, for the individual who has it, of the reality of the power with whom communion is shared. Nonetheless, one may be deceived; and thus, religious experience too needs the support

[14] *Ibid.*, p. 258.

of the other activities of the mind. But when the Being with whom religious men believe they are in communion is recognized as supplying the lack felt by science, art, and morality, then it is reasonable to affirm the reality of that Being.

Hence, science, art, morality, and religion require God for their complete satisfaction. Such a God must be the union of absolute power and perfect love if, on the one hand, the existence of the world is to be explained and, on the other hand, if the mind's moral quest is to be made intelligible. The universe can be considered rational, then, only if it is rooted in the will of a personal being whose purpose for good is the justification for the existence of the universe. The creative activities of man's mind are satisfied when, and only when, united in communion with a Divine creative mind. That such communion exists is the testimony of religious believers of all ages; and when their experience is placed alongside of the demands of the mind, such a belief is justified.

The chief obstacle which stands in the way of accepting an all-powerful will directed toward good as the ruler of the universe is the fact that so much of the world's history seems contrary to the development of goodness. The problem of evil in the world threatens the whole case for theism. The details of this issue are explored in the following chapter; suffice it to state at this point that it is precisely because of the problem evil poses to the theist, both theoretically and practically, that Temple regards Christian theism as the only adequate theism. Evil is not simply defeated through the life, death, and resurrection of Christ; it becomes itself the occasion of God's triumph. Evil is overcome, but what is more important is that in overcoming evil a greater good is achieved than would have been possible without it. Nor is the evil of the world merely explained abstractly; it is God's goodness which overcomes evil, and this is accomplished by God taking the evil of the world on Himself in the supreme act of sacrificial love through Christ's death on the cross.

The fact of Christ, then, supplies what is lacking to satisfy the activities of intellect, imagination, and will. The principle of unity which intellect demands, ordering the world, making it rationally coherent and intelligible to man, is provided when such a unifying principle is seen to be rooted in a loving will such as the dogma of the Incarnation suggests. Likewise, the actual embodiment of an ideal that symbolizes the meaning of life which art grasps, but cannot produce, is offered to man for his contemplation in Jesus Christ whose life, death, and resurrection reaches to the full depths of the tragic in life such as to satisfy the aesthetic response of man and in so doing expresses the image of the Principle of Unity that art suggests. The same is the case with regard to morality. Each man seeks a life of love in a fellowship of men bound together by love, but no one is able of himself to act in a loving way to bring about his own transformation or that of others. Once again the fact of Christ supplies what is needed: "The dogma of the Incarnation, which is that fact interpreted in the light of its consequences, gives to man's moral effort alike the impetus and the goal which it requires."[15]

The creative activities of man's mind expressed through science, art, morality, and religion each seek a unifying principle which none can supply. These four lines of argument converge without meeting until God incarnate in Christ is accepted as the fact required to join them together. That the Incarnation is a fact may be denied, in which case scepticism triumphs, but for those who accept the evidence of the New Testament that God was in Christ it supplies what man needs. Man's search for God ends in God's act of self-revelation, indicating that it was His activity at every stage along the way which made the quest itself possible.

A number of assumptions are evident in Temple's argument: first, he assumes a certain ideal as alone satisfactory to the activities of man's mind and, then, equating the ideal of traditional Christianity with it, he further assumes that the latter ideal supplies what is needed. Thus, for example, the basis on which philosophical theism is dismissed as inadequate to cope with the problem of evil would seem to be the assumption that a particular conception of God is necessary and hence any other conception is *a priori* inadequate. None of these assumptions, however, has been sufficiently demonstrated nor adequately related to the requirements of experience.

3. *Truth, beauty, and moral goodness as providing intimations of a personal God*[16]

Another argument for a personal God can be found in Temple's writings, similar to the one just noted yet stressing not so much the need for God to complete man's search for unity in the creative

[15] *Ibid.*, 352.

[16] The best summary of this argument is found in Temple's *Nature, Man and God*, pp. 246–254.

activities of the mind as the need for God in order to make intelligible the awe man feels before the authoritative claims of truth, beauty, and moral goodness. That is, the experience man has of value exemplified by the august claims which truth, beauty, and goodness make upon him gives intimations of a power transcending the universe whose will it is that sustains these values and by whom the individual feels confronted in his quest for these values.

There is an authoritative quality about all of the experience man has. The judgments man makes about his experience are themselves based upon and corrected by experience. Similarly, the individual seeks to be freed from an appeal to others as authorities for his beliefs and to become more reliant upon his own reflective judgments. But authority is not escaped in this way, for the individual comes under the authority imposed by the quest for truth.

When mind apprehends truth, it recognizes in that act something akin to itself.[17] But the mind also recognizes in truth an object worthy of reverence that is not appropriate to the apprehension of an isolated fact. When such a fact is viewed as integral to a system of truth, then it too takes on the quality appropriate to reverence.

To conceive truth in this way seems to Temple to be an intuitional judgment which cannot be established by argument; the individual either agrees with it or he does not. What can be stated in defense of such an attitude toward truth is that the claim truth makes upon the individual takes on the special quality attached to obligation arising from personal relationships as distinguished from the obligation one feels toward impersonal values. Just what this special quality is Temple does not clarify, but the point he is making is evident: the reverence one has toward truth, even that of a materialistic scientist toward the truth of the physical world, is justifiable only if the universe is the expression of a personal mind.

Such a feeling toward truth may, of course, be due to cultural influences extending from a period when belief in such a Supreme Mind was prevalent. But insofar as most men feel a special reverence for truth, this feeling must either be recognized as implying a personal mind or be discarded as illegitimate. Paradoxical as it seems, some persons as a result of their felt obligation to truth reject belief in a personal mind such as would justify their reverence for truth. Thus Temple concludes:

[17] See *ibid.*, pp. 130, 156; also below, Chapter 11.

We have here then an intimation, though it is no more, that what the mind confronts in its search for Truth, and in the claim of Truth upon it, is something more than an intelligible system of uniformities; it is a Mind akin to itself, though so vastly greater as to be the controlling principle of that vast realm of being which our minds laboriously and very gradually apprehend.[18]

When one examines man's experience of beauty, a similar authoritative claim is made upon man which is commensurate only with mind confronted by mind. In the experience of beauty the intimation of mind is even more evident. One feels a reverence toward an object apprehended as beautiful such as would be justified only if one were communing with another mind; but also the act of apprehension itself feels like such communion. There is no difficulty on this issue with regard to works of art created by man. The work of art is expressive of the artist; it is not due to chance or mechanically produced. But, must not the same hold true of the beauty of nature? Must not beauty be a communication between two minds to be satisfying? Temple's own experience leads him to answer in the affirmative: "*There is more in Beauty than Beauty alone. There is communication from, and communion with, personal Spirit.*"[19]

A third intimation of a personal mind as the source and sustainer of values is gained from one's experience of the claim made by moral goodness. Morality means respecting another as a person and striving to love another as one loves oneself so as to foster personal fellowship. To do what is right means to act on the basis of love and for the sake of promoting love.[20] The personal quality of morality is thus unmistakable. Also, in fulfilling a duty, particularly a difficult and demanding duty, one has the feeling of entering into an already existing reality which has a claim upon one such as only exercised by persons. To take the insight of those who are ethically most sensitive, a failure to fulfill one's duty becomes a violation of a claim held to be sacred. Such a feeling of reverence toward one's obligation is justified only by a theistic philosophy.

For no Law, apart from a Lawgiver, is a proper object of reverence. It is mere brute fact; and every living thing, still more every person exercising intelligent choice, is its superior. The reverence of persons can be appropriately given only to that which itself is at least personal.[21]

[18] *Ibid.*, pp. 251–252.
[19] *Ibid.*, p. 253. Temple quotes approvingly on this issue from Arthur James Balfour, *Theism and Humanism* (New York: Hodder & Stoughton, George H. Doran Company, 1915), pp. 67–102.
[20] See below, Chapter 11; in Temple, see especially, *Nature, Man and God*, pp. 190–196.
[21] Temple, *Nature, Man and God*, p. 254.

Thus, truth, beauty, and moral goodness give intimations of a personal mind which for Temple justify a theistic interpretation of experience. To doubt the intimations of these feelings which are more persuasive than the sensations of touch or sight is to throw in doubt all of one's convictions.[22]

Temple's conclusions based upon this argument are much more modest than those drawn from the preceding arguments. The superiority of theism over humanism, in accounting for man's value-experience, is held to be established, though he does not clarify what version of theism he believes is established by this argument. He does recognize that such feelings of reverence are not self-evidently genuine to everyone, and thus another empirical line of argument is submitted which likewise leads to theism.

4. *A Supreme Mind as the necessary ground for the occurrence of mind in the World-Process*[23]

The most empirical argument for a personal God proposed by Temple is found in his Gifford Lectures. A Supreme Mind is held to be the most adequate hypothesis to account for the occurrence and significance of mind in the World-Process. In the Gifford Lectures this argument is joined with the evidence based upon man's intimations of a personal God arising from his reverence for truth, beauty, and moral goodness, and together they constitute Temple's most philosophically convincing case for the theistic hypothesis.

Temple directs his attention to an examination of experience in general, apart from any specifically religious experience claimed to be revelatory of a transcendent God. It is noted that mind arises and develops within the course of the World-Process. The occurrence of minds within the process and as a part of it is indicative of the process itself; that is, the process must be such that it can give rise to minds.

The basic characteristic of mind when it emerges is its capacity to apprehend the process of which it is a part. At its most rudimentary level it is simply a means of fostering the organism's adjustment to its environment by selecting among objects presented to it those most likely to satisfy the needs of the organism. At its highest level of personal being mind directs the organism by selecting the ends to be

[22] The word "feeling" used in this context is for Temple closer to the German *Ahnung* (presentiment) than to *Gefühl* (a sense of feeling, a sensation); see *ibid.*, p. 255.
[23] See *ibid.*, especially Lectures V, VIII, X.

sought as well as the means for attaining them.[24] Mind, then, though a product of the process partially transcends the process through awareness of it and the ability to apprehend at least part of it. Thus, though the immensity and grandeur of the universe are not to be diminished, neither should one overlook the significance of the fact that man can to some extent know the world of which he is a part. Insofar as the astronomer knows the existence and location of heavenly bodies while they do not know him, he is superior to them.

The implications of the fact that the process should produce in one of its members the capacity to know the process are far-reaching. To consider mind when it occurs as an emergent, not reducible to previously existent entities and neither the product of chance nor of teleology, may be all right when the parts of the process are viewed separately; but when one considers the entire process, then mind must be presumed to be accounted for either by the most primitive entity in the process or by the process in its totality. In either case, mind must be grounded in the process, and hence, the process itself must be interpreted as in some sense "mental." In any case, what needs to be explained is the process as a whole including mind as an element in it.

Three alternatives are suggested as possible solutions for the origin of mind within the World-Process: (1) mind developed as a result of chance circumstances, none of which in themselves contain an element of self-consciousness; (2) whatever gave rise to existence in its various manifestations injected mind as an additional creative act into the World-Process; (3) mind must have been present from the beginning, but in such a rudimentary form that it was unintelligible. The first alternative seems entirely inadequate. The disparity which exists between non-conscious physiological functions and conscious organisms is so great that to suppose the former is the cause of the latter is to render the notion of causation meaningless. To state that when an organism becomes sufficiently complex, consciousness will "emerge" is simply to evade the issue. It is "like supposing that the mechanical robot at a street corner will automatically turn into a policeman if the traffic is sufficiently congested."[25] In such a view mind remains a brute fact unexplained by, and unintelligible in terms of, the rest of the process.

A choice between the second and third alternatives need not be

[24] See above, Chapters 4 and 6.

[25] *Ibid.*, p. 199. The illustration is taken from John Wood Oman, *The Natural and the Supernatural* (Cambridge: The University Press, 1931), p. 45.

made, since in both cases mind is involved from the start. There are, however, advantages to choosing the third view since it preserves the continuity of the process which the first alternative stressed. Hence, it is the third alternative Temple chooses as the more reasonable hypothesis. To test it on the basis of the implications resulting from such a belief now remains.

Previous analysis of mind has revealed that its distinguishing feature is its capacity to transcend and to view the process of which it is a part. By forming concepts (or "free ideas") not tied to an immediate sensation the mind can apply ideas gained from the past to the future and even form conceptions of future experience it would like to have but which have not been experienced. In so doing the mind conceives the process as an organic unity so that the past is a determining factor of the present; and, likewise, the future modifies both past and present. The mind thus attains a degree of superiority to, and independence of, the process; and, though the mind never completely transcends the process, it transcends it to the extent that the process becomes encompassed by mind and mind by process. Mind, then, is capable of "selecting the direction of its own attention, and thereby determining the action which it initiates, even in the physical sphere."[26]

Three points warrant careful consideration when an explanation of the process itself is sought: (1) if it is true that the mind initiates activity, including physical movement, then the universe cannot be considered a closed system ruled by its own laws. When freedom of the mind is admitted, regardless of how slight a difference it makes in the total process, the closed system of the physical world must be denied; (2) whatever explanation is offered to account for the process must include mind as a part of the process. "Its explanatory principle," Temple writes, "must contain the ground of freedom as against naturalistic determinism."[27] The character of the universe must be such that the event of free minds within the process is in accordance with that character; (3) whatever it is which is held to explain the universe must itself require no further explanation; that is, the ground of the universe must be self-explanatory. It is precisely for this reason that the universe cannot be explained by physical laws. Such laws explain present occurrences by tracing their connection with past events, but then these too need to be explained. Furthermore, what is

[26] Temple, *Nature, Man and God*, p. 255.
[27] *Ibid.*, p. 256.

the source of the physical law since it has no efficacy of its own, and why this type of law and not another?

In light of these three points what explanation of the World-Process best satisfies the requirements? Temple suggests:

> When Mind, determined by Good as apprehended, initiates activity, no further explanation is needed. The enquiring mind, confronted with an example of what it perfectly understands as the essential characteristic of its own being, is completely satisfied. Whenever the subject of enquiry is traced to the action of intelligently purposive mind, the enquiry is closed; Mind has recognized itself and is satisfied.[28]

On the basis of this explanation it is not at all surprising or incongruous that mind should arise in the process, since the process is itself grounded in mind. Furthermore, purpose is a self-explanatory principle, indeed the only self-explanatory principle known to man.[29]

Thus culminates the quest for a satisfactory solution to the World-Process on the basis of empirical evidence. Temple defines the solution as theistic: "*To adopt the hypothesis that the process of nature in all its range is to be accounted for by the intelligent purpose of Mind is Theism.*"[30]

But another question arises demanding an answer: is the mind acknowledged to be the power behind the universe contained solely within the World-Process? Temple answers this question in the negative. The immanence of Mind has been established; it remains to show how such a Mind is also transcendent.

Insight into the question is gained when one considers the fact that any explanation of the world must reveal *why* the process developed as it did and *how* such a development could occur. To recognize an immanent being in the process as the ground of possibility for the process is not to account for the totality – mind plus process. To explain adequately why the total process is as it is necessitates attributing to the immanent principle qualities which go beyond both mechanism and organism to Personality.

It is on this issue that Temple departs from Whitehead's philosophy of organism, from whom he has drawn heavily up to this point. The principle of organism implies the unification of the whole which serves as the determining factor in action, but what is required is that the agent be capable of self-determination both prior to and during the course of an action.

[28] *Ibid.*, p. 257.
[29] See above; Chapter 6.
[30] *Nature, Man and God*, p. 257.

This point warrants further consideration. Pointing out how the Organic theory proposed by Whitehead surpasses the mechanistic interpretation, Temple also suggests that an adequate conception of personality must go beyond the Organic theory:

> Organic differs from mechanical reaction in that the reaction is determined by the whole organism as a unity .... But while the organism as a whole and its vital needs thus determine the reaction of its several parts, it is the organism as it is at that moment which exerts this determining influence. There is nothing transcendent there. But in the self-determination of a personality something, which as yet is not, is envisaged as determining that which is. The future self does not exercise efficient causation upon the present self; ... it is the apprehension of what shall be, or at least what may be, which exercises efficient causation over the self in its choice of conduct.[31]

Thus, at the personal level of existence the future becomes a prominent factor in decision such as is not the case for an organism. The present moment in which choice is made, furthermore, needs to be conceived as itself a span of time such as includes more than simply physical movements or organic reactions; determination is made in the moment by reference to one's ideal of what one would like to become. This means that the "self, which frames ideals of itself, is certainly something more than appears in its actions."[32] Hence, a person can never be reduced to, or equated with, his conduct; he always transcends his conduct at least in reference to an ideal he has of himself not yet realized but guiding his actions in the present. This is the freedom of self-determination which requires a self that transcends its own actions.

A word of comment is in order. Temple's criticism of Whitehead in regard to the significance of the future as envisaged by the self in the choices it makes in the present would not seem to be justified. Whitehead's emphasis on "subjective aim" is almost identical with Temple's view of a future ideal. Statements made by Whitehead on mentality as it operates in higher occasions seem to have been overlooked by Temple.[33] However, in emphasizing the moment as enduring through time, Temple comes closer to a legitimate criticism of Whitehead's atomistic view of occasions, even higher level occasions.

In any case, Temple's point is clear: whatever accounts for the World-Process must account for the fact of self-determination based

[31] *Ibid.*, p. 261.
[32] *Ibid.*, p. 262.
[33] See, for example, Whitehead, *Process and Reality*, pp. 164–165; *The Function of Reason* (Boston: Beacon Press, 1958), pp. 26–34.

upon self-transcendence as occurring within the process. The principle of organism fails to do so unless qualities are attributed to it that usually are reserved for personality.[34] It is the principle of personality which is adequate. Personality is, as already noted, self-explanatory, thereby avoiding an infinite regress. Further, personality as the highest principle the process reveals is adequate to account for all that appears; hence, the difficulties involved in trying to explain the higher by the lower are avoided. Still another point in its favor is the way personality acts in the present but in light of the future so that efficient causation is combined with rational coherence.

> When a person acts purposively his several actions cohere on one intelligible scheme, while in each action the present choice, which is at that stage expressive of the constant purpose, is an efficient cause of the changes effected in the environment.[35]

The adequacy of personality to explain the World-Process is most clearly evident in the manifestation of personality in action. The manifestation which is most significant, because of its remoteness from the mechanical or the organic, is in terms of fellowship or love. This indicates the necessity for other persons (or personalities) in order for personality to realize itself fully. Thus, the power behind the World-Process becomes not only purposive mind, but a mind whose actual purpose is love. This completes the survey because persons appearing within the World-Process are explained by the same principle (i.e., personality) as is the process itself. Value and creation are both made intelligible on this basis. Temple concludes: *"The explanation of the world is to be sought in a Personal Reality, or to use the historic phrase, in a Living God."*[36]

Temple has presented one of the strongest lines of argument for God based on empirical analysis available. It represents an extensive development of what is sometimes called the epistemological argument for God.[37] There are some questions, however, which remain unclarified. It is doubtful if the optimism of Temple's theism is any more justified than the optimism Whitehead exhibits, though Temple argues

[34] On this point Dorothy Emmet, one of Whitehead's interpreters, states: "Whitehead leads us finally to the conception of a logical-aesthetic order, and Temple is, I think, justified in his criticism that much of the quasi-personalist language which Whitehead uses about this at the end of his *Process and Reality* goes beyond what is warranted by his own theory"; Dorothy Emmet, "The Philosopher" in F. A. Iremonger, *William Temple . . .*, p. 528.

[35] Temple, *Nature, Man and God*, p. 263.

[36] *Ibid.*, p. 265.

[37] See F. R. Tennant, *Philosophical Theology* (Cambridge: The University Press, 1930), II, 61.

for the superiority of his own position at this point.[38] Further, it needs to be made explicit that Temple's argument has not been shown to establish *Christian* theism. Indeed, even a modified deism is acknowledged by Temple as satisfying the minimal requirements. Finally, there is unacknowledged disparity between Temple's conclusion that this argument leads to a living God as the best explanation of the process and his statements in other writings that one cannot infer a Living God, that is, that philosophical discourse does not lead to God. Hence, Temple presents a philosophically defensible case for theism, but not without some ambiguity regarding alternative positions and the kind of theism he believes has been established.

This completes the philosophical case for theism as developed by Temple. But as was noted at the beginning of this section, and explicitly stated in the course of some of the arguments presented, philosophical theism does not stand alone as evidence for God; it is supported by, and supports, the direct evidence for God afforded by religious experience.

C. THE EVIDENCE OF RELIGIOUS EXPERIENCE

1. The meaning of religious experience

Although Temple contends that the philosophical evidence for theism is convincing, belief in God is not to be construed as a matter of intellectual assent to sophisticated philosophical discourse. Indeed, for the religious man the existence of God is based upon his own direct experience of God.[39] Nor is such experience confined to a few individuals or to a few moments in one's life. Too often religious experience is conceived exclusively in terms of the ecstasy of the mystic or confined to specific moments when one becomes conscious of God's presence. Even William James must be criticized on this point.[40] There are such moments of special illumination for some people, but it is false to restrict religious experience to special experiences and isolated moments.

Such an approach tends to emphasize religious experiences, rather than the testimony of religious experience as a whole. For the person who believes in God this means all of his experience.

[38] See Skelton, "The Problem of Evil in the Works of William Temple," p. 71.

[39] See Temple, *Faith and Modern Thought*, p. 4.

[40] See William James, *The Varieties of Religious Experience* (New York: Longmans, Green and Co., 1902); in Temple see *Christus Veritas*, p. 36; *Nature, Man and God*, p. 334.

It is the whole reaction to circumstances resulting from that belief and from that acknowledged relationship that should be uppermost in our minds when we speak of religious experience and its significance – the apprehension by the psycho-physical organism of its environment as (amongst other things) divine.[41]

Furthermore, even one who shares no belief in God is not without experience of God, though he does not recognize it as such. If the source and sustainer of the universe is Divine Will whose purpose for good is expressed through the world, then one's consciousness of value as absolute and the experience of absolute obligation which it imposes constitute experience of God.[42] Knowledge of God is gained in this way apart from any explicit religious orientation, though many do acknowledge this to be an experience of God. A sense of absolute obligation to something which the individual prizes and toward which he feels reverence would seem to be universal. Furthermore, to the extent that one feels the constraint of moral obligation or the joy of love, he is having intercourse with God whether recognized as such or not.

Religious experience, then, in its most general form is the experience of something ultimate or absolute in the presence of which one feels reverence and awe.[43] That one could go through life without ever feeling reverence toward something that he takes to be his moral superior or without ever feeling awe toward the universe itself which gave him life seems doubtful to Temple. Concerning the implications of this universal experience of awe and obligation, Temple states: "If his reverence and his awe are justified, they imply a Reality fit to be their occasion. If he is genuinely subject to the obligation, that implies a universe in which obligation has a place."[44]

Even the experience more directly termed religious experience has a universal import and is not to be equated with special visions or trances. Defining the nature of religious experience in this narrow sense, Temple states:

By religious experience I do not mean an ecstasy or an extraordinary thing that happens to a few people here and there, but simply that impulse, which comes upon most people at some time, to throw oneself back upon a Power greater than oneself, and the sense, the perfectly sure sense, that that Power has received one and is supporting one.[45]

[41] Temple, *Nature, Man and God*, p. 335.
[42] See Temple, *Christus Veritas*, pp. 35, 95.
[43] See *ibid.*, pp. 39–40. There is an affinity here with Tillich's view of religion as one's ultimate concern; see Paul Tillich, *Systematic Theology*, I, 11–15.
[44] Temple, *Christus Veritas*, p. 39.
[45] *Faith and Modern Thought*, pp. 7–8.

For Temple, the chief characteristic of religious experience, when it is acknowledged as such, is the feeling one has of being confronted by a Being who knows him more intimately than anyone else and whose power supports him even in times of distress. Religious experience is, therefore, inspiration in which one feels that he is in direct communion with God. Evident at this point is the difference between knowledge arrived at by inference based on a chain of reasoning and knowledge by direct acquaintance. Philosophical discourse provides the former, religious experience the latter: "All philosophy culminates with the Divine; only religious experience can give us God."[46] Individuals can be understood only by means of direct experience. The same is true of God: He also is known best through a personal relationship with Him. Thus in religious experience it is God Himself who is revealed and not some proposition about God.[47] Though Temple does not state it explicitly in this context, the implication is that God is revealed to be personal. Indeed, Temple is sufficiently certain of the personal nature of God that he never seriously considers any other option.[48]

The experience of God is thus direct but mediated.[49] The character of the person, the religious heritage which is his, the circumstances under which it occurs – all condition the experience he has and his interpretation of it. Because one has a religious experience does not mean one has interpreted it correctly, still less that the experience itself offers a solution to particular problems. The individual has received inspiration and felt that he was in the presence of God; the content which he ascribes to the experience may or may not be correct.

> In inspiration we are given, not solutions but new data .... It is contact with God; not understanding of God, but living in vital union with Him: and it is possible that the man who has the most vital communion with God will be least able to make a scientific theory of that experience.[50]

2. *The insufficiency of religious experience*

The difficulty which religious experience poses arises precisely at this point, namely, its incommunicability and the possibility of self-

[46] *Ibid.*, p. 31–32. The contradiction between this statement and the argument for God proposed in *Nature, Man and God* has already been noted above.

[47] See Temple, *Nature, Man and God*, p. 354. The implications of this for an interpretation of revelation were noted in Chapter 8.

[48] See W. R. Matthews, "William Temple as Thinker," in W. R. Matthews and Others, *William Temple: An Estimate* ..., p. 15.

[49] For a more recent exposition of this view, see John E. Smith, *Reason and God* (New Haven: Yale University Press, 1961), pp. 170, 181–182.

[50] Temple, *Faith and Modern Thought*, pp. 43, 44.

deception regarding the experience itself. How can one refer meaningfully to religious experience as providing communion with God to another man who has had no such experience? Furthermore, to the claim that God is met in religious experience the psychologist may reply that the experience is itself due to one's expectations and vivid imagination, or to group hypnosis.

The validity of religious experience is challenged in a way not true of man's other experiences (e.g., sight and hearing). In reply to these challenges Temple, reaffirming his realistic epistemology, states that all perceptive experience involves the apprehension of something that is given. "We do not have experiences and infer the object which occasions them; the experience *is* the apprehension of the object."[51] However, still undetermined is the nature of the object given in each case. This can be determined only by critical reflection which necessitates moving beyond what has been given in order to interpret it correctly. All human experience involves such interpretation. Furthermore, the reflective process is a fuller articulation of what was given; it is not theorizing about some fact given to it. Religious experience is the same at this point as any other experience which claims to provide an apprehension of reality.

Nonetheless, because of the charge of illusion brought against religious experience, there is need to justify its claim to apprehend reality through independent argument substantiating the claim that God exists. Indeed, as already noted, Temple asserts that religious experience alone is not sufficient to make a case for theism. Religious experience needs to be put to the same test and examined in the same way as all other experience claimed to be an apprehension of reality. Its claim cannot be held validated until this has been done, but neither should its claim be rejected on an *a priori* basis which denies the possibility of validation.

Hence, the evidence of religious experience is precarious and seeks philosophy for support. At the same time, religious experience because it is direct and not inferential provides intercourse with the Living God, which philosophy can never attain. The complete case for theism thus rests upon both the evidence of general philosophy and the evidence of religious experience.

A basic ambiguity seems evident in Temple's position on this issue. Religious experience is necessary to complete and confirm the philosophical argument for God, but religious experience itself can be

[51] Temple, *Christus Veritas*, p. 38.

substantiated only on the basis of the validity of the philosophical argument. They support each other, but what supports them both? That is, Temple confuses philosophical justification for the existence of God with philosophical justification for the existence of the object of religious experience. But the object of religious experience has not been established as the God of philosophical theism. To do so would necessitate a thorough analysis of religious experience as well as a correlation of the nature of God arrived at by philosophical discourse with the nature of the object with whom one believes to be in communion in religious experience. Neither of these analyses has been provided by Temple.

Temple is, nonetheless, convinced of the theistic hypothesis on the basis of these converging lines of argument. But to trace the cause of the universe to a personal God whose power sustains it and whose goodness guides it requires an explanation of the evil evident in the world which seems to contradict either God's power or His goodness and, in fact, to jeopardize the entire theistic hypothesis.

It has already been noted that a tension is evident in Temple's position in his attempt to show that general philosophy leads only to the Divine, not to God; also, he is never content with the conclusions of philosophical argument, but always supplements them with the assumptions of, and evidence from, the Christian faith. However, it is in the attempt to answer the problem of evil that Temple the philosopher becomes most explicitly Temple the Christian apologist, and the theism to which philosophy leads is replaced by a metaphysics of the Incarnation.

CHAPTER 10

FROM THEISM TO A METAPHYSICS OF THE INCARNATION

A. THE GOOD OF EVIL

Using the hypothesis of a God whose purpose it is to create the world and man so that good can be achieved, the philosopher can proceed to explain the facts of experience. However, one fact resists such an explanation, and that is the fact of evil. The error, suffering, and sin in the world seem to defy the contention that the world is created and sustained so that goodness can be realized. How is evil, then, to be explained?[1]

Temple rejects any attempt to solve the problem of evil which would limit either God's goodness or his power. To limit the goodness of God is to eliminate God as the principle of explanation, since the adequacy of theism resides in the self-explanatory character of purposive will directed by good. Is the other alternative, limiting God's power, satisfactory? Temple thinks not, but it does have the merit ot not reducing evil to illusion. However, to strive to limit God's power while retaining His perfection in goodness is to deal too abstractly with the nature of God. No ultimate distinction between God's goodness and His power can be made. Furthermore, on what basis can one claim that God's power is limited if His will sustains all that is? In any event, to limit God's goodness or power when confronted by the problem of evil is really to admit defeat and give up the quest for a rational explanation of the universe.[2]

Temple correctly sees the necessity for dealing with God's nature as a unity but then draws the unwarranted conclusion from this that

[1] Temple's most complete account of the problem of evil is presented in *Mens Creatrix*, pp. 261–292; but see also *Faith and Modern Thought*, pp. 114–146; *Christus Veritas*, pp. 191–199, 253–273; *Nature, Man and God*, pp. 356–377, 500–520.

[2] See *ibid.*, pp. 264–267. See the reference to Temple on this point by David Elton Trueblood, *Philosophy of Religion* (New York: Harper & Brothers, 1957), p. 243.

the notion of a God with unlimited power and perfect goodness constitutes that unity. What, rather, seems to follow is that Temple brings to the facts of experience an ideal conception of what God must be like to be God and then proceeds to find an explanation of the facts which is most in accord with the ideal. This ontological approach becomes increasingly apparent as his solution to the problem of evil unfolds.

Temple suggests that there is an alternative solution which avoids reducing both evil to an illusion and God to finitude; it consists in recognizing that evil is evil but that the good of the world is itself greater because of the evil which must be overcome. When particular forms of good are examined, it becomes evident that the difficulty involved in attaining them constitutes an inherent part of their excellence. What costs one something is valued more highly than something which does not. Thus moral victory, as a prime example of good, is possible only if there is an antagonist; only if there is a real struggle can victory be claimed.[3]

But this means that a world in which evil is overcome and victory won is a better world than one which contained no evil to be overcome. It is for each man to decide whether his value judgment confirms this claim. For Temple, "evil overcome by good is often justified."[4] The problem of evil is solved, then, not in thought but in action.

Perhaps, the following statement provides the best clue to Temple's approach to the problem evil poses for the theist, revealing his usual candor in such matters:

> *The reasonable attitude is not that which says "This is good, therefore it must be real," or "This is evil; how can it be explained?" but that which asks concerning every situation that arises how good may be won out of it, and how even what is now evil in it be made subservient to good.*[5]

The problem, according to Temple, is not to account for evil occurring in the world operated by an all good and all powerful God; rather, the problem is for man to respond to evil in such a way that good can be derived from it. It is not the efficient cause of evil that is sought but the final resolution of it.

For Temple, then, evil loses its decisiveness when viewed as a necessary component and even as a necessary means for the actualization of the greatest possible good. Evil is conceived as an instrument essential for the realization of the greatest good which goodness itself ren-

[3] See Temple, *Mens Creatrix*, p. 152.
[4] *Ibid.*, p. 269.
[5] Temple, *Nature, Man and God*, pp. 220–221.

ders possible. Value to become actual requires a personal being who is aware of his existence and who responds appreciatively to certain objects in his world.[6] This means that value must be realized in and through individuals; goodness must be an achievement, something which is won or conferred as a result of struggle. The basic principle by which Temple justifies the three main types of evil is now evident: error, suffering, and sin are a part of the struggle which engages man as he strives toward truth, beauty, and moral goodness.

If truth is to be attained, then it must be by man's own efforts. Furthermore, the act of discovery is a greater good than if no intellectual effort had to be expended. Therefore, error in the form of an improper synthesis of one's experience must be a possibility to which man can succumb, since it is in the elimination of error that man finds his highest intellectual satisfaction. Error arises only in the act of synthesis, for Temple, when one asserts the "identity of different objects";[7] error never occurs when one merely analyzes the content of his experience. Error is, therefore, a necessary element in the actualization of intellectual value.[8]

Value can likewise be discovered in suffering. First, suffering elicits sympathy from others, thereby making it a positive gain both to the sympathizer and to the sufferer. Second, there is value received from suffering when one endures it gladly for the sake of a worthwhile cause. Finally, suffering offers to man a dramatic challenge to exhibit courage, or what is even more ennobling, to exhibit love for another despite the personal suffering such acts might entail.[9]

Hence, suffering is not intrinsically evil, since it is a necessary condition for the realization of some aspects of character which are supremely good; e.g. heroism and self-sacrifice.[10]

Temple admits that this view does not fully satisfy all particular cases of suffering as, for example, the tragedy of one entrapped in evil by the situations which elicit conflicting obligations, or of an Othello whose virtue renders him powerless to cope with an Iago. In such cases Temple falls back upon his religious faith, asserting that eternity alone offers the possibility of ultimate justification. Summing up his solution to the fact of suffering in the world, Temple states:

[6] Temple's value theory is developed more fully below in Chapter 11.
[7] Temple, *Mens Creatrix*, p. 274.
[8] See *Ibid.*, pp. 277–278.
[9] See Temple, *Mens Creatrix*, p. 278.
[10] See Temple, *Foundations*, p. 220.

All we can claim is that we have found a principle on which, where we can trace its operation, suffering becomes a necessary element in the full goodness of the world; that in some cases this principle can actually be traced; that in others its action must be assumed if we are to maintain the rationality of the world.[11]

Though it is an immense and audacious affirmation to claim that the fulfillment which sacrificial love provides, if not on earth then in heaven, does justify suffering in principle, the only alternative to it is an unintelligible world. There are, in fact, only three consolations which can be offered for the anguish of the world represented by the approach of the Epicurean, the Stoic, and the Christian. In the face of pain the counsel of the Epicurean is that life will end soon, and then there will be no more pain; the Stoic advises heroic endurance in the face of pain, indicating that the wise man concentrates his attention on other matters; the Christian simply points to Christ and his suffering. That life is short and pain brief is some consolation to one in pain; that wise men forget their pain is no consolation to the unwise; but that God himself suffered as a man is real consolation to man when he suffers.

Sin offers a peculiarly difficult problem. It is rooted in a perversion of the object of self-will which is the same will necessary for all goodness. As such, sin seems inexplicable in a universe claimed to be the medium of God's purpose for good. But even as suffering can be the occasion of eliciting the greatest love possible by a sacrificial act for another which thereby renders the suffering meaningful, so too sin can be the occasion for man's experience of greatest love when he surrenders himself to the love of another.

But the self-surrender cannot be complete if there is not the utmost opposition that can be quelled. Love whose return is achieved by struggle is better than spontaneous affection, not accidentally but essentially; for the specific ardour of the struggle enters into the fibre of the love itself. In fact a sinful world redeemed by the agony of Love's complete self-sacrifice is a better world, by the only standards of excellence we have, than a world that had never sinned.[12]

However, Temple contends that these resolutions of the problem of evil remain speculative and inconclusive. On the basis of them alone it might seem better to some persons to accept the irrational and inexplicable elements which evil introduces into the world. What is needed is a fact of history that demonstrates the sacrificial and redemptive love of the Supreme Power of the universe. The Christian Gospel testifies to just such a fact as is required. The presence of evil

[11] See Temple, *Mens Creatrix*, p. 280.
[12] *Ibid.*, p. 286.

in the world is finally removed as a challenge to God's goodness and power when one turns to history and sees in the life, death, and resurrection of Christ the sacrificial love of God, taking the evil of the world on Himself so as to serve as the dramatic and actualized event which could elicit from man the love he needs to win him to goodness. In Christ, then, the source and sustainer of the universe can be seen actually engaged in the work of redeeming man and the goodness of the whole is vindicated. The theory proposed by reason that the governing principle of the universe is a Personal Being whose purpose is love is now demanded by the facts of experience as well. Thus, for Temple, the Incarnation taken as a fact of history which illuminates all of history provides the most adequate basis for metaphysics. A transition is made from the position of philosophical theism to a metaphysics of the Incarnation, or what is called at one point, "a Christo-centric metaphysics."[13]

Before exploring the details of this Christian metaphysics, some comments on the exposition thus far are in order. Despite his criticism of views which deal abstractly with evil, Temple has analyzed the problem only in an abstract way; particular sufferings of individuals remain unjustified though guidance for practical problems is what distinguishes Christian philosophy from other varieties. Furthermore, that good can be derived from evil is indisputable, but this only produces an instrumental good and lets go untouched the problem of intrinsic evil. The argument that an instrumental good may be derived in the future from what is now evil is just as valid conversely stated; that is, if what is now evil may be altered in the future so as to be viewed as really good, then, following the same reasoning, what is now considered good may become evil at some future time. Once again Temple has posed the problem in such a way that a choice must be made between scepticism and Christian theism so that the intelligibility of the world is identified with the latter and irrationality with the former. Indeed, one is asked to assume intelligibility in order not to lapse into scepticism. Other alternatives (e.g., finitism) surely warrant more careful consideration from the philosopher than Temple provides. Finally, the transition from philosophical theism to a Christian metaphysics is a procedural one for purposes of exposition, since the adequacy of Christian theism is assumed throughout; this assumption is made explicit in the next section.

13 Temple, *Christus Veritas*, p. ix.

B. A CHRISTOCENTRIC METAPHYSICS

Though the present study is not concerned with Temple's theology, as such, inasmuch as certain theological concepts become for Temple the cornerstone of his metaphysics, then his theology is relevant.[14] Such is the case with regard to the interpretation and significance of the Incarnation, and the form which it takes as expressed by the Atonement. According to Temple, the Incarnation and the Atonement provide fundamental insight into the nature of the Supreme Spirit and, therefore, are germane to the present investigation.

The power and love of God have been seen to be guiding and controlling the universe. If man is to fulfill his own nature, then he must respond to this power and love. Also, man as a personal being is free in that he is determined by what seems good to him. That is, the individual follows his apparent good, but is unsatisfied with anything less than the supreme good.[15] Thus, he cannot be coerced into goodness without goodness itself being forfeited. The Supreme Spirit cannot command the allegiance of finite spirit without sacrificing the voluntary devotion that is sought; God must win man's loyalty and love. The true nature of the Supreme Spirit, therefore, must be made known to man in a form which man can understand and to which he can respond appreciatively. Man needs redemption and not merely progress.[16] Furthermore, since man is a personal being, the mode he knows best is that of a human person; and thus if God is to reveal Himself fully to man, He must do so by taking on the limitations of human personality without succumbing to the temptations of finitude. There must come into existence a person for whom his apparent good is always the supreme good.

This is the significance of the Incarnation: Christ becomes for all mankind the manifestation of the eternal truth of God in a particular moment of time and in the form of a particular human being. In so doing Christ also made available the release of a new power or influence in the world, called by Christians the Holy Spirit, by showing the true nature of Divine love. By living a life of love Christ exemplified God's love concretely, calling all men to a life of love; then upon the cross and in the resurrection which followed, Christ demonstrated God's

[14] As already noted, a sympathetic and more thorough treatment of Temple's theology is represented in Fletcher, *William Temple: Twentieth Century Christian.*

[15] See Temple, *Nature, Man and God*, pp. 519–520; also above Chapter 7, and below, Chapters 11 and 12.

[16] See Temple, *Nature, Man and God*, p. 513; also below, Chapter 12.

conquest of death and of the sin which caused his own death. Through the cross man may come to know what sin costs God and at the same time know that his sins are forgiven. Hence, man's sin which seems most contrary to God's goodness and power is seen to be itself the occasion of the triumph of goodness: "God in Christ has not merely defeated evil, but has made it the occasion of His own supremest glory."[17] God supplies the classic example of the alteration of the value of events in the cross and the resurrection by transmitting tragedy into triumph and thereby offering the key to an interpretation of the world.

The meaning and the mode of the Incarnation are revealed most explicitly in these events. It is what the Christian refers to as the doctrine of the Atonement. Commonly viewed as the means by which the sin of man is forgiven, the atonement is for Temple "the mode of the Deity of God" as well.[18] Hence, the central declaration of the Christian faith, more fundamental even than that "the word became flesh" (John 1:14) is expressed by the author of the Gospel according to John in these words: "*God so loved the world that he gave his only begotten Son, that everyone that believeth in him may not perish, but have eternal Life.*"[19] The highest spiritual quality known to man, sacrifice means doing or suffering something for another which apart from one's love for him would not be done or suffered. In the Incarnation, the characteristic activity of God is shown to be sacrifice. God is the sovereign ruler of the universe, and what Christ reveals is that the cross is God's earthly throne. The only object adequate for God's love is the world itself, and in order to redeem it He willingly sacrifices Himself.

> So God vindicates His own Deity. Only such a God can be the God of the world we know. For the Name of God signifies the union of perfect goodness and absolute power. We should have to deny the one or the other if we could not believe in the Cross and Resurrection of Jesus. He reigns from the Tree. Because, and only because, His goodness is so perfect as to include self-sacrifice, His power is known to be supreme and all-controlling.[20]

The ideal conception of God which has been operative throughout Temple's presentation of the problems of philosophy is now made explicit. God is not God unless He is both perfect in goodness and absolute power. It is such a God that Christ reveals. Accordingly, just

[17] Temple, *Mens Creatrix*, p. 322.

[18] *Ibid.*, p. 255.

[19] John 1:14; it is Temple's own translation in his *Readings in St. John's Gospel: First and Second Series* (London: Macmillan and Co., Ltd., 1945), p. 48.

[20] Temple, *Christus Veritas*, p. 273.

as philosophy needs God to satisfy the theoretical demand for a principle of unity, so religion needs Christ to satisfy the practical demand for assurance and specific guidance. But can one justify the acceptance of Christ as the complete revelation of God? It cannot be done on philosophical grounds alone, though the hunger of philosophy for a specific revelation which would make the world intelligible offers some justification. Indeed, when the ultimate principle of explanation is conceived to be a personal God, then revelatory acts are not merely possible but probable. In this way philosophy can show what is needed but cannot assess the adequacy of a revelation claimed to supply the need. It is not clear in Temple's presentation at this point why philosophy cannot assess the adequacy of a revelation-claim if by accepting it the world becomes intelligible.

To base one's understanding of the ultimate principle of explanation on the evidence of God's revelation in Christ is to live by faith and not by knowledge alone, but it is, Temple contends, a reasonable faith. From the standpoint of reason the Christian faith is an hypothesis which must be tested in both thought and practice. It is neither a self-evident premise from which deductions can be made nor a conclusion legitimately inferred from empirical facts. Though resting in part on both of these methods, what Temple now seems to be suggesting is that it is not proved by either one or both together. Ultimately one must act by faith, and the acceptance of Christianity is no exception. Action, not thought, is decisive in enabling one to commit oneself to life as worthwhile. In any event, personal security is the assurance that results from such faith and does not consist of the logical certainty that results from knowledge. Such assurance is won by personal loyalty and not by rational discourse; and the test of its adequacy is not in logic but is in the experiment of living.[21] The Christian hypothesis may not be true; there is no way of being absolutely certain, but what does seem evident to Temple is that it alone offers an intelligible account of the universe. The universe may be inexplicable and, hence, the Christian faith unfounded; but if the universe is intelligible, then Christ alone supplies the principle of explanation. The choice is between complete scepticism or Christian theism. Hence, Temple proclaims "the philosophy of the Incarnation as the only tenable metaphysics."[22]

[21] See Temple, "My Point of View" reprinted in *Religious Experience* ..., pp. 105–106; *Nature, Man and God*, p. 278; *Mens Creatrix*, p. 4; and, *Repton School Sermons* ..., pp. 101, 104–105.

[22] Temple, *Nature of Personality*, p. 96; cf. also, *Mens Creatrix*, pp. 292, 253; *Christus Veritas*, pp. 7–8; *Nature, Man and God*, pp. 266, 520.

Temple's aim as a philosopher is, therefore, the construction of a comprehensive interpretation of the universe as a whole from the perspective of Christ's revelation of God. However, the comprehensive scheme Temple seeks is oriented more toward practical guidance than it is toward theoretical understanding and in such a way that the two aims seem severed. Nonetheless, later in life when time and energy were concentrated on the practical affairs of the Christian church, Temple raised doubts about the feasibility of this task. Whether these later reflections represent a fundamental change in position or simply a change in emphasis has already been analyzed in the first chapter of the present study. What needs to be stated at this point is that Temple is justified in taking a certain datum of experience as the clue to an interpretation of all experience. Success in the latter task is sufficient justification for the choice, but to narrow the choice of alternatives to scepticism or Christian theism does not seem justified. Nor does it seem legitimate to sever practical guidance from theoretical understanding. Can guidance that is lasting and true be provided if it is not rooted in understanding?

C. SUMMARY AND CONCLUSIONS

In this section Temple's conception of personality – human and Divine – has been developed at length, as well as the application of his conception of the ideal of personality to some of the major problems of metaphysics in an effort to render an intelligible account of the universe. Five main points may be noted as constituting the basic arguments and conclusions of Part II.

1. Personality as the key to reality

The picture which modern science presents is that of a physical order which existed long before the appearance of mind and of value. But once mind and value appear in the World-Process, then the process itself cannot be explained except by reference to them. A mindless and valueless universe cannot produce a universe that contains mind and value without destroying the unity of the scheme conceived as strictly physical. However, if the process is itself the expression of mind for the sake of what is considered good, then mind, value, and the physical order are all intelligible. To explain what occurs by indicating the purpose for its occurrence is to provide a self-explanatory principle.

Hence, the World-Process, which at the beginning exhibits only physical objects, gradually produces life, mind and spirit. The total process including the inorganic, the organic, and the personal levels can best be understood by reference to the highest level. Therefore, personality as the highest level produced by the process offers the best principle for explaining the process.

An explanation of the universe may not be forthcoming; but if there is one, it resides for Temple in the purpose of a personal Being. The universe serves as the medium for the expression of value and produces beings capable of consciously sharing in this value. Thus, process gives rise to personality. How is personality to be conceived at the human level?

2. *The Human Person*

Man is a psycho-physical organism. Mind arises within the organism and is an extension of organic reaction to environment. Though the mind is organically related to the body, it transcends the body through the formation of "free ideas," thus making possible the quest for truth, beauty, and goodness. Mind directs the body by means of a purpose it seeks, and the body is the medium for the execution of the purpose.

Purpose, indeed, is the primary characteristic of human personality. The person is aware of his continued existence in a way not possible to the thing (matter) or the brute (life); and the person can, through memory of the past and anticipation of the future, identify himself with ideal goals. Personal action is purposeful action in which the total conscious life of the self is unified around some end apprehended as good expressed through the medium of the body.

Just as the self cannot survive alone, neither can he unify his impulses alone. The fellowship of other persons is required in order to attain the full stature of personal existence. Also, persons desire the approval of others. Hence, only a purpose common to the interests and welfare of all mankind is adequate to satisfy the individual person and to unite persons together in a bond of universal fellowship. Fulfillment of self is made possible through service to society. The highest manifestation of personality is attained in the expression of love for others. However, the ideal of a totally unified, self-determined person expending himself in service to the good of others is not attained on the human level.

3. The Divine Person

Personality appearing in the process offers a clue to the explanation of the process. An ideal of personality is suggested minus the limitations of the human person. Such a being would be completely self-determined and totally unified under the guidance of a universal purpose expressed in the form of love of others. Only such a conception of Divine Personality is adequate, to meet the requirements. For Temple this means that God must be conceived in terms of the trinity. Despite the difficulties involved God is held to be a unified Personal Being whose total nature must be described as a triplex consciousness: the ultimate source and purpose of everything (The Father); the creating, governing, and redeeming power of the world (The Son); and the power active in the world effecting the ultimate purpose (The Holy Spirit).

God is the creator of the world. He operates in the world as an immanent principle of variability adjusting His purpose according to changing circumstances. But God transcends the world also and as transcendent He is the self-identical Person whose purpose for the world is unchanging. The personal nature of God indicates the probability of special revelatory acts and the true nature of revelation. The latter does not refer to propositions but to a personal relation shared between human persons and the Divine Person. Further, revelation of a personal God to persons attains its fullest expression when God takes on the limitations of human personality. It is the faith of Christians that Christ is the human embodiment of God.

Human persons as the highest level of existence suggest an ideal of personality as the explanation of the process which includes human personality. The revelation of God in Christ provides a concrete example of the Divine personality in a human life. What evidence can be offered for the existence of the Divine Person?

4. Evidence for a Personal God

The quest for belief in God is for Temple initiated by his own personal experience of a Personal God. However, philosophical argument offers independent evidence for the reality of God. Without attempting to correlate the conceptions of God arrived at by the two approaches Temple assumes that they support each other. Hence, the complete basis for justifying belief in a personal God consists of the converging independent lines of evidence from both religion and philosophy.

Four types of philosophical argument presented by Temple can be briefly summarized. First, theoretical and practical reason combine to demand a principle of unity sufficient to account for the rational coherence and moral goodness evident in the world. Purposive will alone satisfies these demands; in Christ the nature of such a being is given. Second, man's search for unity through science, art, morality, and religion remains incomplete and precarious unless there is a God such as Christ reveals to complete the quest. Each of these activities of man's mind seek and partially grasp a unifying principle, but none can actually supply the principle required. There is, then, a convergence of these four lines but no actual meeting until God incarnate in Christ is accepted as the fact necessary to bring them together. Third, intimations of a personal God are provided in man's quest for truth, beauty, and goodness. If an intelligible account is to be rendered of the awe man feels before the authoritative claims of truth, beauty, and moral goodness, then a Personal God must be posited whose will sustains these values and to whom the person feels related in the pursuit of them. Fourth, the occurrence in the World-Process of mind capable of apprehending the process indicates that the process is grounded in mind. When mind appears, activities are initiated for the sake of an end that mind itself determines. Only a Supreme Mind which is itself determined by what it takes to be good is sufficient to account for the World-Process which includes mind.

When these arguments are combined with the direct encounter with God that religious believers claim occurs in religious experience, the justification for belief in a Personal God is complete. Temple identifies the God established by these converging lines of argument with the God affirmed by orthodox Christianity.

5. *The Person of Christ*

In Christ the nature of God is revealed. Temple argues that such faith is confirmed by the solution Christ provides to the problem of evil through his life, death, and resurrection. The problem is not to explain the fact of evil in a world supposedly existing as a medium for the expression of the goodness of God. The problem is for man to respond to the evil he finds so as to derive good from it. Evil exists in the world because when overcome it makes possible a greater good than would be the case without it. The example Christ gives of God Himself suffering for man's sake offers real consolation to those who also suffer.

Also, the love of God manifested in Christ is capable of releasing man from the bondage of sin. Intrinsic evil remains unexplained, though in Eternity there is hope that inequities will be rectified.

An adequate account of the universe, then, including both good and evil can be provided only if the Incarnation and the Atonement are taken as the central facts. Man needs to make his apparent good what is, in fact, the actual good. In religious terms this means that man needs to be redeemed. Further, if his freedom is to be retained, then he must freely choose to surrender himself to the Supreme Spirit. This requires that man know what is the actual good for him; that is, that he knows what God is like. Hence, God must reveal Himself to man in a form man knows best – the life of a person. Jesus as the Christ is for Temple that person, and the life of love Christ lived demonstrates the love of God and elicits from man a response of love. On the cross Christ shows God's willingness to suffer for the sin of man. In the resurrection Christ shows God's supremacy over death and the sin which produced it. Tragedy is transmuted into triumph. The nature of God is revealed by the cross and the resurrection, and the world is rendered intelligible by reference to them. Such is the faith of Christians.

Temple was not content to show the supremacy of the Christian faith in solving metaphysical problems; he sought to apply his faith to all areas of life and thought, including the problems of personal and social morality and the meaning and goal of history.

PART III

A CHRISTIAN PHILOSOPHY OF PERSONAL AND SOCIAL MORALITY

CHAPTER 11

PERSONAL ETHICS

It is Temple's contention that the ideal of personality as exemplified by God in Christ can be made relevant to the solution of the basic theoretical and practical problems which have plagued moral philosophers. Thus, personality becomes the central concept in solving the problems of personal ethics (Chapters 11 and 12); personality is also operative in society determining the nature and function of the state and of the economic order (Chapter 13).

A. A THEORY OF VALUE

In the course of the unfolding of the World-Process various levels have been noted, each of which exhibits distinctive characteristics. These levels have already been designated as matter, life, mind, and spirit. The movement, thus, is from a material world in which actions and reactions occur more or less mechanically without a human mind to observe them, to the development of living organisms that gradually come to an awareness of the process from which they have arisen. These organisms, aware of their existence, are able to select among the means offered by the environment those which best satisfy their own demands. When the stage of spirit is reached, the ends sought are also selected by the living organism, and the level of a personal being is attained. The distinguishing trait of man as a personal being is the fact that he is guided by an ideal which he envisages and toward which he strives.

It is at the stage when personal beings arise in the development of the World-Process that Value also appears.[1] In the broadest sense, value resides in the way all things fit together in the universe, but

[1] As already noted, this does not mean that value is of secondary importance, only that like personality it appears later in time than matter. See above, Chapter 6.

the mind's capacity for consciously appreciating this relation is unique and warrants restricting the term value for this special experience.[2] Specific values are produced when mind finds satisfaction in certain objects that are apprehended. Thus the fitting together of mind with its environment constitutes value.

The fundamental condition for the actualization of value is the mind's discovery of something akin to itself in its object. Temple notes two aspects to the experience of the mind's discovery of "kinship" with its object: "First, that it finds the counterpart of the principle of its own activities; ... secondly, that with this discovery goes a feeling of being at home with the object, not lost or bewildered in presence of it."[3]

Value becomes actualized, then, when a conscious being, capable of apprehending the world in which he lives, selects certain aspects of that process as objects of appreciation and worth. Temple summarizes the characteristics constituting any value-experience: "We find, then, that for any actual Value or Good there must be two factors in a certain relationship – the 'valuable' object and the apprehending and appreciating subject; and these must meet in an experience which satisfies or is fit for permanence."[4]

Man apprehends the world and discovers in that apprehension certain features with which he feels a kinship; as a result he experiences a sense of satisfaction. The recognition of this sense of satisfaction by the individual constitutes value. Further, whenever anyone claims to experience a sense of satisfaction in regard to certain objects, his claim is final and indisputable. "To every man his own sense of value is final."[5] Likewise, if one finds no satisfaction in regard to certain objects held to be valuable by others, it is useless to argue with him.

The subjective factor involved in value is therefore essential for the actualization of value. This does not mean, however, that value is entirely relative to every individual or that an agreement on values is not possible. What one claims to be valuable he alone can determine based on his own intuition. But one's taste in all areas of life can

[2] See Temple, *Nature, Man and God*, p. 165. Temple seems to be using mind in the generic sense in this context, and means by it a mode of being and activity with distinctive characteristics.

[3] *Ibid.*, p. 165. It has already been shown that the notion of the "kinship" of mind with reality is also fundamental to Temple's argument for God in *Nature, Man and God*; see above, Chapter 9.

[4] Temple, *Christus Veritas*, pp. 32–33. Good here is synonymous with value and is not to be confused with moral goodness which is considered below.

[5] *Ibid.*, p. 24. See also *Nature of Personality*, p. 72, and *Mens Creatrix*, p. 179.

be developed, and through constant experience with certain objects one can begin to appreciate them so that they come to be regarded as valuable. The influence of others is paramount here. If someone whom you admire enjoys Beethoven, you may decide to listen to Beethoven's music and gradually learn to appreciate it. It is of utmost importance in this regard for one to be rigorously honest with oneself as to what is truly enjoyed for itself and what is enjoyed as a means to some other end. The social nature of human personality also serves as a check on any relativistic conception of value. Man's membership in society places upon him the obligation of realizing certain values appropriate to his position.[6]

More significant than any of these factors in ruling out a subjective view of value is the recognition of the significance of objects in value experience. The sense of satisfaction one feels is necessary for value to be recognized, but it is the object which is appreciated and which gives rise to the sense of satisfaction that is held to be valuable. The objective nature of value is thus evident in the very experience of value. Indeed, the satisfaction one receives from the objects appreciated is proportional to his concentration, not on himself or his satisfaction, but on the objects themselves:

> The self is capable of complete satisfaction in proportion as it is left outside the field of its own attention. Value exists for subjects; but the subject finds the value only when completely absorbed in the object.[7]

Actual value, then, is always a relation to mind. It resides neither in the object held to be valuable nor in the subjective experience of satisfaction; rather, value as actual belongs to the subject-object relation itself. However, what is considered valuable is not the sense of satisfaction one experiences, but the object apprehended and appreciated. Hence, it is in the object that value primarily resides. An appreciating mind actualizes the value an object possesses, but once actualized the value is objective. "And the Value once found is in some measure independent of the occurrence in which it is found." [8]

Temple's conception of value is far from clear. A value is actualized only when an object is appreciated by mind. However, when mind appreciates an object, it evidently finds something that was valuable all

[6] See *Mens Creatrix*, p. 180. This point has already been developed in terms of its significance for an understanding of human personality on Chapter 7.

[7] *Christus Veritas*, pp. 28–29. See Brand Blanshard, *Reason and Goodness*, pp. 308–313, 315–316.

[8] Temple, *Nature, Man and God*, p. 208.

the time. If this is true, then, the subjective appreciation has no effect on value. On the other hand, if an object is not valuable until appreciated, then it was only potentially valuable prior to the experience of appreciation. In another connection Temple suggests a distinction that is in accord with the latter alternative:

> Till Mind appeared as an episode in the world process, all other episodes had value in potentiality only, not in actuality – so far at least as the process itself supplied the condition of its actualisation.[9]

However, he does not develop the notion of potential value or relate it explicitly to his theory of value. Hence, the relation of the feeling of satisfaction to the object in which mind finds satisfaction remains ambiguous in Temple's value theory. Among contemporary ethical theorists, Brand Blanshard argues most thoroughly for a combination of subjective (satisfaction) and objective (fulfillment) factors in his conception of the good; however, unlike Temple, Blanshard unambiguously affirms that the good resides in the *experience* of satisfaction and fulfillment.[10]

Nonetheless Temple's point is clear: value consists in the interaction of mind with its environment resulting in the mind's feeling of satisfaction with what it discovers in the environment. The three chief forms of satisfaction customarily referred to as absolute values are truth, beauty, and goodness. Temple summarizes the nature of value and the occasion for the appearance of each of these three values in the following passage:

> The essential condition for the actualisation of Value is the discovery by Mind of itself or its own principle in its object.
>
> When Mind makes this discovery in the activity of contemplation, the form of Value actualised is Beauty.
>
> When Mind makes this discovery in the activity of analysis and synthesis, the form of Value actualised is Truth.
>
> When Mind makes this discovery in the activity of personal relationship the form of Value actualised is Goodness.[11]

Not all of these three values are absolute in the sense that it would always be best to pursue them. For instance, "to forgo the opportunity of acquiring some minute and probably unimportant fraction

[9] *Ibid.*, p. 364; see also *ibid.*, pp. 421–415.

[10] See Blanshard, *Reason and Goodness*, pp. 308–313, 315–316.

[11] *Ibid.*, p. 164. Truth has already been discussed in Chapter 4, and Temple's views on moral goodness will be expounded at length in the rest of the chapter. His views on beauty are not sufficiently germane to the subject of the present study to warrant separate treatment. His definitive statement on the subject is found in *Mens Creatrix*, pp. 93–152.

of knowledge in order to give pleasure to others might be permissible or even obligatory."[12] Likewise, something which is beautiful may have an adverse effect upon some one insufficiently mature to appreciate its true worth. However, with regard to moral goodness the situation is different: it is always better for man to be as good as he can be and never better for him to be worse than he can.[13] Goodness, furthermore, is a distinctively human value which man himself creates. Whereas truth is apprehended but not constructed by man, and beauty is both appreciated and produced with appreciation predominating, goodness is predominantly a human achievement. The distinctive life each individual lives represents "an original contribution to the scheme of things."[14] What contribution a person should make constitutes one of the fundamental problems of ethics confronting each individual.

B. MAN AS A MORAL BEING

1. *The Moral level*

Man has the capacity for both memory and anticipation. He can form concepts of types of experiences which are not actually present to his senses. In this way man formulates a type of experience which he would like to have and toward which he strives, namely, ideals. Principles are thus formulated and accepted as guides to one's conduct. The significance of the future for personality is once again apparent. This capacity of man to conceive of, and be directed by, ideals and principles entitles him to rights as a personal being in a society of persons, and at the same time places upon him duties which will preserve and foster personality.[15] This means further that the moral level has been attained; for ends can be chosen which guide the individual and which are not merely means to a determined end. Finally, it sig-

[12] Temple, *Nature, Man and God*, p. 136.

[13] Temple is confusing in regard to the status of truth, beauty, and goodness. Although he refers to them as absolute values, he indicates that what he really means is that "there are three forms of absolute value – intellectual, aesthetic, and moral," *Christus Veritas*, p. 26, N. 1. Love is held to be the absolute value which is best expressed through truth, beauty, and goodness.

[14] *Ibid.*, p. 32.

[15] Man thus moves beyond claims and counterclaims appropriate at the level of the brute or with regard to the relation of a person to a brute. Since an animal experiences pain, it makes a claim upon man not to cause it to suffer indiscriminately. Rights and duties, however, involve a reciprocity between the participants which demand a degree of self-awareness animals do not seem to have. See Chapter 7.

nifies that man's actions are his own, revealing at once his individuality and the basis of moral responsibility.

Each individual is, therefore, unique, but this does not mean that he is independent of his environment. Growth in both body and mind requires reaction to something else and nourishment from another source. It is for this reason that the influence of others, particularly society, is so significant. Man is moved to act upon, and to interact with, his environment (including other persons) by desire – e.g., the desire for the approval of others. In order to satisfy this desire the individual must be concerned with the needs and wants of others. To act in this way is to seek the welfare of society which is the primary expression of morality, since morality can best be defined in terms of one's social obligations. However, one's obligation is not exhausted by the relations shared with others, even as the self is not exhausted by his relations.[16] The terms peculiar to moral value – namely, duty, obligation, and ought – need to be understood in terms of the personal relations shared by members of society; but before this can be done, it is essential to understand the nature and content of the moral obligation man feels.

2. *Moral obligation as unique but derivative*

An analysis of human conduct reveals the fact that at times individuals feel an obligation to perform, or not perform, a certain act. This sense of obligation is not to be confused with the content of obligation, that is, what one feels he is obligated to do. The imperative which one feels to do (or not to do) something is unconditional, though that which constitutes the obligation is conditioned by his culture and society.[17] Hence, the sense of obligation is unique and represents a dimension of human personality; the content of obligation is derivative, reflecting as it does the various influences of the environment on the self.[18]

[16] Temple changed his position in this connection. In *Mens Creatrix*, p. 182, he tends to identify morality with social obligation, but in *Christus Veritas*, p. 28, n. 1, he views obligation as more basic than social responsibility. The bearing this has on his interpretation of obligation will be noted in the discussion which follows. Dorothy Emmet challenges Temple's assertion that alll obligations are social obligations, apparently failing to realize that he has changed his position on this point. See Emmet, "The Philosopher" in Iremonger, pp. 535–536; also see Fletcher, pp. 153–154, 324–325.

[17] The experience of absolute obligation is for Temple, we have seen, the experience of God; see *Christus Veritas*, p. 95, and above, Chapter 9.

[18] See Temple, *Nature, Man and God*, pp. 168–169.

Man experiences an obligation to do something, and this feeling is integral to his nature as a self-conscious being; what he is to do or to be is determined not by his nature alone but also by his experiences in the social context which constitutes his environment. In this way one can understand both the universality of moral obligation as an experienced fact of human personality and the variety of moral codes which different cultures have evolved. The fact of moral obligation as unique and inherent in self-consciousness must not be blurred or discarded because of the many different types of conduct to which it becomes attached. Likewise, the fact that the content of obligation does vary to such a wide extent from culture to culture must not be explained away because constant throughout is the sense of obligation.

Only when both of these facts are taken together can personal morality be adequately understood and guidance in ethical living provided. The sense of obligation makes morality possible, but it is discerning the nature of the sense of obligation and what constitutes the legitimate object of one's feeling of obligation which pose the moral problems. It is necessary, therefore, to ask what the consciousness of obligation in itself means and, further, what is the proper goal of moral obligation?

C. FUNDAMENTAL MORAL PRINCIPLES

1. The obligation to be conscientious

An analysis of the experience of obligation itself provides only a formal solution to the problem of a choice of the proper object of obligation. What is commanded by the sense of obligation is absolute: one is to will the right; but no guidance is provided in the command as to what it is that is right for one to do.

However, this absolute command to will what one considers right, though devoid of specific content, is nonetheless significant. There is a universal sense of obligation but different interpretations of the content of obligation. The sense of obligation which man feels as absolute and unconditional is not to be attached to any particular command but rather is a command to the person himself always to do what is right. Man's obligation, then, is to be conscientious in the choices he makes and the actions he performs. Obligation in this sense is the correlate of the experience of value, that is "absolute obligation of absolute value."[19] However, such obligation does not specify what particular acts in any situation it is right for him to do.

> Absolute obligation therefore attaches not to the act, but to the will. It is my absolute duty to will the right; but there is no act which it is my absolute duty, independently of circumstances, to do or not to do .... Thus as we search for the proper subject of absolute obligation we are driven back from act to agent, from conduct to character.[20]

On this point Temple's affinity – though not identity – with "the new morality" or situation ethics has correctly been noted by Joseph Fletcher.[21] However, as we shall see, Temple avoids the extreme relativism of Fletcher's situationism by stressing the determinative role played by one's attempt to discover and to fulfill both his place in a given social structure and his place in the Divine Purpose.

Just what is meant by referring to obligation as the correlate of value is not clarified. Perhaps, Temple means that one's absolute obligation is always to express love, the one absolute value. This would be consistent with his emphasis on love of neighbor as the only valid form of the moral law. However, Temple does not make this connection and, hence, what he intended is uncertain.

2. *The optimific principle*

To discover the proper object of man's sense of obligation it has been necessary to distinguish between the imperative one feels to do what is right and any specific act he takes to be right in a given situation. Thus, obligation is more a matter of a man's character than his conduct. But character and conduct cannot be separated in practice, and it is guidance for the latter that is needed. What principle should constitute the basis for determining what it is right for an individual to do in a particular situation?

Following G. E. Moore rather than W. D. Ross, Temple sees the formal solution to this problem as residing in what is sometimes referred to as the optimific principle, namely, "the view that those acts are right which are productive of most good."[22] In view of this principle

[19] Temple, *Christus Veritas*, p. 28, n. 1. Temple's change in position is made evident at this point.

[20] Temple, *Nature, Man and God*, pp. 178–179, see also, *ibid.*, p. 405, and "A Conditional Justification of War" in *Religious Experience* ..., pp. 173–174.

[21] See Joseph Fletcher, *Situation Ethics: The Mew Morality* (Philadelphia: The Westminster Press, 1966), pp. 27, 59–60, and Fletcher, *William Temple*, pp. 55, 147, 151, 156–163, 310.

[22] *Nature, Man and God*, p. 406; see also *ibid.*, p. 180.

one must always consider the total consequences of his actions in terms of whether or not the effects produced are, on the whole, the best for all concerned.

3. Lack of certainty in ethics

What is right, then, in any situation can be stated in principle to be whatever tends to produce the greatest good. But this criterion is inadequate when one strives to apply it in actual concrete situations. In the first place, all the consequences of any act cannot be determined. Secondly, the criterion noted fails to give guidance in distinguishing between different kinds of good. As an example of the difficulty involved Temple offers the following dilemma:

> Most will agree that it is in general better to pursue knowledge than to pursue pleasure, to escape from ignorance rather than from pain. But few would admit that it would be right to choose a course of action that would lead to an increase of knowledge rather than one which would deliver a man (still more a multitude of men) from great suffering, if both could not be pursued together.[23]

One's choice of a scale of values is involved here, and how is one to know which particular value should have priority in any given situation? To be able to decide this would necessitate knowing the total effects of the possible alternative actions, but no such knowledge is forthcoming. There must always be a lack of certainty in regard to the rightness of any specific action taken. The individual is called upon to do what is right, but he can establish that he has fulfilled his obligation only by the risk of action taken which at the time he is not certain is right. Such adventurous action in the moral realm cannot be and should not be eliminated. It is part and parcel of the mature moral life. But for the constant and conflicting choices which confront man, more concrete guidance than is offered in the utilitarianism evident in the optimific principle is essential if morality is not to degenerate into subjectivism.

To affirm conscientiousness as a universal obligation indicates the moral dimension of man's nature, but only serves to pose, not solve, the practical moral problem of what one is obligated to do in a specific situation. Even to suggest that one's obligation is always to produce the greatest good in light of the total consequences is but a formal resolution and contains little specific guidance in determining what course of action offers the best chance of producing the best results.

[23] *Ibid.*, p. 183.

What these analyses have revealed of special significance in solving the theoretical problems of ethics is the necessity for placing the emphasis not on human conduct but on human character. Similarly, perhaps a solution to the practical problem ethics poses of knowing what acts are best in a given context can be solved by concentrating not on the action to be taken but on the agent who must decide. An exposition of the roots of obligation, both as a unique faculty of human personality and the derivative aspects in regard to the content of obligation, may provide the clue that is sought.

D. PRACTICAL PRINCIPLES OF GUIDANCE

1. Social significance of origin of obligation

Moral obligation may be seen to have three primary bases in the emergence and development of human personality in the World-Process.[24] First is the fact of man's status in the universe as one center of conscious awareness in the universe. As soon as the individual becomes conscious of his own consciousness and hence self-conscious, he likewise is made aware that he is one of many such self-conscious centers which the universe has produced and, therefore, that he shares this fact in common with others. A bond more profound than the clash of commercial interests binds men together.

In the second place as soon as a plan of action regarding himself and his own interests is formulated, it becomes apparent to him that others have a claim upon him which he recognizes as binding. And, finally, to achieve the integration of self which he desires he must submit to a purpose which can utilize effectively all his energies. Such a purpose to be fully satisfying cannot be one directed only to himself, for woven into his own being is the influence and guidance of others. He is a social being by birth, training, and inclination, and can thus gain full satisfaction of his entire self only by dedication to a social purpose.

2. Membership in society as a clue to right action

The importance of an analysis of the actual development of an individual's sense of obligation, both in regard to its uniqueness as an

[24] See Temple, *Christus Veritas*, pp. 69–71, and *Nature, Man and God*, pp. 185–189.

absolute command to do the right and what is considered to be right by him, is that it returns the discussion to the concrete realm of individual choice. The content of obligation, since it involves the influence of the individual's total environment, must be viewed in the perspective of the individual's relation to society. What one feels obligated to do does not develop in a vacuum, since from the start each individual is a member of some society.[25] His survival and the realization of any plan he has is to a greater or lesser extent dependent on the other members of that society. The responsibility which is his, then, is likewise to a great extent determined by his membership in society, or what F. H. Bradley labels "My Station and Its Duties."[26] The actual obligations which are placed upon one depend on the role he has to play in the social structure of which he is a member and on the nature of that structure. Thus, the sense of obligation as it is actually manifested in any individual's life may be defined as follows:

> That sense of obligation is the spontaneous reaction of a person who is a member of society towards acts or suggestions which conform to or contradict the standards of conduct which under the influence of experience have come to be accepted in his community.[27]

Temple's conception of actual obligation as determined by one's place and membership in society approximates, though for different reasons, the recent prescriptivist theory of P. H. Nowell-Smith in analyzing the purpose of moral rules. For Nowell-Smith custom and tradition at the social level and habit and conscience at the level of the self account for most of the rules we have and the fact that we keep them.[28]

The theoretical problem of ethics regarding one's duty is thus solved formally by the recognition of one's membership in society and the contribution one can make to that society. As significant as this solution is, however, it fails to answer the questions of how one determines what his place in society should be and how he is to go about making his contribution.

To these issues it will be necessary to return, but for the present another consequence of conceiving obligation in terms of membership in society warrants explication. Does such a position foster a conserva-

[25] Temple's epistemology noted above in Chapter 4 is significant at this point. Man's knowledge of the world and himself is from the beginning based on his interaction with his environment.

[26] See F. H. Bradley, *Ethical Studies*. In Temple see *Nature, Man and God*, p. 189.

[27] Temple, *Nature, Man and God*, p. 188.

[28] See P. H. Nowell-Smith, *Ethics* (Baltimore, Md.: Penguin Books Ltd., 1954), Chapter 16, esp. pp. 230–236.

tive, even reactionary, attitude toward the existing social order so that what is, is held to be right? This does not follow, however, except in the extreme and negative form which states that it is always wrong to take action which would eliminate any society whatsoever. Only the avoidance of anarchy can legitimately be inferred as an unconditional obligation from the necessity of man's membership in society. Indeed, the obligation of individuals to society is to seek constantly to improve it.[29]

It is particularly pertinent at this point to note that what one feels is his obligation will be influenced by the training he receives. Though a sense of obligation cannot be cultivated, the content of obligation can be. In terms of one's loyalty to society, this training should consist in expanding his conception of society to wider and wider communities, encompassing more and more people until all mankind is recognized as having a claim upon him.

Progress, in the form of a change in the existing social order, may also occur by the reflection of an individual member on some of the basic principles accepted by the society and by the application of them in a way not previously done. In this way Wilberforce successfully opposed slavery in England.

Thus, though one's membership in society determines his actual obligation, this does not impede progress or foster stagnation. No society is perfect, and the appeal of the sense of obligation always to seek what is right extends beyond the existing social order in quest of a still better one. This sense of an absolute obligation independent of any one social structure, though always operating through some one society, reveals man's inherent value and worth.[30]

It is the recognition of the intrinsic value of personality which provides the proper perspective from which personal relations are to be viewed. In so doing one recognizes another as a person and recognizes the principle of personality each shares. When one becomes aware of himself as a person and respects others as persons also, the basic principle of morality has been made explicit. As Temple puts it:

> The principle of morality is that we should behave as Persons who are members of a Society of Persons – a Society into which Personality is itself a valid claim of entrance. We are to treat all Persons as Persons, and all as fellow-members

[29] See Temple, *Mens Creatrix*, pp. 207, 211. This would seem to have been Socrates' position in the *Crito*.

[30] See Temple, *Nature, Man and God*, p. 190. Here we may see the significance of Temple's change in position already noted in which obligation is more basic than social responsibility and is the source of it.

with us in the Society of Persons. Actual duties will depend upon actual personal relationship; there is a special duty of parent to child and child to parent.[31]

The primary concern of each person is the best and highest development of the personality of all. Personal goods have priority over all non-personal goods. Society too is for the sake of personal development even as personality cannot fully develop apart from society.

3. *Love of neighbor as the absolute moral law*

These considerations lead to the conclusion that the one expression of the moral law which is truly universal and unconditional is contained in the commandment: "Thou shalt love thy neighbor as thyself."[32] Each person is to count himself as one and only one. The acceptance of this fact and its implications in terms of one's own loyalties and interests constitute the primary moral task for each individual. To love another as one loves oneself is the essential practical problem of personal ethics. Each individual is called upon to be conscientious in his pursuit of what he considers to be right but guided in what is right by his feeling of love for others.

Can such concern for others be realistically asked of the individual? Indeed, does not the fact of self-conscious awareness make it inevitable that what each one considers right and good both for oneself and for others will seem more correct than what others affirm? Can it be any other way if man's individuality as a focus of conscious awareness is to be maintained? Temple succinctly states the dilemma confronting each individual: "He is a being particular and finite called to live by a principle universal and infinite; and his particularity distorts his vision."[33] The self is lifted out of his particularity by loving another as himself and thus he is commanded to love, but love cannot be commanded; it can only be elicited.

4. *The failure of formal solutions*

Thus the solution of the practical problem of ethics is only provisionally solved by the commandment to love one's neighbor. For if this could

[31] *Ibid.*, p. 191. The influence of Kant is evident here especially in the second and third formulations of his Categorical Imperative, or what are referred to as the practical imperatives. In the third formulation Kant states: ' Every rational being must act as if he, by his maxims, were at all times a legislative member in the universal realm of ends." Kant, *Foundation of the Metaphysics of Morals* in the *Critique of Practical Reason and Other ...*, trans. Beck, p. 95.

[32] *Mens Creatrix*, p. 206; *Christus Veritas*, p. 215; *Nature, Man and God*, pp. 195, 406.

[33] *Christus Veritas*, p. 215.

be accomplished by the self alone, then ethics would pose no problem. But it is precisely man's failure to love which causes the problem. Hence, the practical problem of ethics becomes: how can individuals come to love one another? As long as this issue remains unsolved, practical ethics is rendered impotent.

The situation is the same with regard to the theoretical problems of ethics. Man has the obligation to do what is right, and this means to promote the greatest good. However, no help is provided by these principles for deciding what is, in fact, right to do in a given situation. And though the solution was proposed that membership in society provides the clue to right action, this too is only a formal resolution and the guidance most needed was not forthcoming. How is one to determine what his particular membership in his particular society commands of him? Furthermore, to know that one's station in society determines one's duties is important, but what one also needs to know is what one's place is in the society.

The failure to resolve these issues indicates the inadequacy of ethics to solve the problems which are raised by ethics on the level of ethical science alone. To solve them adequately ethics must submit to the insights of religion. "For the problems of Ethics arise out of the relations of finite spirits to each other, but can only be rightly determined by reference to the relation of those finite spirits to the Infinite Spirit."[34]

A comment is in order at this point regarding Temple's approach. Is the alleged failure of ethics to solve its own problems due to ethics or to Temple's statement of the problem and the solution he wishes to impose? Temple has a definite ideal for man in mind; and when philosophical ethics fails to measure up to the ideal, he criticizes it. But it is questionable whether such an approach is legitimate since he is unwilling to modify the ideal in accordance with the demands of experience. The content of the ideal Temple is employing becomes evident in the following chapter.

[34] Temple, *Nature, Man and God*, p. 172.

CHAPTER 12

THE NEED OF ETHICS FOR RELIGION

A. CONVERSION AS THE SOLUTION TO PRACTICAL ETHICS

It is well before proceeding in an attempt to solve the theoretical and practical problems of ethics to state more carefully what man's moral situation is. This entails bringing together in a different way material already presented in preceding chapters.

1. *Man's moral situation as a self-centered being*

Man emerges in the World-Process as the culmination of the process, containing within himself all four levels of reality: matter, life, mind, and spirit. He is a psycho-physical organism. Combining as he does many desires, needs, interests, and aspirations, man possesses a unity which is at first only partial and is always precarious. It is rooted in the unity provided by the physical organism. But part of his natural tendency is to strive toward a fuller unity under the guidance of a purpose to which the total self can respond. Also, one desire man has is for the approval of others, and hence the attitudes and actions of others exercise a significant influence on the individual. But what significance and who in particular will influence him are the individual's choices.[1]

Furthermore, each individual is a finite center of self-consciousness and of value-realization. Value existed only potentially until mind appeared in the process capable of appreciating what is apprehended and thereby actualizing the value of objects.[2] Man not only experiences pleasure and pain; he is aware that he is experiencing them and is able to select among objects presented to him which ones he chooses to pur-

[1] See Chapter 7.

[2] As already noted, unfortunately Temple does not relate the notion of potentiality indicated here to his theory of value; see Chapter 11.

sue and to enjoy. He is able to determine the direction of his attention and action by his awareness that he is attending and by his selection of some objects among those available for his attention. This places man on a moral level, for he can choose not merely the means to a predetermined end but the end itself.[3]

Herein lies the source of both the grandeur and the misery of man. As a center of value-realization man has inherent worth and is able to engage in the quest for truth, beauty, and goodness; but as a finite center of consciousness, man possesses a limited vision of the process of which he is a part and which he partly transcends by his awareness of his status in it. He apprehends the world and appreciates values; but because it is always his apprehension and his appreciation, he is prone to place more importance on himself than on another as apprehender and appreciator and more importance on his ideas and aspirations than those of others, even when his prove unworthy or wrong.

Morally this means that each individual directs his life by what appears to be good to him, that is, by what Temple calls the apparent good.[4] It could not be any other way than this since each individual is a self-conscious center of value experience. But the result is that each tends to care more for what he takes to be good than what others do, and to assume that the apparent good for him is the true good for all. In a passage strikingly similar to Reinhold Niebuhr's analysis of sin, Temple states: "*So he becomes not only the subject of his own value judgements, which he can never cease to be, but also the centre and criterion of his own system of values, which he is quite unfit to be.*[5]

Thus the sin which is man's is the constant tendency to exaggerate the importance of what is his because it is his, quite apart from its actual value as contrasted with what belongs to others.[6] To do this is to act directly contrary to the ethical goal for man which commands him to love another as he loves himself. Man's sin is thus his self-centeredness which tempts him to give priority to his own concerns, whether justified or not.

It is important, however, to recall that it is in the self and the

[3] See Chapters 6 and 7.

[4] See, *Nature, Man and God*, p. 362.

[5] *Ibid.*, p. 365. For Niebuhr man's sin is "his inclination to transmute his partial and finite self and his partial and finite values into the infinite good"; *The Nature and Destiny of Man: A Christian Interpretation*. Vol. I *Human Nature* (New York: Charles Scribner's Sons, 1941), p. 122. Temple and Niebuhr influenced each other; see Craig, pp. 9, 129, 151.

[6] See *ibid.*, p. 370, and *Christus Veritas*, p. 215. For Temple this is the true meaning of original sin.

self's activities that the possibility of any realization of value resides. Hence, "it is self-centredness that is evil, not selfhood. Selfhood is a precondition of all true good."[7] The destruction of the self is not at issue, but rather a recognition and acceptance by the self of its subordinate status in the entire process and the need to place the Spirit of the Whole at the center of its life. But this the self cannot do of itself, for of itself it is and must remain its own center.

2. *The self's bondage to itself*

This same dilemma that man faces can be stated in terms of freedom and in so doing will point up the way of resolution. To be free does not mean that something is uncaused. The latter would make for chaos. Thus the real question concerns the mode of determination and not whether an event is determined or not.[8]

In the course of the World-Process the transition from physical particles to personality is evidenced by an increase in the significance of individuality for the results produced. Movement of physical parts is for all practical purposes determined by external force and only in a small way by the particularity of the part itself. However, at the level of personality the contribution of the character of the person is paramount. As we have noted, the reason for this, making it possible for the self to determine itself, is rooted in the capacity for free ideas. In this way the mind is able to detach itself in a limited but significant way from the needs of the organism so as to contemplate possible ends toward which it can choose to work. Once having chosen them it is determined by them in what it becomes. Hence the freedom which is gained resides in the self's choice of what will nourish its body. Since decision in any given moment is determined primarily by one's character at that moment, and character itself is determined by what ideas and ideals one fixes his attention on, the real freedom man has is in the choice of his attention. Or, to state the same idea in another way, the primary choice made by each individual is in terms of what he will permit to influence him.[9]

Thus, man chooses what to him is his apparent good, which in turn determines what he will be and do. Such freedom can be bondage of the most extreme form if what is chosen as apparent good is not,

[7] Temple, *Nature, Man and God*, p. 376.
[8] See *ibid.*, p. 229; also, see above, Chapter 7.
[9] See *Nature, Man and God*, pp. 230, 384; also *Christus Veritas*, p. 219.

in fact, the true good; for the self is the source of action, but from the self there is no escape.[10]

3. *Quest for values as a means of partial escape from self*

The bondage which is man's due to his freely chosen apparent good may be partially alleviated through the quest for truth, beauty, and goodness. The emphasis in both truth and beauty is on the object perceived, and submission to it is essential if its truth is to be discovered or its beauty revealed. However, escape is partial in that only an aspect of man's self-centered nature is involved, not his total self. In goodness, however, the obligation placed upon the individual is to love another as himself which would mean deserting self-centredness itself. Here one reaches the core of the problem. For man can proceed by gradual steps to concern himself more and more with others, taking their needs into account even as he does his own. But this is still not enough; for no matter how wide the circle becomes and even if it includes all mankind, the individual self is still its center. It is the same with the effort of the individual toward disinterested love. That disinterested love is a possibility for the self is evidenced in the feeling of affection which the child has for the mother and in the willingness of persons to give their lives and themselves to the service of others. But it must be noted that one loves only one person (or at most a few persons) in this way, and to this person one feels a close affinity. The relation is one of lover and beloved with each belonging to the other.

Hence, though real progress is made both in widening one's area of loyalty and in effectively loving another for the other's sake, the self is still at the center. Indeed, if one concentrates on delivering oneself from self-centeredness, that is procuring one's own salvation, then one is apt to be proud of being delivered from one's pride and thereby never fully loses it.[11]

4. *God as the center of the self*

The only conclusion which can be drawn is that if the self is to forget oneself in service to others, then something beyond the self must take

[10] Cf. Temple, *Mens Creatrix*, p. 144, *Christus Veritas*, p. 58, and *Nature, Man and God*, pp. 241, 385.

[11] Cf. *ibid.*, p. 390, with the fourth temptation in T. S. Eliot, *Murder in the Cathedral* (New York: Harcourt, Brace and Company, 1935), p. 44. "The last temptation is the greatest treason: to do the right deed for the wrong reason."

hold of the self which means an abrupt break with one's own spiritual progress, or what religion calls a conversion. The self as one locus of conscious apprehension and appreciation within the World-Process can apprehend and appreciate adequately only if at the center of its activities is the Spirit of the Whole or God. But to make God the center of one's attention is not man's to do.

What is quite certain is that the self cannot by any effort of its own lift itself off its own self as centre and resystematise itself about God as its centre. Such radical conversion must be the act of God, and that too by some process other than the gradual self-purification of self-centered soul assisted by the ever-present influence of God diffused through nature including human nature. It cannot be a process only of enlightenment. Nothing can suffice but a redemptive act. Something impinging upon the self from without must deliver it from the freedom which is perfect bondage to the bondage which is its only perfect freedom.[12]

But man cannot be converted against his will any more than he can will to convert himself. Man must find that the good he seeks is only attained through surrendering himself to God. Sacrificial love alone is capable of effecting this result. "*The one hope, then, of bringing human selves into right relationship to God is that God should declare His love in an act, or acts, of sheer self-sacrifice, thereby winning the freely offered love of the finite selves which He has created.*"[13]

One finite center of self-consciousness must become the focus of God himself, which when adopted by others as their center frees them from partial and incomplete visions. For Temple, God was focussed in a finite, human center of conscious awareness in the person of Jesus Christ. If man is to make his apparent good the truc good, then he must surrender himself to the God revealed in Jesus Christ.

Even for man to surrender to Christ is possible only because God has so constructed man that he can respond and because God takes the initiative to elicit the response from him. Man's contribution to this process, known in religous terms as grace, is the need for deliverance; the rest is God's doing.

A solution to the practical problem of ethics which commands that each person love all others in the same way he loves himself is, therefore, attainable only when ethics passes over to religion, only when moral philosophy becomes Christian ethics. Conversion of the self from the self's quest for the good to his being possessed by the good which is God, alone suffices to resolve the practical problem ethics poses.

[12] Temple, *Nature, Man and God*, p. 397.
[13] *Ibid.*, p. 400.

5. *Content distinguished from motive of morality*

Thus, for Temple the content of morality is to be distinguished from the motive of morality. Man's capacity to recognize the good and his duty is independent of religion. Man can even know that he ought to love though not be loving. It is the motive to love which religion supplies in the example of Jesus Christ, his love and sacrifice. Christ shows to man the depths of his sin and elicits a response of love from man, thereby changing his will. In this way the individual feels differently. Though man does not learn the difference between good and evil from Christ, what does occur is that his will is changed so that he does not want to do the wrong thing. Hence, though man's moral sense is independent of religion, representing as it does a dimension of human personality, it needs religion to nurture it and make it effective in the world.[14]

Temple shows a keen sensitivity to the moral problem confronting man. Has he, however, in his concern to point the way by which man can escape from an unjustified concern for himself lost the self he strived to save? The account of conversion tends to deny the efficacy of man's will, rendering him incapable of cooperating in his own redemption, in which case human personality is negated. Can man's will be changed independent of man's willing it without sacrificing individual integrity and moral worth?

B. VOCATION AS THE SOLUTION TO THEORETICAL ETHICS

A similar situation arises with regard to the theoretical problems of ethics. In the discussion of the fundamental moral principles it was proposed that man be conscientious in what he wills so as to will always what is right, and that the right is what produces the greatest good. To this was added the view that one's particular duties are determined by his place in society. These solutions, though sound in principle, fail to provide adequate guidance in practice. If each individual has a specific vocation to fulfill which will when realized develop his capacities to the maximum and at the same time render the greatest good to society, then the problem is solved in both theory and practice. An ethics of vocation offers, then, the clue which is sought.[15]

[14] See Temple, *Kingdom of God*, pp. 57–59, 64, 66, 101, 103. Also cf. the discussion of the limitations of moral philosophy in Thomas, *Christian Ethics and Moral Philosophy*, pp. 370–372.

[15] See Temple, *Nature, Man and God*, p. 407. The doctrine of divine will operating in

The individual can by a careful examination of his capacities and the opportunities society affords determine what his vocation is. That it may also be determined by consciously aligning oneself with the Spirit of the Whole, or God, is the testimony of religious believers. These points need to be explored more fully.

1. Right and good as identical

The apparent distinction between an act, as the consequences following from an individual's choice, and an action, as the choice itself including the reasons for initiating the consequences, may be removed. In practice one cannot decide which act is right by examining the total effect of the act and choosing that one which produces the best possible consequences, for such calculation is impossible.

Each one must rely upon the logic of his own nature, being what he is and the possible consequences being what they are, to guide him to choose what is best for *him* to do in that particular situation. Moving beyond W. D. Ross' distinction between the right and the good, Temple affirms that what is right for one to do and what is good for all merge so that what is right is his obligation and what is good is the fulfillment of the obligation. "Right is the Good as presented to mind practical; Good (as applied to an act) is Right as presented to mind contemplative."[16]

2. Man's inner logic as guide

Another clue to the actual problem confronting the individual as he attempts to live morally is the recognition of how he must go about fulfilling his obligation. For though man's obligation is to the entire human race, in practice he can only fulfill his obligation by serving particular men living in particular societies. What he can and must always keep in mind is how his service to limited groups will foster mankind as a whole.

A man must in practice serve his family, his city, his firm, his trade union or what not; the over-riding obligation to the entire spiritual fellowship can in practice

history and determining the events of history including the individual's vocation implicit in this view will be briefly considered in what follows and examined more thoroughly below in Chapters 14 and 15.

[16] Temple, *Nature, Man and God*, p. 409. The identification of right and good in this way presupposes that history is the unfolding of a divine purpose. This issue is developed further in Chapter 15. See W. D. Ross, *The Right and the Good* (Oxford: The Clarendon Press, 1930).

only be expressed through the prohibition of any service to the narrower unit or structure which involves injury to the wider.[17]

That is, he must check each narrow loyalty by the wider one.

However, the claims made upon the individual and his own demands on himself must remain divergent unless there is a Supreme Mind ordering the various structures without and within the moral agent. If there is such a Supreme Mind ordering all that exists, then the individual can discover what it is right for him to do through following what fulfills his own true nature. This follows because there would be a logic of conduct immanent in each individual as part of the Divine ordering of events assuring him of the rightness of his act. Therefore, conscience defined as "the spontaneous verdict of a man's moral nature,"[18] though not completely reliable, should be followed since it is more apt to reflect the inner logic of his being. However, in following conscience one should be guided by the total effect one's choices have on others. Conscience provides the source of right action; the actual production of goodness provides the test.

By following the inner logic of one's own being a person is relieved of the impossible task of trying to discern which act is right by examining the supposed consequences of each. The time such a procedure would entail renders it impractical for most choices in any event. But this does not mean that one can or should fall back on a mere subjective interpretation, thereby fostering fanaticism. For an objective check is contained in the obligation to pursue that course which, in fact, produces the best results. The point is, an individual's best means of determining what he should do is by reference to his own conscience but the test of the choice resides in the total effect that results. Hence, man's "duty is both to intend and to accomplish the good."[19]

The task of the moral philosopher, then, can only be to present the general principles of goodness, never to suggest what is good for any individual in the many specific situations he faces. No deductions regarding a specific choice can be made from the general principles proposed. Each individual must seek his own solution, and even the guidance of a sympathetic friend should never be considered definitive.

There is an element of hazard and adventure to the ethical life which cannot be eliminated. But this may now be viewed as the risk of a confident faith of one who strives to discover and to fulfill his place

[17] Temple, *Nature, Man and God*, p. 409.
[18] *Ibid.*, p. 179.
[19] *Ibid.*, p. 410.

in the Divine Purpose. Ethics once again is supplemented by religion, and the speculation resulting in understanding is supplemented by religious practices cultivating a deeper personal devotion. "As the general ethical problem finds its solution in general religious principles, so the personal problem of each individual finds its solution in personal religious practice. In the life of personal devotion to God, known as Righteous love, the answer to problems of conduct otherwise unanswerable may be found."[20]

Temple's departure from Fletcher's situationism should now be clear: though both men emphasize that the absolute obligation to do what is right is relative to circumstances, Fletcher places the burden for determining what is right (most loving) on the individual deciding in the situation; whereas Temple's relativism is tempered both by his conception of actual obligation as determined by one's place and membership in society and by his confident faith that through fellowship with God man can come to *know* what he ought to do.

Temple has made a shift in the meaning that he gives to moral obligation without indicating that a change has been made or offering a justification for it. Before, he defended a non-cognitive theory in which the experience of obligation did not provide the content of what one ought to do. He now affirms a religiously oriented cognitive theory of obligation in which man can know *what* it is right for him to do and not merely *that* he ought to do what is right. Thus for Temple the problems of personal ethics can be fully solved only from the perspective provided by the Christian faith. The same is the case with regard to the problems that arise when the person is viewed in relation to society.

[20] *Ibid.*, p. 411.

CHAPTER 13

CHRISTIAN SOCIAL THOUGHT

Temple's understanding of Christianity led him to affirm three basic social principles as applicable to any social structure.[1] An exposition of these Christian social principles is the logical place to begin an analysis of Temple's views on human personality and society followed by the application of these principles to the two major social orders, namely, the political and economic orders. In what follows no attempt is made to present an exhaustive treatment of Temple's views on social issues; what is offered is an exposition of the significance the principle of personality has upon Temple's social thought and some of the applications he made to crucial political and economic issues.[2]

A. BASIC SOCIAL PRINCIPLES

1. *The sacredness of personality*

When man is conceived in Christian terms, then there is an inherent worth in each man based on the fact that he is a child of God, created by the love of God and for the sake of communion with God. The notion of personality itself, Temple argues, is derived from Christian thought about God and man's relation with God.[3] Each person, therefore, is to be respected simply because he is a person and quite apart from any

[1] See Temple, *Christianity and the Social Order* (Harmondsworth, Middlesex: Penguin Books, Ltd., 1942), pp. 61–74. In earlier writings on the subject four principles were noted; cf. *Christus Veritas*, pp. 203–207; *Personal Religion and the Life of Fellowship* (London: Longmans, Green and Co., Ltd., 1926), pp. 66–68; *Essays in Christian Politics and Kindred Subjects* (London: Longmans, Green and Co., 1927), pp. 9–18. The difference involved is explained in the exposition of the principles.

[2] For a more complete analysis of Temple's social and political philosophy, see Robert Craig, *Social Concern in the Thought of William Temple*; John D. Carmichael and Howard S. Goodwin, *William Temple's Political Legacy: A Critical Assessment* (Naperville, Illinois: Alec R. Allenson, Inc., 1963), and Fletcher, *William Temple*, pp. 147–227.

[3] See *Essays ...*, p. 79.

usefulness he may have to society. Temple is unequivocal in his assertion of the primacy of personality over society and the institutions of society: "The person is primary, not the society; the State exists for the citizen, not the citizen for the state."[4]

Certain consequences follow from this emphasis on man's inherent worth. Each person is to be provided with the opportunity to develop his capacities to the fullest possible extent, requiring the best possible education for each child. Having aided its citizens to fulfill their capacities, the society must then provide them with every possible opportunity to determine for themselves how they will live their lives. Nor is this simply a matter of not interfering with them; it entails respecting their thoughts, words, and deeds. Citizens should, so far as possible, be free to choose their personal activities and at the same time be held responsible for the choices made. Freedom and responsibility are thereby encouraged, which in turn allows for the unfolding of personality: "It is the responsible exercise of deliberate choice which most fully expresses personality and best deserves the great name of freedom."[5]

Only as one is free to express himself is he able to realize himself as a person. The goal of the political order of society is thus clear: it must establish and maintain freedom for the citizens within its domain. Such freedom does not imply simply the absence of external restraint, or a freedom *from* something. This type of freedom too readily leads to slavery to one's momentary impulses. The individual needs to be freed from his own impulses as well as from those of others which would hamper his own best development. As previous discussion has shown, true freedom requires the ability to formulate and execute a purpose to which the whole individual is committed. Personal freedom in this sense entails restraint both externally and internally since it involves control, determination, and direction by the self. "To train citizens in the capacity for freedom and to give them scope for free action is the supreme end of all true politics."[6]

Furthermore, man as a finite center of self-awareness thinks and acts from his own perspective of the world, and hence it is to be expected that he will not always use his freedom in a way that fosters the freedom of others. Man's self-centeredness thus points up the necessity for, and significance of, law in society.

[4] Temple, *Christianity and the Social Order*, p. 61.
[5] *Ibid.*
[6] *Ibid.*, p. 62.

The function of law is primarily negative in that it puts restraints on certain acts which infringe on the freedom of others. However, the real value of law is in the liberty which it makes possible for everyone. In this respect the restraint which law encourages may also have a positive effect on the individual by guiding him into channels of conduct that develop certain potentialities and thwart the development of others.[7] In this way the person is stimulated to realize those qualities which foster fellowship, another basic social principle.

2. *The principle of fellowship*

A person must be free from unnecessary restraint so as to fulfill his own nature. Each one is to be respected as a person in his own right; but one must respect others as persons too, and the use each makes of his freedom should be for the sake of all and not himself alone. Fellowship must be freely chosen and thus cooperation presupposes freedom. But unless persons who are free do choose to cooperate, their freedom readily results in anarchy and the eventual loss of freedom for all. Hence, if freedom is to be effective, then each individual needs to exercise it for the sake of the common good.

On the positive side, fellowship has been shown to be requisite for the development of personality itself.[8] Man is naturally and necessarily social. Beginning in the social unit of the family, man's life continues through other social units as the school, community, state, church, trade or profession. The individual is, in fact, largely determined by the influence of these groups and constituted by his relations to them. This does not mean that he contributes nothing himself, for that is the error of determinism; but it does mean that to remove the particular social relations is to eliminate the individual who actually exists.[9] The freedom which an individual enjoys must, therefore, be viewed in terms of the social units in which he participates. The family is the basic unit since in this fellowship the individual is born and nurtured; therefore, a responsibility falls on the community to make available adequate housing, health, wages, and leisure for its families so as to afford the proper conditions for family living. Industry too is to be viewed in terms of public service and not profit only.

Temple approves of Maritain's distinction between individuality and

[7] See Temple, *Church and Nation*, pp. 65–71, and *The Church Looks Forward*, p. 174.
[8] See above, Chapter 7.
[9] See Temple, *Christianity and the Social Order*, p. 64, n. 1, and above, Chapter 7.

personality.[10] Individuality indicates that each one is distinct from everyone else, but personality relates the members one to another since one can become a person only through social relationships. Accordingly, if the state is to fulfill its function, then it must promote the social units in which citizens are grouped and see that they become agencies for the development of personality. The richer an individual's personal relations are, the more fully personal he can become. Thus, society is for the sake of personality even as personality finds its fulfillment in society. There is, then, a duty on the part of everyone, both individually and collectively, to serve the welfare of all.

3. *The duty of service*

So long as man is not simply an individual distinct from others but is also a person who needs and desires the fellowship of others, then he must live his life so as to serve society. The primary means by which this is accomplished is through one's chosen vocation, though the use of one's leisure in voluntary service is also significant.

The relevance of vocation in solving the theoretical problem of personal ethics was argued in Chapter 12; what needs to be stressed at this point is the service rendered to society through vocation. The individual is called upon to choose a vocation that develops his capacities to the maximum and also renders the greatest good to society. It does not follow that one's vocational interests are to be ignored; what does follow is that the choice itself should be determined by the principle of service to society and not merely on the basis of personal satisfaction or monetary reward.

The practical difficulty which such an obligation poses is that not everyone can choose an occupation. Circumstances beyond the control of the individual (e.g., the labor market) too often dictate what work one will do, if any; therefore, society is obligated so to order the economic life of the community that such a situation will not arise. Thus, not only individuals but the social units of society have the duty to serve society as a whole. This means that the narrower loyalties which one normally serves (e.g., family) must be checked by the wider loyalty (e.g., nation) cultimating in mankind itself.

Suppose one is caught in the practical problem noted above, so

[10] See Jacques Maritain, *Scholasticism and Politics*, trans. ed. by Mortimer J. Adler (New York: The Macmillan Company, 1941), pp. 56–67. In Temple see *Christianity and the Social Order*, p. 67.

that there is not available to him a vocation which fulfills his capacities, and the only work offered is dull and distasteful? If this is the case, then the person might accept the job and perform it as an act of self-sacrifice so as to serve society and in such a way that he fulfills himself through the sacrifice. However, Temple hastens to add: "Of course, this does not justify an order of society which offers to many men only such forms of livelihood as require a miracle of grace to appear as forms of true vocation."[11]

The relevance of self-sacrifice as a basic social principle needs to be carefully examined. When it is not possible to serve society and also fulfill one's own needs and aspirations, the power of self-sacrifice to transform both self and society must never be minimized. Sacrifice is, in fact, the only true means of gaining victory in any dispute. For to win by subduing another by force is to elicit his bitterness toward you; whereas sacrifice of oneself for another, even an enemy, is to elicit a response of love from him and convert him to a friend. The willingness to serve society even to the point of self-sacrifice is the highest value as illustrated by Christ on the cross.

However, self-sacrifice cannot be proposed as a separate social principle because of the impossibility of applying self-sacrifice as a principle, inasmuch as no one fully accepts it for oneself and because social groups are even less prone to accept it.[12] The difficulty is most apparent when one (e.g., a father) strives to impose on others (e.g., his children) standards which are not accepted by them. In such a case the result is that the children become alienated both from their father and from the standards he sought to impose. Self-sacrifice by its very nature can never be imposed on others. It is one thing to choose to do something which will result in the loss of one's life because of a principle believed in; it is quite another thing to act in this way when the lives of others are also at stake. Sacrifice of self, to be sacrifice, can only be self-imposed. The ideal of self-sacrifice needs to be set before men, but it is for each to decide if and when the ideal is to be actualized.

> We see then why a man cannot without more ado take as his guide for the treatment of his fellows the Christian standard that service to the point of self-sacrifice is our truest welfare. Let him live by that as far as he can; and let him invite others to join him in that enterprise; but let him not force that

[11] Temple, *Christianity and the Social Order*, p. 71.

[12] In earlier works Temple does propose it as the fourth principle, but in *Christianity and the Social Order*, pp. 72–74, he combines sacrifice with service. I find the shift from four to three principles quite reasonable, but Fletcher does not think Temple has adequately explained the change; see Fletcher, *William Temple*, pp. 196, 333.

standard on his fellows, and least of all on those dependent on him. They will always have the opportunity to act on it if they are so minded.[13]

There is problem enough to get oneself and one's groups to acknowledge the duty to serve society as a whole and not merely their own self-interests. Hence, to establish justice in the sense of "the securing of rights and interests of individuals in the most equitable manner"[14] is, perhaps, as high an ideal as can be expected to be realized on a social level. This is not to forsake sacrificial love as the ultimate ideal, but it is to recognize that justice is the necessary means by which love is expressed on a group level. Thus Temple asks: "Is it not the fact that in problems concerning the relations of corporate groups of men, the way of love lies through justice?"[15] Love in this case becomes the motive power for the establishment of justice.

Freedom, fellowship, and service constitute the three fundamental principles on which any social order must be founded, and for Temple they are rooted in a Christian understanding of man as a child of God created for eternal fellowship with Him. The aim in principle of a Christian social order has now been suggested through the realization of these principles and is summed up by Temple as consisting in "the *fullest possible development of individual personality in the widest and deepest possible fellowship.*"[16] But these are general principles. How is a state to be viewed both in origin and present practice so as to make possible personal development and social fellowship? What type of economic order is consistent with these aims? These and other questions must now be explored.

B. THE POLITICAL ORDER

1. *Society as a natural product*

There are basically two theories regarding the origin of society.[17] According to one theory, man is, as Aristotle affirmed, social by nature and, therefore, the development of a government in some form is a natural outgrowth. The other theory, of which Hobbes is the classic exponent, holds that man is essentially selfish by nature, and hence

[13] Temple, *Christianity and the Social Order*, pp. 73–74.
[14] Temple, *Citizen and Churchman* (London: Etyre & Spottiswoode, Ltd., 1941), p. 76; see also *ibid.*, p. 79.
[15] *Ibid.*, p. 78.
[16] Temple, *Christianity and the Social Order*, p. 100.
[17] See Temple, *Christianity and the State*, pp. 43–44.

society itself is constructed on the basis of a contract agreed upon by the individuals. According to Hobbes the origin of society is identical with the origin of government. In order to gain protection and security from the predatory instincts within each individual leading him to desire everything he can get, men agree to restrict these natural rights and to place power in the hands of a sovereign ruler who will enforce the laws agreed upon. Hence, the sovereign comes into power through the contract which is made by the participating members but is not himself bound by it.[18] As ingenious as this theory is, it is patently false. It rests on a view of man as an isolated individual, but the facts of the evolution of the race and the individual's own development point to his necessary interrrelation with his environment, particularly fellow human beings. Further, there is no indication historically that men ever actually took the steps of forming a contract leading to an absolute sovereignty as the theory suggests.

These difficulties are avoided in the view which takes society as a fact of human nature and government as a fact of human history. Man is essentially social, and hence there is no need for a contract to bind him to others. The form that society takes need not be speculated on, for one need but examine what forms actually developed.

Though the contract theory renders an inadequate account of the origin of society, there are some basic truths in it which need to be incorporated into an account of the state's origin and function. There is a necessity for restraint within the state not only to protect one from the conduct of others, but to protect oneself from one's own conduct that would not be beneficial to society. "We are all of us tacit partners to the compact that we will not do injuries in order that we may enjoy security against suffering them."[19] Further, the contract theory rightly perceives that there arises the need from time to time to alter or even abolish the existing form of social order: and if the state is viewed as a construction by its members and rests on their consent, then they have the right to change it. This leads to still another insight of the contract theory: namely, the chief political problem within the state is discovering a proper balance between the obedience of its citizens to the law and the fostering of their individual freedom.

Nonetheless, the social contract theory is inadequate and inaccurate.

[18] See Thomas Hobbes, *Leviathan*, ed. with an introduction by Herbert W. Schneider (New York: The Liberal Arts Press, 1953), Chaps. XIII, XIV, XV. In Temple see *Christianity and the State*, pp. 46, 61–65.

[19] *Christianity and the State*, p. 47.

To agree to live in society is not a contract made explicitly or implicitly by man; it expresses a dimension of human personality. Society can only be explained if man is social by nature. But if social unity is to be maintained, then some means must exist for preserving it; and some officials must be designated whose function is to employ these means so as to guide the society toward the aims which it professes. When these means are sufficiently developed and the officials provided with sufficient power, then both law and the state come into being. The error into which man has been led historically is the assumption that the geographical boundaries of a state were essential to its operation so that the exclusiveness of the state became intertwined with its function as a unifying agency. Previously this was the case since sufficient means of communication were lacking to bind peoples across territorial boundaries.

The starting point, then, of any political theory is man's essentially social nature: man is always found in some communal organization. This social fact of man is apparent in sexual union which gives birth to the individual, and in the necessity of an extended period of parental care for the young. Hence, "the family is the root fact, and however far civilisation advances, it grows like a tree from that root."[20] Each individual from the start is conscious of his unity with the group which protects and cares for him, and of the difference between his group and other groups. "Thus the sense of community grows from within and is strengthened from without."[21]

As a matter of historical fact the real problem has been not that of isolated individuals relinquishing some of their freedom for the sake of banding together; rather the social solidarity of the group to which one belonged was so complete that little, if any, freedom was permitted the individual.

It was the differentiation of the individual with his own rights as distinct from the group and its rules that had to emerge gradually. This movement was fostered by the developing complexity of the group and hence the need for specialists in law, religion, merchandising, and so forth. In this way associations grew up within the community but distinct from the state, thus requiring that society be distinguished from the state. Too often the state is identified with society so that all which society accomplishes through, and sometimes despite, the state is attributed to the state. But if state, associations, and society

[20] *Ibid.*, p. 101.
[21] *Ibid.*

must be distinguished, then the nature of each and their relationship one with another have to be explained more fully.

2. *The state as the necessary organ of society*

Temple, combining the views of Unwin and MacIver, interprets society (or the community) as the basic and natural development of man's social nature, the natural groupings in which men are joined together.[22] A consciousness of unity pervades such groups fostered by mutual need and ties of affection, as illustrated by the family. Society, then, is prior to both the state and to any association. Further, because associations of individuals develop with the society, the life of the society is more than the state and independent of it. Moreover, the distinguishing feature of the state is not the fact that it can use force to maintain social unity; this is a right it has by virtue of its unique function as the special organ of the community from which one cannot readily remove oneself. If one is opposed to the requirements of a particular state, only two alternatives are open: (1) that of becoming a citizen of another state, (2) separating oneself from civilization. The state thus exercises a universal authority over its citizens which is carried out by means of the force entrusted to it. Law, not force, therefore, characterizes the state.[23]

Associations as distinguished from the state, represent the forms taken by the social life of the community as the society develops. The state is not such a development, for it is integral to the community itself and serves as the necessary instrument of the society. The only accidental qualities of the state are its geographical determination and hence its extension. National sovereignty is the necessary means by which both liberty and order are possible. Social life itself, then, is dependent on the law and order the state affords though it carries on a life independent of the state. "*The state is a necessary organ of the national community, maintaining through Law as promulgated by a government endowed to this end with coercive power the universal external conditions of social order.*"[24]

[22] Cf. R. M. MacIver, *Community: A Sociological Study* (2d. ed. rev.; London: Macmillan and Co., Ltd., 1920) and *The Modern State* (Oxford: Oxford University Press, 1926); George Unwin, *Studies in Economic History*, ed. with an introductory memoir by R. H. Tawney (London: Macmillan and Co., Ltd., 1927). In Temple see *Christianity and the State*, pp. 109–110.

[23] See Temple, *Christianity and the State*, p. 114. Here Temple disagrees with Unwin; see *ibid.*, p. 110.

[24] *Ibid.*, pp. 123–124. See MacIver, *The Modern State*, p. 22; and also, Blanshard, *Reason and Goodness*, p. 402.

The state, then, is to be conceived as the necessary organ of the community, its existence derived from and its authority conditioned by the community. Ultimate political loyalty, therefore, is not due the state but the community itself, though the state is, under normal conditions, necessary; and hence loyalty is due it.[25] Nonetheless, since a state can be administered improperly, resulting in the necessity to alter it, the priority of the community must be maintained. No particular type of state is required to serve as the community's unifying organ. However, when the citizens of a community are capable of it, representative democracy is advocated as the best form of government because of its educative effect on personality by fostering both freedom and responsibility.

It must be remembered that it is for the sake of the community of persons that the state exists. Though man is social by nature, he is not merely social, and still less is he merely political. He seeks truth, enjoys beauty, and aspires goodness. The pursuit of these values cannot be prescribed by the state. The state, in fact, exists as the indispensable means for the maintenance of man's social life, but it is the means for the attainment of these ends, not the ends themselves. "The higher values of that life are established upon the foundations which it provides, but are themselves beyond its cognisance."[26] Thus the state, acting as it does through law for the sake of preserving the conditions of well-being, has universal jurisdiction over its citizens but only in respect to these conditions and not to the total life of its citizens. The state is sovereign, then, but only with regard to law and even then only so far as it fulfills its function of maintaining peace and justice. The state is to provide the conditions which make possible the fullest development of its citizens.

In terms of the basic social principles enumerated, the principle of fellowship provides the basis for the state's origin; and the problem which a state poses is the preservation and promotion of the principle of freedom by encouraging its citizens to serve the best interests of the entire community. If the state fails to guard the rights of its citizens and even hinders their expression in the associations formed, then the individuals and the associations must rise up against the state. "For in such a case the state is impoverishing the common life which it exists to preserve and to foster."[27] The state cannot dictate to its

[25] The ultimate loyalty of the individual is not to any historical order for Temple, but to the Kingdom of God which is beyond history. See *Christianity and the State*, p. 174.

[26] *Ibid.*, p. 126.

[27] *Ibid.*

citizens what to believe or how to worship. The individual citizen can, in fact, be free only in and through the social units of society. Thus, if his actual liberty is to be preserved, the state must promote and protect these associations, allowing them freedom to develop a life of their own.

At the same time the association formed must be made responsible for their activities and need to be regulated by the law at those points where the well-being of the state is at stake.[28] Particularly pertinent here is the relation of the state to the economic groups operating within but also extending beyond its borders. This will be taken up later in the chapter; but the point to be understood at this stage is that the associations within the state possess power and are responsible for the exercise of that power. More than any other group within the state, voluntary associations develop the social life of the citizens, thereby aiding the state in fulfilling its function of fostering the development of personality; nonetheless associations, like individuals, can act for selfish purposes so as to infringe upon the freedom of non-members. The task, then, is to make these associations responsible agencies for the welfare of the total community, that is, agencies of service. Thus, Temple espouses a doctrine of Functionalism in regard to the structure of social life in a society: "Within human society we must aim at establishing that relation of the various functions or activities to one another which corresponds to their contribution to the general well-being."[29]

Thus the state must strive not only to promote freedom but to encourage its citizens to exercise their freedom in service to society, both individually and through their collective organizations. In this way all three social principles are taken into account in the analysis of the state's origin and function.

> Such a scheme as has been outlined gives the fullest possible scope to Personality; for this reveals itself largely in special affinities and in the associations which embody these. To increase the scope of these associations is thus a potent method of fostering the growth of Personality. The same policy plainly recognises and rests on the Fact of Fellowship, for fellowship is chiefly realised through those same affinities and associations. But above all it stresses the Duty to Service; for it takes associations originally self-centered and sometimes even selfish, and bids them take counsel for the common good.[30]

[28] This is true of a church when, for example, it owns property. See Temple, *Christianity and the State*, p. 127.

[29] *The Hope of a New World*, p. 67; see also W. G. Peck, "William Temple as Social Thinker" in *William Temple: An Estimate . . .*, p. 74.

[30] Temple, *Christianity and the State*, pp. 138–139.

What is the responsibility and function of the state to other states and to the total community of mankind?

3. The international community

In order to understand adequately the relations which should prevail between states it is imperative to keep in mind the nature and function of the state just noted. Each state exists for the sake of acting on behalf of the welfare of all its citizens, past, present, and future.

At this point a difference must be noted between the disputes individuals have one with another and disputes between nations. The interests of the citizens which the state exists to serve cannot be sacrificed in the same way one might choose to sacrifice oneself and one's own interests. And while it is quite true that what is morally wrong for the state to do cannot be politically right for that same state to do, it is not necessarily the case that what is morally right or wrong for an individual to do is the same for the state. The agent and the circumstances must always be considered in any ethical choice.[31]

A state must, therefore, be certain that it reflects the will of its people when it acts, for example in a time of war. It cannot take lightly its role as trustee to the community it represents and to the world-wide community as well. Confronted by the threat of war, the nation can choose to capitulate to the demands, thereby avoiding war, only if such a course is the will of the community it represents and such a course of action would serve the best purposes of the wider community.

> Trustees have no right to inflict self-sacrifice on their clients .... Furthermore, not only is the State a trustee for the community, but each national community is a trustee for the world-wide community, to which it should bring treasures of its own; and to submit to political annihilation may be to defraud mankind of what it alone could have contributed to the general wealth of human experience.[32]

Hence, there are essential differences in the problems that arise between individuals and between nations, and in the way they can and should be handled. To blur these differences hinders the promotion of peace and justice. Not only are the disputes of a different nature, but so too are the aims and purposes quite different. The principles

[31] See *ibid.*, pp. 150–153, and Fletcher, *William Temple*, pp. 172–173. Temple is being consistent here with his view of vocation as a special calling of each individual, and thus what is right for one individual to do may be wrong for another.

[32] *Christianity and the State*, p. 156.

on which a nation acts within and without its borders cannot be equated with those that motivate and guide individuals.

The internal function of the state is to foster the fullest development of individual personality consonant with maintaining social unity and social fellowship; its external function is the development of a community of nations while retaining the integrity of each separate nation. Thus, the problems and aims of a national state externally are the reverse of those internally: "Within the nation, unity (broadly speaking) is given; the problem is to foster independence; among the nations, independence is given and the problem is to foster unity."[33]

However, the unity of the national states and the function they serve must not be lost even in the movement toward internationalism. Turning again to the historical method of analysis, Temple argues that the mutual relations of one state to another can best be understood by reference to the origin and development of the state itself. The guarantee of any state is law, not force, and the foundation of the state is the desire and necessity of its people for a community.[34] Force is the state's means of maintaining law.

The sovereignty of the state may be considered in regard to two main issues: (1) the right of the state to ask its citizens to die, if necessary, in the fulfillment of its commands; (2) the supremacy and full sovereignty of the state illustrated in its relations to other states since each one admits no superior beyond itself. The first of these two points Temple accepts; the second he rejects.

Since the state is the necessary means for preserving the community, if the state collapses, then the life of the community is also endangered. Though man's intellectual and cultural interests and all those activities comprising his social life are more precious to him than his political interests, nonetheless the latter are the indispensable conditions for the former. "Therefore the State is, in principle, . . . justified in calling on its citizens to die, and even to kill, for the preservation of what is necessary to it as the indispensable instrument of the nations' life."[35]

The second point, however, can be defended only from an exclusively nationalistic perspective. Even as the nation arises from, and exists

[33] *Ibid.*, p. 157.

[34] What MacIver (inverting Rousseau) calls the General Will *for* the state, see *The Modern State*, p. 11. See Temple, *Christianity and the State*, pp. 119, 159.

[35] *Christianity and the State*, p. 162; see also "A Conditional Justification of War" in *Religious Experience*, pp. 171–178. The individual can be called upon to kill but not to hate; see *ibid.*, p. 175. Also see *Hope of a New World*, p. 81. Temple defends the right of the citizen to refuse to participate in war as a result of personal convictions, though he does not agree, for the most part, with such a view.

for, the community of individuals who comprise it, so too the nation fulfills itself best externally by cooperating with, and operating through a community of nations. Temple concisely sums up the issues at stake: "The State is an organ of community; community has mainly been territorially demarcated into nations; therefore the State has been national. Community is become very largely international; therefore the State must become international also."[36]

Thus, the state's own logic points beyond itself to an international organization. This would mean consciously and historically establishing a real social contract such as Hobbes noted; however, the contract would not be between individuals for the sake of forming a society but between nations for the sake of establishing an international organization as the organ for the already existing international community. Evidence of the existence of an international community is most noticeable in the economic realm where territorial borders become secondary to the needs and demands for the interchange of goods and services. The role of economic groups in their relation to the state, the function of the economic order itself, and the relation of this order to the social principles affirmed must now be stated.

C. THE ECONOMIC ORDER

1. The necessity for economic freedom

The state is the guarantor of law and order in the society for the sake of fostering the personality of its citizens. As such, it regulates the lives of its citizens, but there is little direct personal contact between the state and the citizen. For the most part the state when functioning properly has an indirect effect on the people. With regard to the economic order, it is quite the opposite since the work which individuals do to earn their livelihood directly controls their daily life. The regulations which accompany their particular jobs "invade their very homes and tell them when they may get up and when they may go to bed."[37] Furthermore, whereas in a political democracy the citizen now has some voice in the regulations enacted through duly elected officials, for a long time the worker had no representation in determining the economic regulations that controlled him. Even with the

[36] *Christianity and the State*, p. 171.

[37] Temple, *Mens Creatrix*, p. 222; also see *Church and Nation*, p. 82.

development of unions, the workers can affect the regulations over them only through the threat of a strike.

What is at issue here is not merely the wages workers receive, important as they are, but rather the tendency to treat workers not as persons but as "hands." "A hand is by nature a 'living tool,' which is the classical definition of a slave."[38] The labor a man renders has been separted from the man's total nature as a personal being; this is an unwarranted abstraction, for the labor a man performs is inseparable from him as a person: "I may sell my coat and another man may buy it without in any way affecting my personality; but I cannot thus sell my labour for my labour is simply myself labouring."[39]

Such injustice cannot be rectified by charity, for this misses the point which concerns the total personality of the worker and his right to be recognized as a rational and responsible being. The root of the difficulty is that the economic order still claims a sovereignty which the political order has relinquished. Though no longer ruled by the crown but by duly elected representatives of the people, the state may still be dominated in its economic life by the private capitalist.

To treat a worker as a "living tool" is to defy the principle of freedom and the sanctity of human personality. Furthermore, to grant a man political freedom does not insure the full freedom necessary for the expression of one's capacities if economic freedom is denied. One must be free to order his life if he is to become a fully personal being; and this means being able to choose a vocation consonant with his abilities and the social needs; it means further having a voice in the work to which he becomes committed. Despites the increase in living standards and improvement in working conditions, there is still this one great lack in the economic life, namely, the absence of worker representation in the policy of the company for whom he labors most of his waking hours. The case for political freedom is now widely accepted, but full freedom for the worker cannot be said to exist until economic freedom is also a reality. An evolution of industrial freedom with responsibility must take place in which the workers have a fair share not only of the company's earnings but also in the formulation of the company's policy. "Before we can be said to have a free society it will be essential that the control of industry shall pass largely into the hands of those immediately concerned."[40]

[38] Temple, *Christianity and the Social Order*, p. 87.
[39] Temple, *Mens Creatrix*, p. 223.
[40] *Ibid.*, p. 222.

Similarly, too much work offered to a person today is monotonous, and far from stimulating his faculties, it actually deadens them. Nor is it justified simply to reply that one gets out of something just what is put into it, for some labor is degrading and dehumanizing. The person must be willing to serve his fellowman, but in so doing he should also have the possibility of fulfilling himself. If a person is to find a vocation which will both develop his capacities to the maximum and render the greatest good to society, then the labor market must make such opportunities available to him. Particularly pertinent would be the provision for fruitful labor at times of enforced and extended unemployment. What are the implications of granting economic freedom to the worker and of taking an active interest in his vocational opportunities, in terms of the purpose of the economic order and its relation to the other orders of society?

2. *Economic productivity as a means to cultural productivity*

Temple turns to the notion of natural law for the light it sheds on an understanding of the orders of society and the proper relations between them. By natural law is meant "the proper function of a human activity as apprehended by a consideration of its own nature."[41] With the application of this definition to economic activities, the proper function suggested by an analysis of their nature indicates that "the reason why goods are produced is that men may satisfy their needs by consuming those goods."[42] Accordingly, production does not exist merely or even primarily for the sake of the profit it can bring to the producers but to satisfy the needs of the consumer. This does not mean that profit is wrong but that profit is one result, in the form of monetary rewards, of meeting consumer demands.

> But it is possible none the less for these two to get into the wrong order, so that the consumer is treated, not as the person whose interest is the true end of the whole process, but only as an indispensable condition of success in an essentially profit-seeking enterprise.[43]

The difficulty involved is in no small measure due to a false conception of the economic process as an isolated and independent sphere of activity to be judged on its own principles (e.g., productivity and profit). This runs directly counter to its natural function in the scheme

[41] *Christianity and the Social Order*, p. 77.
[42] *Ibid.*, p. 78.
[43] *Ibid.*

of things. "The economic process is not an end in itself; it and all its parts are primarily a means to something that is much more than economic – the life of man."[44]

The economic order is to be judged not only on the basis of producing and distributing goods – though even here it may succeed in the former while failing in the latter – but also on the effect such production and distribution have on the personality of those concerned and their relations with one another. An economic system which is effective in the production and distribution of goods, but which in that very process dulls the individual's faculties and fosters hostilities among the citizens, must be condemned as morally ineffective.

In actual practice both the necessity of producing for consumption and the necessity of making a profit if one is to continue to produce must be considered, and a reasonable balance between them maintained. The difficulty in maintaining a proper balance is that the indispensable condition for production is that the producer make a profit.[45] Goods can be produced even when the consumer's interests are not taken into account or are artifically stimulated, but these goods cannot be produced if there is no profit. This leads Temple to formulate a general principle stating the proper relation between consumer needs and producer's profit. "For economic production there *must* be profits, there *ought* to be regard for the consumer's interest, and it is wrong to sacrifice that interest to the increase of profits above a reasonable figure."[46]

What is reasonable in such a case is not made explicit. However, in another connection Temple suggests that industrial disputes be settled by an impartial tribunal, and this would seem to be the reasonable approach he has in mind.[47]

In the same way the economic order is to be related to man's cultural life. Just as the state exists to foster man's personal life but is the necessary means for maintaining the freedom and order requisite for such a life, so too the economic life is the *sine qua non* for providing the physical and mechanical means that make possible a full personal existence. Poetry cannot be written or appreciated if men are starving. Nonetheless, economic production is a means to the end of cultural productivity.

[44] *Ibid.*, p. 79.

[45] It is for this reason that the state might do well to subsidize certain commodities so as to keep the price at cost or less and within the economic reach of most people. See *ibid.*, p. 81.

[46] *Ibid.*, p. 82.

[47] See *ibid.*, pp. 76–77, and *Citizen and Churchman*, p. 72.

The whole equipment of life with food, houses, clothes, furniture, and so forth is for the sake of the personal life, the family life, the cultural development, the human fellowship which is thus made possible .... The means (industry, commerce, etc.) is to be judged by its success in promoting or facilitating the true ends of human life – religion, art, science, and above all, happy human relationships.[48]

At stake here is nothing less than the development of personality itself. If the person and the unfolding of his capacities are sacrificed for production and profit, then for whom are the goods produced and for what purpose is profit procured? It is to pervert the natural priority evident in the reason for the existence of both the person and his economic activity. But if the proper perspective is to be attained, then certain specific steps must be taken.

If the development of the person and not the gaining of profit is the true goal of the economic order, then the family which gives birth to and nurtures the person is the primary social unit. This means that families should be provided with adequate housing for their needs and within their financial means, and that ample leisure time be afforded so that they can pursue activities of interest. In particular this requires that the worker be given days off with pay at regular intervals. The state should further assist families by providing allowances (e.g., food, clothing), supplementing wages when necessary due to the size of the family. Basic bodily needs of the young must be cared for, including diet, exercise, and education. "Respect for the sacredness of personality in all citizens will lead us to demand that no child shall be condemned to grow to maturity with faculties stunted by malnutrition or by lack of opportunities for full development."[49]

Other specific steps can and must be taken before an economic life consonant with the basic social principles already enumerated can be said to exist.[50] But basic to the changes that must be effected is a clear grasp of the natural order that prevails in the relation of the economic order to the total life of the person. As the previous discussion of this indicated, the problem is that the means and ends involved have become inverted.

48 *Christianity and the Social Order* p. 82. In this way Temple sought to relate both the principles of freedom and order and the radical and conservative temperaments; see *ibid.*, and Fletcher, *William Temple*, pp. 163, 170.

49 *Christianity and the Social Order*, p. 88.

50 Temple enumerates specific proposals which he feels can serve as a start in the right direction and as a basis for further investigation. The limitations of the present study do not warrant exploring the details of his exposition of this issue, as significant as some of them are. Cf. e.g., *ibid.*, pp. 99–100, 101–121; *The Church Looks Forward* (New York: The Macmillan Company, 1944), pp. 146–169.

It is clear that, in the natural order of things, God's order, the object of all industry is the supply of men's wants .... But in our world, goods are produced, not primarily to satisfy the consumer, but to enrich the producer. The profit-motive predominates over the service-motive; and this inversion of all that is right is gone so far, that now finance controls production instead of production controlling finance, and the consumer, for whose benefit alone production really goes on at all, becomes no more than an indispensable condition of successful business enterprise.[51]

Not until the priority of personality and its fullest development are accepted in the economic order more radically than is now the case, and expanded politically beyond national borders to an international organization, will the aim of a Christian social order be possible of realization. However, in this quest for a just social order the end for which it is sought must not be forgotten. A social order founded on the principles proposed is desired for developing man's spiritual nature. Furthermore, there should be no illusion about the type of social order that can be attained on earth: it can never be perfect or permanent. But more important is recognition of the fact that the social order, no matter how ideal, is never an end in itself. This is so because man's true destiny is beyond any temporal order, residing as it does in the Kingdom of God beyond history. Any social order constructed on earth is to be judged in terms of its adequacy in preparing man for eternal life. This was Plato's insight in *The Republic* and separates social theories into those which take into account man's immortality and those which do not.[52]

D. SUMMARY AND CONCLUSIONS

Before considering Temple's Christian philosophy of history it is worthwhile to summarize the basic arguments of the three chapters in Part III, indicating briefly Temple's value theory and the solutions he proposes to the problems of personal and social morality.

1. *Actual value as a relation between mind and object*

The fitting together of everything in the universe constitutes value in the widest sense, but the special correlation between mind and its environment warrants restricting value to this relationship. Hence, Temple's fundamental conception of value is the mind's discovery

[51] Temple, *Hope of a New World*, p. 17.

[52] See Temple, *Christianity and the State*, pp. 3–12; also cf. *Plato and Christianity*, pp. 32–37 and *Essays ...*, p. 39.

in its object of something akin to itself. Actual value is the relation between appreciating mind and valuable object. Implicit in Temple's theory of value are two different conceptions of the meaning of value without a clarification of the relation between them or an attempt to synthesize them into one coherent value theory. On the one hand, he affirms an objective interpretation in which objects are valuable independent of man's appreciation of them; on the other hand, he suggests a modified objectivist theory in which values exist only potentially until man actualizes them in his own experience of satisfaction. A similar ambiguity resides in Temple's analysis of the practical and theoretical problems of ethics.

2. *Ethics as a life of devotion to God*

As a center of value realization in the world man is guided by his apparent good. He is free in that he is not determined by forces outside him or momentary desires; he is not free in that he is determined by what he considers good. True freedom and full value realization could be attained only if his apparent good were, in fact, the real good, only if God and His will motivate the individual's action and the goal toward which he strives. But how is man to will that the real good become his apparent good? Similarly, the absolute form of the moral law states that one should love his neighbor as himself. But how can one will to shift his center of concern from self to another?

Thus, the practical problem of ethics is held to reside in man's will and not in his actions. It is a problem of character and not conduct: one can know what he should do but not will to do it. Further, he cannot begin to will it until he wants it, and he cannot want it until he wills it. Man must be presented with the real good – the ideal of love of neighbor – in a form which will elicit from him a response of love. That is, man needs to be converted. It is Christ, the human embodiment of God, who provides the dramatic expression of love which man needs. By surrendering his will to God's will as manifested in Christ man is enabled to love as commanded. Such a transformation of character is an act of grace to which man contributes only the need to be transformed.

The theoretical problem of ethics concerns man's obligation to do what is right. What promotes the good of all mankind constitutes the definition of what is right. How is one to know what will best serve mankind? In discerning what is the good the individual has as the basic principle of guidance the assurance of a Divine plan for each individual and for history as a whole. Discovering one's specific vocation in the Divine scheme and fulfilling it provides the solution to theoretical ethics. The individual can find out what he ought to do by examining what fulfills his own true nature. Hence, a cognitive theory of moral obligation is affirmed, rooted in one's personal relation to God regarding specific acts, though the only absolute obligation one has regarding all acts is to will what is right.

Ethical decisions are to be made from the perspective of one's personal relationship with God in the attempt to discern God's will for him in a particular situation. As a check on one's subjective inclinations, Temple affirms the need to be guided by the actual consequences of actions taken in promoting the welfare of society. However, the basis of decision remains in conscience and not in the consequences.

3. Society as the means for spiritual development

Temple analyzes society and the institutions of society from the perspective of three Christian principles: freedom, fellowship, and service. The political and economic orders exist for the development of personality, which means that the individual must be free to realize his potentialities. The function of law in the state is significant in protecting one's rights and checking his destructive impulses. A person can develop to maturity only through social relationships; and hence, one's freedom should be exercised in terms of the freedom of others and the fellowship they share together. Necessary in society are the specific social groups which foster the fellowship of its members. At the same time, each individual should strive to serve the welfare of all. Society is essential for personal development, and the richer the society the greater the opportunity for personal fulfillment.

Society, viewed as a natural product, has as its source the social nature of man and as its goal the fulfillment of each of its members. The state is the necessary organ of society enabling it to fulfill its function by maintaining peace and justice. Force is necessary at times in order to preserve unity within and to resist aggression without, however, it is law which is the fundamental characteristic of the state. Since the state is necessary to preserve the unity, peace, and justice which are essential for the development of personality, one should be loyal to the state. But ultimate political loyalty is reserved for the community, and any particular state may be so ineffective as to require being replaced by another form of government. Furthermore, because the state is founded upon society, when the relations among persons extend beyond national borders forming an international community, then the state is obliged to participate in an international organization.

Nowhere are the principles of freedom, fellowship, and service more in need of application than in the economic order. Political freedom in the form of government by representation has been secured for many people, but economic dictatorship or a benevolent monarchy still widely prevails in which workers have little or no voice in the regulations that control them. The sacredness of personality is defiled by the treatment of workers as "hands" rather than as persons.

Each individual has the responsibility of serving his society, but this means that society has the responsibility of providing the opportunity for fruitful labor. The difficulty is that economic productivity is too often regarded primarily as a means to make profit rather than to satisfy the needs of consumers, thereby perverting the natural order in which the satisfaction of needs is viewed as the end and the economic process as the necessary means.

An economic system can be judged by its success in producing and distributing goods; but there is also the obligation to evaluate the economic system on the basis of what it does, or fails to do, for the development of human personality. To achieve the latter goal may require more direct intervention by the state in economic affairs than has been the case previously. Temple does not hesitate to make specific proposals aimed at improving the material and spiritual status of the individual and directed toward regulating the social order in accordance with Christian social principles.

Society, then, exists for the sake of fostering the spiritual development of man. The personal level of existence, though last in temporal sequence, is prior in value, and its significance is independent of, and extends beyond, the historical order. But if man's ultimate destiny is beyond the present historical order, then it becomes imperative to examine the meaning of the historical process for personality and the significance of eternity both for history and personality.

PART IV

A CHRISTIAN PHILOSOPHY OF HISTORY

CHAPTER 14

THE HISTORICAL PROCESS

Temple's interpretation of history begins with an examination of the historical process itself, of the task which confronts the historian in his attempt to understand this process, and of the human forces which operate within history. The historical order, however, can only be understood in terms of its relation to the eternal order; hence, the meaning of eternity and the mutual effect of eternity and time on each other must be explored. A final question is posed and a tentative answer suggested regarding the possibility of individual personality surviving both death and the end of history.

In order to clarify the issues to be discussed, it is necessary once again to begin by bringing together several strands of Temple's thought presented in preceding chapters dealing with the relation of personality to time and to value.

A. PERSONALITY, VALUE, AND TEMPORAL SEQUENCE

A person, as distinct both from a thing and from a brute, is characterized by the capacity for conscious experience which encompasses more than the present fleeting moment.[1] The person is aware of his existence in the present but also remembers his existence in the past and anticipates his existence in the future. He is, thus, conscious of the continuity of his existence. Furthermore, the present experience of a person is itself a time-span involving duration.

The person is capable of being aware and of retaining in his awareness a series of events extending over a period of time. In a drama, for example, there is a succession of scenes and acts, but the audience grasps the series as a unit in the course of the play's unfolding so that at

[1] See Chapter 7.

the end of the play the beginning is also "present." Art in this way provides a clue to the conception of an "Eternal Now" by giving to man "in a selected and deliberately ordered portion of experience, an illustration of what might be extended over the whole of it if our faculties were sufficiently developed."[2]

Similarly, the future is anticipated by man in the present to the extent that he is lured on in the present by a goal which he is striving to realize in the future. The most distinctive trait of personality is revealed in such purposive activity.

With the emergence in the World-Process of the person conscious of his existence and capable of selecting certain objects for appreciation, value also appears.[3] When a person finds satisfaction in objects which he apprehends, then he has experienced value. Also, the value which is experienced may become partially independent of the situation in which it occurred so as to influence the evaluation of other events.

In like fashion one can often gain new insight into the meaning of past events as a result of viewing them from the perspective afforded by the lapse of time from when the event occurred. Thus, though an event which transpired sometime in the past cannot be altered in regard to the details of the event, the interpretation of the event and the value (or disvalue) attached to it may be altered. That is, viewed from the present context one can appreciate the past event in a way not possible at the time and thereby elicit from it a character not previously discerned. In this way something that was evil may come to be interpreted as integral to a series of events which is good. The evil event in the past is not now good, but it is conceived as a necessary element of what is considered good.

Thus, for Christians the crucifixion of Jesus of Nazareth was evil but in the perspective of the ensuing events has come to be interpreted as an integral element in God's redemptive act which is good. Apart from the truth of this particular instance, however, the principle involved remains valid; viz., "that the future does not merely disclose in the past something which was always there, but causes the past, while retaining its own nature, actually to be, in its organic union with its consequences, something which in isolation it neither is nor was."[4]

Nor does this mean that only the instrumental value and not the

[2] Temple, *Nature, Man and God*, p. 205. The influence of Josiah Royce is evident here; cf. *The World and the Individual*, II, 145: "In our own experience of a time-span of consciousness we have the analogy of eternal consciousness when expanded indefinitely."

[3] See Chapter 11.

[4] Temple, *Nature, Man and God*, p. 210.

intrinsic value (or disvalue) of a past event can be altered in this way since distinctions are not, in fact, ultimate. Both past and present are real only in relation to the whole of which they are successive moments. The value of a past event when considered in separation from the present and the future is not its real value, since this can only be determined in light of past, present, and future, that is, until the completion of the series of which it is but one moment. The series may in principle, Temple contends, extend to all eternity. If this is the case, then, "the evil thing remains in itself evil, but whereas it was a bad thing that it should happen it is a good thing that it did happen."[5]

Is this more than a rhetorical alteration of the past as Temple himself confesses?[6] Because good results follow from an event does not alter the character of the event, whatever that may have been, no matter how long a period of time is included. If it does, then the event had no distinctive character at the time it occurred; and if this is extended to include all historical events, then the reality of the process is destroyed. Eternity alone becomes real.

Nonetheless, for Temple, the past is alterable so far as its value is concerned. The significance of this insight for the present problem is that whatever meaning history displays can only be determined in reference to Eternity. So too with the person; as an episode in the historical process the events of his life are part of the historical order, but his true destiny can only be known in light of his relationship to and significance for, Eternity.

Granting the emergence of the personal level of reality in the course of the World-Process as distinct from the levels of thing and brute, the question which arises is the meaning of the total process and man's status in and beyond the historical process. Before these questions can be answered, however, another one must be considered: How is man, standing as he does within the process of history, to apprehend the meaning of the process as a whole?

B. THE INTERPRETATION OF HISTORY

1. The historical method

Temple notes that historical awareness as it is now known is a recent development. Contemporary events have been recorded by man

[5] *Ibid.*, n. 1.
[6] See *ibid.*, p. 209.

throughout the ages. However, an attempt to record and grasp an understanding of any large block of time can perhaps be dated only back to Gibbon's work. The Darwinian theory of evolution with its emphasis on viewing present species in terms of their developmental history gave added impetus to the importance of historical sequence.

Today the historical method is accepted procedure in all fields so that an event or idea is not held to be understood until it is viewed in its historical context and in light of its historical antecedents. One of the changes wrought by this emphasis on historical method has been the attitude toward change itself. Whereas stability was assumed by former generations, change is taken for granted now and is held to be essential to life. The latter attitude is accomplished by a widespread belief in progress.[7] The content and validity of this belief will be noted below.

The historical method is the logical conclusion of an awakened historical consciousness on the part of man. It aids him in his understanding of events within history. But how is history itself to be conceived?

2. *The historian's task*

Temple offers both an objective and subjective definition of history. Objectively viewed, history consists simply in the totality of all the events in history. What has actually occurred in the historical process constitutes the content of history. However, if man is to understand what has occurred in history, then he must apprehend and interpret these events. It is the interpretation and apprehension of history which constitute the subjective conception of history. The two views are, of course, inseparable so far as man is concerned and pose the problem which confronts the historian.

An understanding of the events of history, particularly when the events under consideration are those which involve man's will either through initiation or modification, necessitates a combining of all three of the basic activities of the mind, viz., the intellectual, the aesthetic, and the ethical. That is, the historian must draw upon all three of these disciplines. His use of the evidence must be scientific. Accurate and careful recording are basic and essential. But a mere listing of events even in sequential order is not the extent of the historian's task; for he is also obligated to bring together these events and relate them in

[7] See *ibid.*, pp. 428–429.

such a way as to constitute a meaningful whole. It is not the recording of the occurrence of events alone that makes history, but rendering their occurrence in such a manner as to show their significance. Thus the historian is led to the aesthetic activity of the mind, both in regard to apprehension and expression of the events and their significance.

However, it is an impossibility inherent in the historian's task to be able to gather and record all of the events which occurred in the period which he is studying. Even if he could, the recording itself would become so massive as to render the task meaningless. Hence, he is forced to select. But what is to be selected and how? Some standard or criterion is necessary. Since such a governing principle will be used to pass judgment on the relative merits of human activities, the historian has moved into the realm of ethics. Thus Temple concludes that, "science, art and morals are all involved in the study of history."[8] Nor can such an investigation avoid philosophy, "for the principle of selection among events, and the suggestion or articulation of the significance of those selected, can hardly be detached from ultimate questions concerning the nature of reality."[9]

C. THE FORCES OPERATING IN HUMAN HISTORY

1. *Personal and universal fellowship*

Turning to an analysis of human history, two basic unitary principles may be seen operating as the goals of human action, viz., personal and universal fellowship. Temple describes the history of man as "the effort of men to achieve individual unity, and the groping of men, sometimes conscious, more often unconscious, towards the unity of universal fellowship."[10]

Here is the struggle between the liberty of individuals and the order of society already noted. Much of history certainly reflects the effort to achieve some balance between these two principles. A hasty survey of history seems to indicate that there is a force operative in the historical process itself which will eventually produce these two unities through the formation of some international organization joining the nations of the world. Toward this end man must certainly work. But

[8] *Ibid.*, p. 428.
[9] *Ibid.* For a similar interpretation on this point see W. H. Walsh, *An Introduction to Philosophy of History* (London: Hutchinson's University Library, 1951), pp. 16–17.
[10] Temple, *Christus Veritas*, p. 76.

if the goal of history is identified with the achievement of such an international organization, then all who died before its appearance have no enjoyment of it and do not share in history's goal. Furthermore, can such a goal of history be claimed reasonable when it is made contingent on man's success or failure in working toward this end and on the planet's continued existence until it is attained? Such an interpretation of human history would not seem to penetrate deeply enough into man's nature either in terms of motivation or aspiration.

2. *Self-interest*

The struggle which the history of man exhibits is not merely between individual liberty and social order, but first and foremost within the individual himself in an attempt to determine and to satisfy what is to his own self-interest.

Following Plato's analysis of the soul in *The Republic*, Temple finds three principles operating within every man: desire, pride and reason.[11] Each one has a necessary place within the life of the individual and society, but the difficulty is maintaining the proper harmony between them so that each fulfills the function for which it is intended. In order for physical life to be sustained certain basic desires of the organism must be satisfied (e.g., hunger, sex, thirst). Since the satisfaction of these desires is necessary, one might as well satisfy them in a way that is enjoyable. But it is one thing to eat in order to live and in so doing to eat what one enjoys; it is quite another thing to live in order to eat so that the choice of food is dictated solely for its pleasure. Desire in this case has become lust or evil desire, and would lead one simply to ignore others, rather than either cooperating or competing with them. Ignoring, competing, and cooperating constitute the three possible relations between human beings for Temple.[12]

Self-respect or pride also serves to foster the interests of the self by curbing desires which are detrimental to the total interests of the self and by "claiming for the individual his right to live his own life and to find scope for the exercise of his abilities."[13] The necessary emphasis of the individual on himself and his abilities leads to the relationship of competition between individuals, which in turn may become a battle for positions of honor, fame, power, and wealth. No

[11] See *ibid.*, pp. 79–81.
[12] See *ibid.*, pp. 78–79.
[13] *Ibid.*, p. 80.

longer is each interested in the recognition due him based on his abilities; the impulse now is to get for himself all he can.

The satisfaction is different with regard to reason, for the rational principle involves the whole personality in the quest for absolute values (e.g., truth, beauty, goodness). Furthermore, in satisfying the principle of reason one cannot ignore others, for they are helpful partners in the same quest; nor need he compete with them, for success in this realm by one means the success of all. The true status of the individual as a member of the community is hence made evident, and each cooperates with one another. However, life requires more than reason alone: "But reasonableness, while always a good, is not a sufficient equipment for the perfectly good life; there must be the energy of desire and the assertiveness of Pride – both directed and controlled by Reason – if the full richness of human life is to be realized."[14]

All three principles, therefore, serve essential functions within the life of the individual.

There is, then, a psychological stratification within the individual similar to the stratification of reality. "Desire (like Matter) is the indispensable foundation; but it does not display the purpose of its own being until we see it organized by Pride and controlled by Reason."[15] Once again the higher level requires the lower for its existence, but the significance of the lower is only evident when controlled by the higher.

It is the interaction of these principles as worked out among both individuals and nations which provides the actual history of the human race. The external struggle evident in history for individual unity and universal fellowship is, therefore, rooted in, and a manifestation of, the internal struggle within man and its resultant consequences for the relations among men. Hence all the forces operating within history which might lead to the realization of the two unities are rooted in self-interest.

Thus, when an individual learns to be a responsible citizen, he is motivated by the realization that his own existence is dependent upon the welfare of his family and nation. There *are* other forces also at work. Unselfish love is manifest in certain acts by parents toward their children (and vice versa). The sacrifice of self for others (e.g., a soldier in wartime) and the promotion of values in which all can share do exist. The traits of personality reflected in such acts could become dominant so that the possibility for the realization of the two goals of

14 *Ibid.*
15 *Ibid.*, p. 81.

unity cannot be eliminated; but all the while the interest in self remains, even when the other-regarding motives operate.

The self-interest is never overcome. Nor can it be overcome by the self alone, for it is rooted in the basic fact which makes human history possible, viz., that man is a conscious center of apprehension and appreciation. Values are thereby made possible but can only be actualized in the individual's own experience. This means, furthermore, that each one will seek his own values and tend to underestimate those sought by others. There is, therefore, an initial bias toward self-seeking and pride. Nor is this the end of it, for man's awareness of his actions means that he knows when he is seeking his own interest to the detriment of the interests of others. At one point, in fact, Temple conceives the real meaning of history – so far as "its politics, its diplomacies, its wars, its intrigues, its aspirations" are concerned – in terms of "the conflict of God's love with man's selfishness."[16]

Temple concludes that man's progress on earth does not exhibit a movement from self-interest to dis-interested love, but rather the progress is "the substitution of enlightened selfishness for stupid selfishness."[17] He goes on to state: "Of any emancipation from selfishness itself, or any attainment of perfect fellowship in self-surrender to the absolute good, our historic progress hitherto gives no promise whatsoever."[18]

Therefore, though education is necessary and valuable, the goal to which man is directed demands more than education; he needs conversion as well. The same is true in regard to political progress and social reform. Both are necessary and desirable, but man needs redemption more. And more than peace and security, man needs eternal life. Man and history taken alone or together are incomplete; they need the indwelling presence of God for their completion. This leads to the basic question for a philosophy of history: What makes history intelligible?

D. PROCESS AND RESULT

Temple reasons that the meaning of any process is to be found either in the process itself (i.e., in the course of its unfolding or development)

[16] Temple, *Personal Religion* ..., p. 26.

[17] Temple, *Christus Veritas*, p. 88.

[18] *Ibid.* Toynbee seems to agree at this point; cf. Arnold J. Toynbee, *Civilization on Trial* (New York: Oxford University Press, 1948), pp. 260–263. Also a similar view is presented by John Baillie, *The Belief in Progress* (New York: Charles Scribner's Sons, 1951), pp. 211–220, 227–235. However, both Toynbee and Baillie conceive of history as revealing a greater unfolding of grace, at least in the sense of general influence and wider opportunity.

or in the result at which the process eventually arrives. Both of these views are, in fact, necessary with regard to the meaning of history. To look only at the result of history for history's meaning is to make precarious the rationality of history at any given point in history. Further, if the result proves to be some concrete event in history, then all who died prior to the event are deprived of participating in its significance. This renders the historical process morally irrational. And yet, if meaning is to be discovered in the historical process, then the apprehension of it must be made from a perspective which transcends the process as a whole.

It is not made clear, by Temple, why those who died prior to the result of history cannot share in its significance. Granted that they cannot share in the result itself as an historical event, there is no reason why they cannot share in its significance through anticipation of the result. Also, to the extent that they contribute to the realization of the event that gives meaning to history, they are participating in its significance.

The conclusion to which Temple is led is that history can be rendered meaningful only in relation to eternity and, similarly, that history must be a part of the content of eternity.

> History is fully intelligible only in the light of eternity. But, on the other hand, eternity must be conceived as requiring the actual historic process as part of its own content; for otherwise we render history unmeaning by the very means through which it is thought to secure its significance .... As we must regard history in the light of eternity, so we must conceive eternity in the light of history. History and eternity must be so conceived as to interpret each other.[19]

What, then, is the relation of history to eternity and of eternity to history?

[19] *Christus Veritas*, pp. 89–90.

CHAPTER 15

HISTORY AND ETERNITY

A. RELATION OF TIME TO ETERNITY

The attempt to clarify the relations of time and eternity can appropriately begin with an examination of the meaning that history has for eternity. Temple suggests three main views which have predominated in this regard. All three present partial truths taken separately; Temple proposes a fourth view in which he strives to bring together the truths of each of the other three while eliminating the falsities.

1. Significance of the temporal for the eternal

First is the view generally attributed to Plato and best summed up in the Platonic dictum: "Time is the moving image of Eternity."[1] The temporal process is conceived as proceeding from the Eternal without, however, affecting the Eternal. The only meaning which history has is that which is derived from the fact that it is an expression of, and flows from, the Eternal. However, from the standpoint of the Eternal, history is itself meaningless. The movement of time alone is explained, but the temporal world remains a mystery.

There is a sense, Temple affirms, in which this view is true. For the world is not necessary to God in the same way in which God is necessary to the World. This is illustrated by a very simple mathematical formula: "The World − God = O; God − World = God."[2] Though the formula is an oversimplication, it does contain the significant truth that God is self-sufficient. How coherently Temple is able to maintain the self-sufficiency of God while at the same time stressing the meaning of history for God warrants careful consideration.

[1] Temple, *Nature, Man and God*, p. 434. In Plato, see the *Timaeus*, 37 d.
[2] *Nature, Man and God*, p. 435.

In the second interpretation of history, the opposite extreme of the first view is proposed: Eternity is conceived as "the integral totality of Time."[3] History is frankly acknowledged to have eternal significance. Man himself is caught up in the historical process. The future and what it may produce cannot be determined on the basis of the past or the present. Further, the past and present cannot be properly interpreted either, since they can only be seen as discrete movements and events and not as a connected whole. When all of the parts are placed together and are viewed as a whole, then the true meaning will be revealed; and what, for example, seemed evil, when viewed as separate parts, now become good when the whole is grasped. In this way both religious hope and moral judgment are preserved.

Essentially this view is an appeal to ignorance.[4] What evidence is there for supposing that the unknown future will produce good? The empirical evidence points to the contrary since the past and present exhibit an unbalance between evil and good in the world at any time. If it is proposed that God will correct the situation through an act of divine intervention, then man's freedom and responsibility become an illusion. The entire historical process is reduced to a projection of the nature of God; and one has returned to the first view.

The third view of history freely acknowledges that history is nothing more than passing episodes in relation to Eternity. In this view both history and Eternity are accepted as "primitives." Neither one can be derived from the other; rather a relationship is established between them.[5] God has brought time and the world into existence simultaneously and He will bring them to a decisive end together. However, spiritual beings who lived in the world will at its termination resume their existence conditioned by the lives they led in response to their opportunities.

Such a view Temple considers to be more mythological than philosophical. Thinking is manifested in terms of pictures rather than carefully worked out thoughts. Nonetheless this view adds a new dimension to the meaning of history by affirming a definitive historical climax and the ushering in of a new order. History not only exhibits an ever wider application of the Eternal principles, extending beyond earthly existence into life immortal, but also points toward another and

[3] *Ibid.*, p. 437.

[4] Temple states the difficulty clearly and cogently at this point, but as we have seen, he still proposes a strikingly similar solution to the problem of evil; see above, Chapter 10.

[5] For a lucid and persuasive exposition of a more sophisticated variant of this view see W. T. Stace, *Time and Eternity* (Princeton: Princeton University Press, 1952).

different community of persons. Entrance into this fellowship is determined by one's earthly life.

Defects are, however, evident. The relation which history and the Eternal share is entirely external, and no adequate reason is offered why history was initiated by the Eternal. Further, the Eternal enjoys only an incomplete supremacy over history. Although, attempting a synthesis of the first two views, the third one fails because it ends in cancelling out both in the synthesis proposed.

Temple proposes to synthesize the significant elements of all three views without succumbing to the above fallacy. No final or absolute conclusions are to be expected in such an endeavor; the difficulties encountered by each of the views are inherent in the very attempt to understand the Eternal from the perspective of the temporal. Man is not capable of conceiving of the relation between the temporal process and the Eternal except by analogy.

Despite the failure of the three views, each one contains significant elements which must be incorporated in any true view. "In the first, the complete and all-controlling supremacy of the Eternal; in the second, the ultimate importance of History and its moral choices; in the third, the expectation of a climax of History inaugurating a new world-order." [6]

Nonetheless, each view is inadequate as it stands, and a synthesis which combines the best of each one needs to be constructed.

The creative artist at work provides the best analogy of the relation of the Eternal to the temporal, as is offered in the experience of a dramatist writing a play.[7] For here history is seen in a miniature form. Once the author creates the characters and places them in the drama, their conduct is based on the personality the author has created and in this sense is beyond the dramatist's control. However, he can at any moment destroy them simply by ceasing to write. The play is entirely dependent upon him in this sense, while he is in no wise dependent upon the play (i.e., for his existence). But he can remain a dramatist only by continuing to write plays, and thus the play and the characters are in the real sense important to him. What Temple fails to recognize is that if the dramatist must continue to write plays, then he is dependent upon the play for his existence as a dramatist. Temple is involved here in the fallacy of logical abstraction.

[6] Temple, *Nature, Man and God*, p. 441.

[7] Cf. Temple, *Mens Creatrix*, pp. 359–360; *Christus Veritas*, pp. 90–91, 187–189, 275–577; *Nature, Man and God*, pp. 441–443.

Another analogy is that of a human father and his children. The latter owe their existence and most of their environmental influences to the father. They respect and obey him. However, the control of the father over his children is not through coercion, but through love. The children are free to disobey.

Both analogies are, of course, incomplete. In the first the characters have no real existence, and in the second the father is himself subject to the same finite conditions as his children. However, taken together they offer penetrating insight into a true understanding of history.

Temple affirms that the beginning of an understanding of history is God, Eternal and Perfect in His being. God has created the world; hence, his purpose constitutes the meaning of history.[8] By relating the view of God as creator to the analogies above, Temple connects creation "with the sheer satisfaction of creative activity ... and with the desire for self-communication."[9]

The inorganic world becomes, then, the expression of God on the level of quantitative relationships. On one planet God's creativity expresses itself in another form, so that beings are brought into existence who have additional powers such as self-consciousness, reflective thought, and love. Through these powers, these new creations may enter into the mind of their Creator and appreciate His work. Such beings are a part of nature but are not wholly determined by it. Although dependent on God, they are controlled, not as the natural order is, but, by means of, and according to, "the law of their being which He has imposed on them; He must control them through what appears to them good and their power to appreciate it – that is, through their unforced affection and will."[10]

Hence, in regard to these beings God as immanent in history does not know prior to any choice what response will be made. However, like the dramatist God is not entirely in the action of his players but also transcends them and as such He is certain of knowledge (past and future). "To Him the contingent is still contingent, as not being compelled by its own past; yet the whole is necessary, and therefore also all its parts; and the whole is the expression of His will. So He knows the contingent as contingent and yet knows it with certainty."[11]

There is a basic ambiguity here which Temple does not resolve: if

[8] See William Temple, "Christianity as an Interpretation of History" reprinted in *Religious Experience* ..., pp. 259–260.

[9] *Nature, Man and God*, p. 443.

[10] *Ibid.*

[11] *Ibid.*, p. 445.

the contingent is known as certain, then it must be necessary; and if necessary then it cannot be contingent. Temple acknowledges that, on this issue, one is led to something which for finite minds is impossible to penetrate. However, he argues, the difficulty occurs just where it is to be expected since man is finite, namely, man's attempt to comprehend the nature of God. The interpretation which Temple offers suggests a form of Christian trinitarianism.[12] God as the Eternal Being of the universe communicates Himself; indeed, the Word, which is the self-expression of His mind, is co-eternal with the Being of God. Man's response to the Divine Word recognized as the good is itself the operation of what Christians call the Holy Spirit within man, enabling him to respond to the Divine Word. However, man's response to the Word, though itself made possible by the activity of God in man, is not mechanically evoked. Hence, Temple affirms that man is free and that God operates through man, but the rational justification for both assertions is not indicated.

The question arises, what effect, if any, does history have upon the Eternal? That is, is God as the Eternal Being unaffected by what occurs in the temporal process which he has created?

2. *Effect of the temporal on the eternal*

Two answers must be given to the question of the effect history has upon the Eternal. There is one sense in which history makes no difference to God. This is in the sense that history consists in successive events; whereas there is no succession for the Eternal. However, from another perspective history does affect the Eternal, for it indicates what the Eternal is. If history were otherwise or were not, then the Eternal would be different from what He is.

Putting this double interpretation in terms of the Christian faith, the birth, death, and resurrection of Christ did not add (or substract) anything to God, but through these historical events and the historical person of Christ God was provided a new channel by which to deal with man. Thus a new relationship was made possible through divine love, but the love of God remained the same. This is not to take lightly Christ's earthly existence, however, for it was made necessary by God's

[12] See *ibid.*, pp. 445–447. Cf. also the sermon on "The Holy Spirit and the Blessed Trinity" in *Fellowship with God* (London: Macmillan and Co., 1920), pp. 130–144; and the final chapter of *Christus Veritas*, "Love Divine: The Blessed Trinity," pp. 274–285. The case for, and explanation of, a trinitarian conception of God was developed in Chapter 8.

nature. If history were devoid of Christ's love, then God's nature would not be what it, in fact is. "*The eternal is the ground of the historical and not* vice versa; *but the relation is necessary, not contingent – essential, not incidental.* The historical is evidence of the eternal . . . as a necessary self-expression of a Being whose essential activity is at once self-communication and self-discovery in that to which He communicates Himself."[13]

Despite Temple's ingenuity, fundamental questions remain unanswered in his interpretation of the effect of the temporal on the Eternal. Must there not be succession in God just as there is succession in history, if history is to be meaningful? Likewise, if the ontological reality of time is denied, then is not history rendered devoid of meaning?

Temple is led to conclude that though an understanding of human history must remain partially veiled to man, certain principles of interpretation may be noted based on the nature of value which has been presented. Hence, for Temple the ultimate meaning of human history is to be "found in the development of an ever wider fellowship of ever richer personalities. The goal of History, in short, is the Commonwealth of Value."[14] From the standpoint of traditional Christianity the Commonwealth of Value is akin to the fellowship of saints.

> It is a Harmony of Harmonies, for it takes into itself all lesser loyalties and fellowships .... It is the peace of eternity, wherein all successiveness is comprised and all discords are resolved. We have called it the Commonwealth of Value; its Christian name is the Communion of Saints; its perfection is in eternity, but to bring its divided and warring members into that Harmony and Peace wherein alone it is actual is the purpose which gives meaning to History.[15]

Thus Temple has preserved the deepest intuition of religion, noted in the third view above, in which history is conceived as culminating in a new order. This new order supplants the old, and yet the old is a necessary condition to the new. The transition from the historical order to the new order beyond history provides an illustration of "one of those unities where the principle of unity is in the whole,"[16] so that what came before can be fully understood only in light of what comes after. Man's life is much like a play of which God is the author and man the character He creates as a result of His love. Through His love,

[13] *Nature, Man and God*, p. 448.
[14] *Ibid.* The Commonwealth of Value is, as already noted, Temple's attempt to solve the problem of ethics by suggesting an ethics of vocation.
[15] *Ibid.*, p. 426.
[16] *Ibid.*, pp. 450–451.

God guides these finite persons from their initial concern for self into the fellowship of cooperation, that is, the Commonwealth of Value.

Such is the meaning which history displays for Temple.

> *The end is not predictable from the beginning; and the beginning can only be understood in the light of the end. Consequently our apprehension of the Meaning of History is very meager. But we apprehend these two points. It can only have meaning at all if Eternal Life is a reality; and the meaning then is one which we do not so much discover as actually make.* For human History is nothing other than ourselves; and we make its meaning by living out its process in the power, already available to us, of the Eternal Life which is at once the source of that meaning and its culmination.[17]

Thus, the completion of the purpose which is manifested within the historical process can only be accomplished in a realm which transcends it. Further, if there is such a realm, then it has significance not only for the end of history but also for the historical process at any stage along the way. The relevance of Eternity for an understanding of history is clearly evident; but, what is meant by Eternity and what concrete effect does it have on the temporal?

B. RELATION OF ETERNITY TO TIME

1. Significance of eternity for the temporal process

By "eternal" Temple does not mean simply everlastingness. Rather, he defines Eternal as a "unitary synthetic apprehension of the whole process of Time and all that happens in it."[18] Such an experience is an extension to the point of perfection of what man experiences in his own consciousness as a partial transcendence of time.

Various other interpretations of the Eternal and its relation to the changing temporal have been offered. In much of Oriental philosophy the Eternal is emphasized to the point that change becomes an illusion and the temporal, meaningless. This is the inevitable outcome of an exclusive emphasis on the eternal. However, the reverse emphasis made by materialistic views is even more disastrous; for, at least, the eternal has meaning for the mystic, whereas there is no meaning for the materialist. Meaning cannot be found in the mere succession of events.

Human experience is, in fact, more than merely the apprehension of a series of discrete events; "it is always a unitary apprehension of a

[17] *Ibid.*, p. 451.
[18] *Christus Veritas*, p. 187.

successive manifold."[19] The poet perhaps offers the best illustration. For the reader to discover the true meaning of the poem, it is necessary to read the entire poem. But there is a sense in which it is equally true for the poet. For the thoughts of the poet are apprehended by him only as he articulates them. Hence, the meaning of the poem even for him only becomes actualized during the process of its composition. Temple feels that an important conclusion is to be drawn from this analysis: "It means that *there exist series of successive parts, so ordered that when regarded forwards no necessitating ground is discernible, but which are seen to be governed by an immanent necessity when regarded backwards, from the view-point of the completed series.*"[20]

Thus in the poem referred to above it is evident that no line (or lines) *must* be. Not until the end of the poem is the necessity of each line present, but then necessity is apparent: "In order to be that poem, and express that meaning, it had to consist of exactly that series of words arranged in that order, with that rhythm."[21]

This same principle is to be seen to operate in the lives of some people. Though many choices are present along the way and in each instance it is never possible to predict precisely what will follow, when viewed from hindsight a definite unity is discovered. This is due in such instances to certain constant elements in the person's character.

This is true as well in the life of a nation, though in a more incomplete way. Hence, a poem, a man's life, and the history of a nation all illustrate this same principle of the unity of the successive. The conclusion to which Temple is drawn is that "there is found as a feature of history an element which may properly be described as an immanent purpose."[22] One basic task of the historian, then, is to make evident the immanent purpose in regard to the period of history or the movement with which he is dealing.

> He is not called upon to formulate the immanent purpose of a nation's life, or of a civilization or a culture. But he is rightly expected to set forth the facts which he narrates in such a way that they are felt to express a more or less constant tendency which gives unity to them. He must not be content to compile a chronological table; he must make a story of it, and a story must have, at least, coherence, which is a form of unity.[23]

[19] Temple, *Nature, Man and God*, p. 430.

[20] *Ibid.*, p. 431.

[21] *Ibid.*, p. 432. This analogy of the poet or dramatist may also be found in *Mens Creatrix*, pp. 357–360, and *Christus Veritas*, pp. 187–189.

[22] Temple, *Nature, Man and God*, p. 433.

[23] *Ibid.*, pp. 433–434.

The importance of Eternity for the temporal order cannot be exaggerated. The temporal order must always be viewed against the background of Eternity. Descriptions of the end, for example, may vary; but if there is an eternal order, then the present historical order must end. It means further that nothing (including the winning of a world-war) is as significant for man as is his relationship to that which characterizes the eternal realm. The qualities which Eternity exhibits are the important ones; and, for Temple, this means that love is the sovereign power in the universe. The love which is supreme in history is conceived in terms of the sacrificial act of Christ on the cross, so that the cross of Christ as the manifestation of God's love in history constitutes the focus of history. Thus Temple states: "The eternal Spirit is love; the eternal goods are love, joy, peace, loyalty, courage, wisdom, beauty, knowledge. These are the true goods; that man is truly successful, that nation is truly great, which has these things in abundance."[24]

2. *Effect of the eternal on the temporal*

If, then, history is the unfolding of the purpose of the Eternal Spirit, what will eventually prevail in history must be in accord with that purpose. Selfishness cannot succeed, therefore, in a universe operated by eternal love. Service is rooted in the ground of history. This does not mean that the individual (or nation) choosing to serve will necessarily profit from it on earth; only that the opportunity to serve will always be available. In fact, service may entail suffering for the server; but if it is done in the spirit of love, then one can rejoice that he is considered worthy to be called upon to suffer.[25]

To claim that love is the sovereign power in history will seem to some better homiletics than philosophy, but for Temple it is sound philosophy as well as persuasive preaching: "Philosophers seek to know the nature of reality and the right way to live; Christianity offers the answer to both enquiries in one word – Love; and if we accept the hypothesis, it works both in theory and in practice, in the sense, not that it makes all clear, but that it progressively, if never completely, reduces chaos to order."[26]

[24] *Christus Veritas*, p. 190.

[25] Temple seems to betray a callousness here in regard to human suffering. Cf. also Nels Ferré, *Evil and the Christian Faith* (New York: Harper & Brothers, 1947), p. 107: "To accept suffering as a gift from God *to be used for others* is hard, but suffering so accepted opens the door to a new world and to the real God."

[26] *Christus Veritas*, pp. 190–191.

The objection which immediately is raised against such a view is the difficulty of finding traces of divine love in the historical process. Though man continues to learn more effective control over the natural order, there is no hope that he can completely control it. Accidents which are beyond the domain of his powers and which destroy his plans will always plague him. But if this is true, then how can it be maintained that the universe reveals the unfolding of a loving purpose?

Part of the difficulty involved is the tendency of some to refer any event not readily explainable by scientific knowledge to a special act of the Eternal Spirit. In one sense this interpretation is correct since "all that exists is the self-utterance of God's will."[27] But it does not follow that the particular event is a special act of will. Another difficulty arises in regard to the meaning of accident in this connection. Temple defines accident as "an interference with human purposes due to the action of natural forces, known or unknown, but incalculable in their bearing on the purpose interfered with."[28]

Nonetheless the sceptic might reply that God could intervene at those times when the natural law is working counter to the purposes of man so that the good might be achieved. Temple believes that God can and does intervene in specific incidents, though its occurrence cannot be proved beyond question, and hence no philosophic world view should be built upon it. He admits further that such acts on God's part are exceptions and that the problem is intensified by the belief. If God does intervene on one's behalf occasionally then why not always?

What is at issue when the question is stated in this way is one's scale of values. It seems unfair at first blush to think that God would spare the life of one boy in battle because the boy's father prayed for him and allow another to die because the latter's father failed to pray. But this is to misconceive a number of factors involved. If it is really best for either boy to return home safely, then the father's "prayer might be the condition needed for the realisation of this best result."[29] Perhaps, more significant is one's attitude toward death. If death is viewed as the greatest evil that can befall man, then, of course, the death of one boy and the continued life of the other will seem unfair. But to view life and death on these terms is to fail to interpret earthly

[27] *Ibid.*, p. 192.

[28] *Ibid.*, p. 193. The problem of accident constitutes one aspect of the problem of natural evil. Human suffering not due to accident was considered in Chapter 10. For a complete discussion see Skelton, "The Problem of Evil in the Works of William Temple."

[29] Temple, *Christus Veritas*, p. 196.

existence in light of eternity. The real tragedy of untimely death falls upon those who survive the lost loved one, not the one who dies. Finally, the supposed unfairness involved does reveal one example of the fact that each person gains or loses as a result of environmental influences, particularly the home in which he grows up.[30] Thus the one boy must suffer for his father's failure to pray quite apart from whether he lives through the war or not. Such, at least, is the case if eternity provides the real meaning of temporal history.

However, only a partial answer is provided in this way. What must be added is the very purpose of human history itself which has been shown to be the fullest development of personality in a fellowship of persons bound together by mutual love and under the guidance of the Eternal Spirit. It is toward this end that the evolutionary process moves. Therefore, the fundamental problem confronting each individual is that of detaching himself sufficiently from the temporal so as to become aware of the Eternal. Accident plays a major role in dramatizing this fact to the individual and disciplining him to take cognizance of it.

God does not, then, choose to destroy life through widespread devastation; rather he has created a world in which such accidents are incidental to the orderly process. When accidents do occur that frustrate the purposes of man, God stands ready to turn them into an occasion for further spiritual growth. Goodness, it must be remembered, means service to, and love of, God, so that nothing which happens in the natural order can prevent the individual from serving God and thus from being good.

A false conception of God may also be at fault. Though God is personal, indeed the only perfect personality, man's relationship to Him is not to be conceived in the same way that one person stands in relation to another person. God is the source of all life and His love the source of all love. Only in Him, then, does one find one's true nature and the proper relationship with others. It is in this perspective that the love which the death of a friend elicits must be viewed.

> The call to a deeper love of God which comes through the death of a friend is not the call to forget the friend and to love God instead; it is a call to realise more deeply what our love for our friend really was and is – an activity of God in us – and to rise from the temporal relationship of a "natural" friendship to an

[30] It is because the environment is so significant for personality development that the state should strive to provide the proper conditions for the development of its citizens, as was noted in Chapter 13.

apprehension of the Eternal Love in which that friendship lives on in spite of the friend's death.[31]

If, then, what is best for man is not happiness defined as what makes him comfortable, but participation in a universal fellowship, this can be attained by the individual only through his choosing it. An individual centered in his own self-interest must be shown what is to his own best interest. What survives in the long run in history will be that which is in accord with the purpose of God in history. Judgment is, therefore, evident in history.

The judgment of God in history is a fact of history, but it is not to be conceived as signifying the destruction of all those individuals and nations who fail to fulfill His purpose. God's aim and actions are for the sake of saving man and history, though the actions of man do produce destruction at times. There is judgment, nonetheless, in the sense that individuals and nations who live by principles contrary to divine purpose will be destroyed.[32] The Kingdom of God is present whenever this occurs. However, neither the sovereignty of God, not the reign of His Kingdom are ever fully actualized in this way. Judgment in such cases is for the sake of eliminating the offense and disciplining the offender so as to lead him to mend his ways. It is to win men's hearts to the acceptance of His love that God aims.[33]

The final question to be raised in this context concerns the finality of judgment which occurs in history. That there is such final judgment with regard to the elimination of nations from the historical scene is evident from history itself. The nation of Israel is a case in point: "No 'restoration of the Jews to Palestine' can now affect the finality of the judgment of which the armies of Titus were the instrument."[34]

Similarly, if fellowship with God freely chosen by each individual is the purpose of human life, then the person's right to refuse must be real; and if he persists, his decision must be final. This would seem to entail a failure on God's part which is inconsistent with His power and love, but to state otherwise would make a mockery of both human freedom and responsibility.[35]

[31] *Christus Veritas*, p. 199.

[32] Temple sees providential guidance of the course of history in the lives of Alexander the Great and Napoleon. See Appendix V, "On Providence in History," in *Church and Nation*, pp. 201–204.

[33] The basic social principles of freedom, fellowship, and service, and the ideal of sacrifice – proposed inChapter 13 – offer guidance in the kind of life expressive of God's purpose in history.

[34] Temple, *Christus Veritas*, p. 208.

[35] See *ibid.*, p. 209. As Temple notes, this view represents a change in position from the universalism proposed in *Mens Creatrix*, pp. 290, 357; see *Christus Veritas*, p. 209, n. 4. The

A further question concerns whether time itself will end. Human knowledge yields no definitive answer to this question. That there are relative ends to so-called periods in history (e.g., the ancient world), there can be no doubt. But if history can be conceived simply as the succession of events, there is no reason presently evident why such events must ever end. However, there is every reason to believe that *human* history as known on earth will come to an end. At that time the Kingdom of God will be fully established and all of those who respond to God's love will participate in it. That some will not, due to their desire for another kind of life, must be maintained in principle, though the details cannot be worked out in practice.

The establishing of that kingdom on earth is not the issue which confronts man. It exists whenever and wherever an individual views the temporal in terms of the Eternal, taking as his values those of eternity. One must live in time as a citizen of eternity.

Man's meaning, then, is not to be found in the World-Process from which he arises and in which his earthly life is lived. His true meaning demands a new creation in which a new order is ushered in. So far as man in history becomes a new creature and shares in the new order, he is already to that extent a citizen of the Kingdom of God beyond history.

Personality which has its inception in the World-Process has its completion in a realm beyond the process. This is the conclusion to which an analysis of history leads. But the conditions which make possible one's entry into life eternal have yet to be made explicit.

C. PERSONALITY AND ETERNAL LIFE

1. *The imperative of immortality*

There can be little doubt about the ethical imperative of life after death for man if personality and its fulfillment are held to be central to the purpose of history. To call upon man to seek what is true, beautiful, and good, to ask that he be willing to serve society even to the point of self-sacrifice when all for which he has worked will eventually come to naught in the dissolution of his earthly abode, is to render his actions meaningless and to command the irrational. "If at the end there is to be nothing but cold dead cosmos – which might as

possibility remains, of course, that man's freedom and God's love will both be maintained; see *Nature, Man and God*, p. 470.

well be chaos – then, though their presence shines like a jewel in the prevailing gloom, yet it were more creditable to the Determiner of Destiny that virtue and love had never bloomed."[36]

To have virtue and love make an appearance upon the historical scene in the life of a personal being as the culmination of a process which began with inanimate things, only to have the process reverse itself again so that personal beings and their concerns are irrelevant, is to make a mockery of the total process. Furthermore, it directly contradicts the ethical ideals of man to which the process itself gave rise.

Similarly, the religious aspirations of man are defied if the life of love to which he is called terminates with his brief span of existence on earth. He has been led to believe that love manifested in and through personality is the governing principle of the universe, only to discover that his own personal existence is but a means in the furthering of some end beyond him, or simply the sport of a deceiving deity.

Therefore, if the ethical ideals and the religious aspirations of man are not to be cruelly discarded, then persons in whom these ideals and aspirations have become manifest must have at least the possibility for eternal life. Such is the hope of man for eternal life. But what, then, is the basis of such hope as man does have for continued existence after death, and who can rightly expect the fulfillment of this hope?

2. *Faith in God as the basis for immortality*

Man's interest in immortality is varied. The ethical and religious imperative of immortality noted above carries with it an authentic note which reaches to the very depths of man's nature. However, for many, eternal life is desired because they simply do not wish their present lives to end. Still others wish for immortality because they want to be with loved ones from whom they are now separated by death.

The only adequate basis for eternal life is that which is consistent with the purpose of man in history, namely, to serve and glorify God. It is faith in God which constitutes man's real hope for immortality even as service to God is his purpose. Equally evident is that God whose essence is the union of power and love would not allow man in whom love is most fully expressed to perish. The immortality of man is thus a corollary to faith in the Eternal love of God.

[36] Temple, *Nature, Man and God*, p. 453.

God can only be known by man through his relations to man and the world. If he treats man as a thing without feelings or purposes of his own, when man has in fact both feelings and purposes requisite to the level of a personal being, then God cannot be conceived as the union of perfect love and power. Hence, though man on his own right has no claim on immortality, nonetheless, when he places his trust in God's love, immortality follows as a necessary consequence. Such is the paradox of religious faith: "We must spiritually renounce all other loves for love of God or at least so hold them in subordination to this that we are ready to forgo them for its sake; yet when we find God, or, rather, when we know ourselves as found of Him, we find in and with Him all the loves which for His sake we had forgone."[37]

To desire eternal life because the contemplation of death is distressing or because the thought of separation from friends is depressing is but an example of one's self-concern which immortality could only exaggerate further. But if one desires God and desires to be used for God's glory, then immortality provides a greater opportunity for service than this life affords and hence is justified.

When these considerations are recognized, then it becomes evident that experimental proof of man's survival after death for which psychical research affords some hope is both unnecessary and undesirable. The hope of continued existence would in such an event become a matter of intellectual perceptivity, and the life of faith which is man's essential business on earth and in heaven would be made all the more difficult.

It is worth noting at this point how far Temple has moved in such a pronouncement as this from the aim of philosophy to understand the nature of the universe. It is one thing to analyze the evidence of psychical research and conclude that it is insufficient to prove man's survival of death; it is quite another thing to hope that such evidence is not forthcoming. The latter may be sound religious faith, though that is debatable, but it is clearly antithetical to the philosophical attitude. Though Temple does not urge that psychical research be stopped, his confession that he hopes for its failure reflects quite the opposite of an open-minded approach to man's knowledge of the world. Since the statement occurs in his two major discussions of eternal life, one of which is his Gifford Lectures, it must be taken seriously.[38]

[37] *Ibid.*, p. 458.

[38] See "The Idea of Immortality in Relation to Religion and Ethics" (The Drew Lecture for 1931), reprinted in *Religious Experience* ..., pp. 115–116, and *Nature, Man and God* (The Gifford Lectures for 1932–1933, 1933–1934), pp. 458–459.

Temple finds another basis for immortality in the ethical life of man. He is called upon to seek the good quite independent of what benefits he might receive. Indeed, the highest good is that of sacrificial love. One best finds his own true self by losing himself in service to others.

Immortality is not justified for one who does good deeds in order to avoid being punished in hell, or for one who does good deeds with the expectation of being rewarded in heaven. Fear of punishment and the hope of rewards are not devoid of moral value as Kant supposed, since they serve a disciplinary function; but they can be only preparatory steps to the stage where the good is sought for its own sake.

In ethics too the problem has been shown to be that of shifting the center of interest from concern for self to concern for the good; and fear cannot accomplish this since it is a self-centered emotion. Hence, one cannot get to heaven by striving to avoid going to hell. Nonetheless, when the good is done for its own sake, then immortality becomes a necessary corollary of such goodness in a world which is under the control of a good God so that there can be a proper balance between goodness and happiness.

One final strand needs to be woven into the fabric of faith which constitutes man's hope for immortality. It is based upon the uniqueness of each individual as a center of conscious experience making possible a variety of values to be realized in the world, and also on the distinct vocational calling of every individual by which he actualizes certain values in his life.

In asmuch as the solution to the theoretical problem of ethics resides in each one discerning what type of work offers the best combination between his abilities and the needs ot society, this means that to the extent this is achieved a contribution is made to the totality of value in the universe which no one else (including God) could make. If such an individual does not attain eternal life, then his unique value experience and the distinctive contribution he makes to the universe are lost. But it is the purpose of God in creation that just such individual fulfillment through service should occur and that value should be actualized. To permit the loss of value which the finite spirit alone embodies would, therefore, be self-contradictory.

When you bring together the Purpose of God and the uniqueness of each individual soul, the doctrine of immortality follows as a necessary corollary; for it is impossible that God should allow the universe to be impoverished, and it is certain that the destruction of a unique, and therefore irreplaceable, spirit could be nothing other than its impoverishment.[39]

[39] Temple, *The Faith and Modern Thought*, pp. 166–167.

Furthermore, since each individual makes a unique contribution to the total value of the universe, each one needs the contribution of the other for his own perfection. Eternal life thus takes on the character of a community of selves each enriching the life of everyone else by means of his own distinct individuality and his own unique value experience, and at the same time each being enriched by the individuality and values others contribute.

Man's hope for immortality is thus both dependent on, and subordinate to, his faith in God. Man is not immortal by nature, nor does immortality necessarily follow for the individual who has attained a certain level of ethical achievement. It is, and can only be, a gift of God. But as a gift it is a necessary corollary to faith and to God's purpose for good in creation. It is in making explicit the implications of these conclusions that the character of eternal life becomes evident.

3. *Eternal life as fellowship with God*

Temple accepts the Christian doctrine regarding eternal life which emphatically affirms man's resurrection from the dead and not the immortality of the soul. It should be noted that Temple so interweaves philosophical discourse with Christian affirmations on this issue that it is not always evident to which he is appealing. However, in regard to the nature of Eternal Life he is clearly asserting what he considers to be Christian doctrine based on New Testament teaching.[40] Whereas non-Christian religions seek for ways to enable man to escape from the evils of earthly life, Christianity seeks to transform the evils of this world so as to make them the occasion for good.

Though Temple explicitly distinguishes between resurrection and immortality, precisely what he means by the distinction is not clear. He does indicate that life after death is not the mere survival of man's rational soul. Eternal life involves the transformation of man in entirety so that he can enter into a new order as a new being. Presumably this means the elimination of man's self-centeredness. However, Temple nowhere clarifies what he means by resurrection or how this would differ from immortality, and he continues to use the two terms interchangeably.[41]

[40] See *ibid.*, pp. 165–172, and *Nature, Man and God*, pp. 460–466.

[41] See *Nature, Man and God*, pp. 452–472. Also, he retains as the title of a lecture, "The Idea of Immortality in Relation to Religion and Ethics" though in it he affirms resurrection; see *Religious Experience* ..., p. 117.

Man's life on earth is viewed by Temple as preparation for the new life lived beyond this terrestrial existence. If man merely survives death without transformation, then there is no guarantee that he might not eventually be annihilated. The point is, that man is called not to survival merely, but to a quality of life which is characterized as fellowship with the God revealed in Jesus Christ. Suffering and death take on a different meaning in such a view; for sacrifice, even self-sacrifice, becomes the means by which one realizes his true self.[42]

Heaven is not to be thought of as a place where rewards are bestowed upon those who have been faithful and punishment meted out to the unfaithful. It is, rather, a type of relationship one shares both with God and one's fellowman in which the intrinsic joy of love and the inherent misery of selfishness are both experienced for what they are.

> Indeed, objectively regarded, Heaven and Hell may well be identical. Each is the realisation that Man is utterly subject to the purpose of Another – of God who is Love. To the godly and unselfish soul that is joy unspeakable; to the selfish soul it is a misery against which he rebels in vain. Heaven and Hell are the two extreme terms of our possible reactions to the Gospel of the Love of God.[43]

Eternal life, collectively considered, is a Kingdom of love in which finite spirits who love are united together under the rulership of the Eternal Spirit, the source and goal of love; it is the Commonwealth of Value.

But granting that the ultimate conditions for eternal life reside in God and that the Christian conception of this life suggests a new order in which a new being enters, the question remains whether any philosophical basis for such a life can be discovered in man's nature. That is, does the interpretation of man as a psycho-physical organism provide any possibility of his surviving death? What are the conditions within human personality which make it a possible candidate for eternal life?

4. *Capacity of man for eternal life*

One characteristic of man which distinguishes him from all other living organisms was found to be his capacity for forming concepts (or "free ideas") independent of sensory impressions. In this way he is able to gain a partial detachment from the World-Process and secure a life of his own. His conduct can then be directed by ideals which he has formed of future goals to be realized and toward which he strives.

[42] See Temple, *Faith and Modern Thought*, pp. 111–112.
[43] Temple, *Nature, Man and God*, p. 466.

Thus Temple states: "*The mind of a human being increasingly organises itself and its own world apart from the processes which, for the most part, control the body within which, and (at first) as a function of which, the mind has come into being. As mind increasingly takes control of the organism, so it becomes increasingly independent of the organism as physiologically conceived.*"[44]

Two common experiences man has illustrate this independence. One is his capacity to concentrate his attention so completely on some object that he becomes detached from the circumstances of his environment and the conditions of his own body. Similarly, the experience of obligation occurs independently of the organism's own interests so as to call at times for sacrifices of one's interests.

Further, it must be recalled that the ideas one has are not independent of the World-Process, for they arise as a result of the interaction of the self with its environment. It is not that the spiritual man thinks of different objects from the materially minded man, but that he thinks differently about the same things.

> Consequently the ideal attainment of human nature would be a lifting of the physiological organism itself to the status of a free vehicle of the completely spiritual mind. But short of that there is at least indicated the possibility of life for the mind in independence of the physiological functions of the organism. Man is not in his own nature immortal, but he is *capax immortalitatis*.[45]

Therefore, the development of the spiritual elements within the psychophysical organism of human personality by responding to, and sharing in, the fellowship of God makes possible God's gift of personal immortality to otherwise mortal creatures.

Thus, wherever human personality exists, it survives bodily death since it is difficult to conceive of anyone descending to such depths of degradation as to lose the capacity for forming concepts. But if this is true, then, as we have seen, the problem arises of whether everyone enters into eternal life. If not, it would seem to indicate that God's love and power have failed; but if so, then it would seem to indicate that man is not freely choosing according to his own apparent good.

Such a dilemma does not admit solution under the conditions of earthly existence. But there is one type of conduct which can be acknowledged to offer a solution in principle so as to preserve both man's freedom and God's supremacy. That occurs when one chooses to act

[44] *Ibid.*, p. 467.
[45] *Ibid.*, p. 468.

in a way which will produce pleasure for a loved one. The act is freely chosen, but what is chosen to be done is determined by the pleasure of another. Such a union of free choice by man and an act of grace by God in determining what is chosen points the way in principle to a resolution of the problem of universal salvation and human freedom.

> Now the Grace of God is His love made known and active upon and within us; and our response to it is both entirely free and entirely due to the activity of His love towards us. All that we could contribute of our own would be the resistance of our self-will. It is just this which love breaks down, and in so doing does not override our freedom but rather calls it into exercise.[46]

Nonetheless, the consequences of one's choices must be retained. God does not lightly cast aside what man has chosen to do on earth. Whatever act is performed, one must be held responsible for it; and if it is an evil act, then one must repent of it. The hope that everyone will be saved cannot be readily dismissed, and the possibility of its realization has been stated; but at the same time the quality of eternal life to which man is called cannot be forgotten and even less can it be compromised. Man has the capacity for eternal fellowship with God; the realization of this capacity, and this alone, is what God offers to man. On whom it is conferred must remain a mystery, though that it is received is man's legitimate faith.

In conclusion Temple summarizes the basic contentions of his position regarding life eternal:

> Man is not immortal by nature or of right; but he is capable of immortality and there is offered to him resurrection from the dead and life eternal if he will receive it from God and on God's terms. There is nothing arbitrary in that offer or in those terms, for God is perfect Wisdom and perfect love. But Man, the creature and helpless sinner, cannot attain to eternal life unless he gives himself to God, the Creator, Redeemer, Sanctifier, and receives from Him both worthiness for life eternal and with that worthiness eternal life – for indeed that worthiness and that life are not two things, but one.[47]

D. SUMMARY AND CONCLUSIONS

Three major issues have emerged in the presentation of Temple's Christian philosophy of history. By focussing on them we may be able to clarify further Temple's analysis of the meaning and goal of history.

[46] *Ibid.*, p. 470.
[47] *Ibid.*, p. 472; also see "The Idea of Immortality in Relation to Religion and Ethics" in *Religious Experience* ..., p. 123.

1. *The incompleteness of history*

Since mind actualizes value in the world, the value of events is not fixed in time. The full significance of an event may not be apparent until viewed in the perspective of later events. Thus, what was considered bad, may come to be interpreted as a necessary part of a series of events which is good.

The actual events which have occurred in history as interpreted by man constitute the definition of history for Temple. The historian's task is to bring these events together into a coherent whole so as to show the significance of them. Because of the nature of this task, the historian is involved in the disciplines of science, art, morality, and philosophy.

Human history exhibits a struggle between individual liberty and social order which is in turn rooted in the individual's attempt to satisfy his own self-interest. Other motives, such as unselfish love and self-sacrifice, may also be seen at work in history, but none are more fundamental than self-interest. As a conscious center of apprehension and appreciation man actualizes the values in the world and is constantly tempted to stress those which he seeks and to underestimate the significance of the values realized by others. This illustrates man's bias toward pride and why progress on earth can never be complete. Selfishness cannot be eliminated by man alone; he can only replace it with enlightened selfishness.

Hence, history is incomplete taken by itself. Its meaning cannot be found either in the process or the result taken alone; both must be considered together in relation to Eternity.

2. *The Kingdom of God beyond history*

Temple's interpretation of the relation of time to Eternity represents a synthesis of three views which stress respectively, the supremacy of God, the ultimate significance of history and moral choice, and the inauguration of a new order beyond history. The relation of history to Eternity can only be grasped by means of analogies – e.g., a dramatist writing a play and a human father and his children. The true basis for an understanding of history is the affirmation of the Eternal and Perfect God who created the world. The purpose of God constitutes the meaning of history. The entire universe is the expression of the creative activity of God. In man a creature is brought into existence who is guided by his apparent good, by final as well as efficient causation. Man's response to God is elicited through the operation of the Holy Spirit in man.

Because the historical order is the necessary self-expression of God, history does effect God. However, the succession of history does not alter the Eternal, for whom there is no succession. Human history is fully intelligible only when it culminates in a new order beyond history. Temple calls this order the Commonwealth of Value in which the successiveness and discords of history are eliminated. Men are joined together with one another and with God in perfect harmony and peace. Hence, Eternity, defined as a unitary grasp of the whole temporal order, has a significance for the temporal process that dare not be underestimated. Man has a glimpse of what such an apprehension of the time process would mean in the unity of his own conscious experience which encompasses a span of time. The meaning of history, therefore, can only be expressed in the total succession of events; only when the historical process is complete will the full intent become evident. However, an immanent purpose is discernible in the historical process, and to discover its operation in a given period of time is the task of the historian.

The temporal order, therefore, can only be adequately understood in light of Eternity. What occurs in history is secondary to the purpose of God for history. Sacrificial love as demonstrated by Christ on the cross is the sovereign power in history. Each individual is called upon to view all that occurs in history in terms of the opportunity afforded for spiritual development. Hence, accidents which result in human suffering can become the occasion for more complete service to God.

God does judge history in the sense that what is contrary to the divine purpose is destroyed. However, God is concerned with the redemption of history, not its destruction. Human history will end and those who respond to God's love will enter the Kingdom of God.

3. *The conditions for personal immortality*

Though human personality arises within the World-Process, its meaning and fulfillment reside in a new order beyond earthly existence. Heaven is not a place, but a relationship of love shared with God and fellowman.

Man is not immortal by nature; faith in God provides the basis for immortality. If the purpose of God in creating human personality is for the sake of establishing a universal fellowship of love, then it would be self-contradictory for God to allow all mankind to perish. Man exhibits the capacity for immortality in his ability to concentrate attention on an object to the extent that he becomes unaware of the physical environment, including his own body. Also, man's experience of obligation often commands acts which are contrary to his interests. Who will be saved and whether or not all men will enter into eternal life Temple leaves as an open question, while stressing both man's freedom to refuse God's love and the supremacy of God's love. One thing is certain: what man is offered is fellowship with God. That some men enter this fellowship is the faith of Christians.

Just as philosophy merges ultimately with theology, as human personality finds its perfection in divine personality, and as ethics passes over into religion through the demand for conversion and a vocational calling, so too the temporal order is incomplete both in its beginning and its ending and necessitates an eternal order as its source and goal. In each case an appeal is made to some power and being other than that which man and the natural order provide to supply a lack inherent in man and nature.

The exposition of the Christian philosophy of William Temple is now completed. What remains to be done is to evaluate critically his construction of a Christian philosophy and his application of it to solve some of the major philosophical problems.

PART V

EVALUATION AND RECONSTRUCTION OF TEMPLE'S CHRISTIAN PHILOSOPHY

CHAPTER 16

PHILOSOPHY AND THE CHRISTIAN FAITH

In the preceding four sections Temple's Christian philosophy has been systematically and sympathetically expounded. Some brief critical comments have been made at various points for the sake of noting ambiguities and to facilitate an understanding of Temple's position. The task of the final section is to offer a more extensive and systematic evaluation of Temple's contribution toward the construction of a distinctively Christian philosophy. An exhaustive critique of all facets of his Christian philosophy has not been attempted; however, an attempt is made to focus on the major critical points of Temple's position. Where it serves to clarify Temple's views or to sharpen the evaluation, a reformulation of the problem leading to a possible alternative solution is outlined.

The first aspect of Temple's thought that needs to be evaluated is his understanding of, and justification for, a Christian philosophy. Three issues seem to be central in his construction of a Christian philosophy and can serve as the basis for evaluating his views: (1) the metaphysical task of rendering the universe intelligible; (2) the relation of both believing and doubting in making knowledge possible; (3) the nature and possibility of a Christian philosophy.

A. THE METAPHYSICAL QUEST FOR UNDERSTANDING

Temple's philosophical sympathies are with the efforts to construct an adequate metaphysics. Whatever else the philosopher's task may be, as a metaphysician he is called upon to provide as coherent an account of experience as the facts warrant. This means striving to understand man and the world in which man lives. There is, then, an obligation to make sense of the universe; and if this obligation is denied, then to that extent the metaphysical task of the philosopher is forsaken.

In his lament against his own emphasis on a coherent account of experience, Temple does despair, for the time being, of the metaphysical task. However, for the most part, Temple is concerned with the attempt to understand the universe. The difficulty inherent in his philosophic efforts are at once more subtle and more serious than the lament of 1939. For in Temple's case it is not so much his forsaking the metaphysical task to interpret experience as it is a case of not fully taking up the task.

Temple does not begin the quest for truth perplexed about the world and wondering how to resolve the conflicting facts of experience; he starts the quest already convinced of a particular conception of ultimate reality, certain that whatever ambiguities there are can be clarified, and unclear and uncertain only as to whether man can apply these truths adequately to the world in which he lives. He is perfectly willing to adapt his method of presentation to the tenor of the times in order to convey these truths to others, but concerning the truths themselves there is no wavering. W. R. Matthews succinctly states the point in the following passage: "Some of the greatest philosophers and theologians convey to us a deep sense of the profound mystery and tragedy of the being and destiny of man; we feel it is this which has stirred them to think; I do not find this in the writing of Temple."[1] Temple's beliefs were not held tentatively as a result of being based on philosophical probability about which there were serious doubts. He was thoroughly convinced of, and committed to, certain fundamental truths about man and the world.

Therefore, Temple does not approach the metaphysician's task in order to discover the nature of reality; he brings to this task a conception of the nature of reality and tries to show how far philosophy can by its own procedure support his view. Philosophy is also employed to explicate the view of reality he holds. Thus Temple follows an analytical method in which the details of his world view gradually unfold and become clarified in the process of trying to understand the world in terms of it. At times Temple acknowledges this procedure, though he calls it the method of theological philosophy. According to this method, one begins with the assurance of the reality of the Supreme Spirit derived from a personal relation with Him, and the facts of experience are explained by reference to the character of the Supreme Spirit. Further, for Temple, the nature of God is revealed

[1] "William Temple as Thinker," in *William Temple: An Estimate* ..., p. 20.

in the person of Jesus Christ. Hence, he is assured of God through his personal relation with Him and is assured of the nature of God through the person of Christ; at no point does Temple challenge or justify his assurance.

It is no wonder that Temple is critical of the conclusions to which philosophical argument leads. However, does the fault lie with philosophy or in requiring of philosophy what the data of experience do not admit to be possible? Though Temple argues eloquently that probability is all one can hope for in an empirical analysis of the world, he demands certainty; and since philosophy does not provide it, he justifies appealing to religious faith which does. Similarly, while *arguing* cogently for the dialectical method in which fact and theory emerge jointly in the process of interpreting the data of experience and in which conclusions are constantly checked by the facts, Temple actually *employs*, as we have seen, an analytical method in which he starts with a specific conception of reality and proceeds to interpret the data of experience by reference to it without checking his assumptions against the facts.

It is one thing to point out that the conclusions of philosophy are always tentative and that they are constantly subject to modification and revision; it is quite another thing to suggest that philosophy fails because of this and must be replaced by a type of faith which starts with a view of reality accepted as final on the basis of which certainty is provided. There is no apparent reason why the same certainty could not be achieved by assuming from the start that the conclusions reached by philosophy would be absolute and final. Such dogmatism is equally applicable to any set of doctrines and is equally unjustified. One means of distinguishing between the assurance of the fanatic and sound assurance is to put one's inner convictions to the test of explaining the facts of experience.

It is one thing to demand that a philosophy should be relevant to life; it is quite another thing to evaluate the adequacy of a philosophical position solely on the basis of the immediate guidance provided. In examining possible world views, Temple tends to be less concerned with whether or not they present a coherent account of the facts than he is with the practical guidance offered. This is to misconceive the metaphysical task in which guidance for living and an understanding of the world emerge together. Plato stressed the necessity for the philosopher to return to the cave to give guidance to those who had not seen the light. But the point is, the philosopher can offer guidance only as he catches a glimpse of the truth. Just as the best kind of assurance one can have is that which is grounded on an hypothesis established as having a high probability of being true, so too the best kind of guidance is that which is based on an understanding of the world. Similarly, what offers the best guidance for living fosters an understanding of the world. Hence, understanding the world and guidance for living cannot be severed; they represent the joint effort of the philosopher to discover what is true and valuable.

Only in so far as one is in quest of truth to the extent that it can be approximated and only in so far as the method of critical inquiry is employed in which no area of experience is granted exemption from criticism, can the quest legitimately be called philosophical. By these standards Temple's method is not completely philosophical, as he readily admits in affirming theological philosophy, but for other reasons than those he suggests. It is not that he starts with the inner assurance that God as revealed in Christ constitutes the character of reality that renders his approach philosophically suspect; it is his failure to examine critically such a view of reality when put to the test of providing an intelligible account of experience.

Nor is it a question of whether or not one has faith; it is a question of what one has faith in and whether one is willing to examine critically the basis and content of the faith. Faith can be placed in a set of beliefs regarding man and the world to which one clings regardless of the facts of experience; or faith can be placed in one's encounter with reality, the interpretation of which is constantly checked by, and revised in accordance with, the facts of experience. The difference is between faith conceived as assent to specific beliefs and faith conceived as trust in one's relationship with reality. Temple's view of revelation suggests the latter view of faith, and some of the most profound aspects of his thought are representative of this view, but in practice he did not escape from the restrictions of the former view of faith. Kent Bendall and Frederick Ferré debate this problem in an illuminating way: Bendall sees Christianity committed to certain specific propositions; whereas for Ferré the metaphysical model as a whole functions propositionally in a way not true of any one sentence that articulates it.[2] In terms of present assent to certain historical truths of the Christian faith, Ferré states: "Modern Christians are no more bound

[2] See Kent Bendall and Frederick Ferré, *Exploring the Logic of Faith: A Dialogue on the Relation of Modern Philosophy to Christian Faith* (New York: Association Press 1962), pp. 150, 160, 194–201, 203, 208–216.

to the philosophical concepts and assumptions of the past than are any rational agents responsible for living effectively in a changing world."[3]

In conclusion, then, it is not so much a question of where one starts the quest for truth, whether from a religious or a scientific perspective, but rather whether one is willing to subject even the starting place to critical evaluation when the facts of experience require it. Also, the issue is not whether a view provides certainty or probability, but whether it provides both a comprehensive understanding of the world and specific guidance for living in the world.

Thus, though Temple's academic training was philosophical, his interests and outlook were religiously oriented.[4] His interest in philosophy is real, but it is for the sake of the independent support that philosophy can provide for the Christian conviction of which he is personally and epistemologically certain.

B. BELIEVING AND DOUBTING

The notion of certainty plays a prominent role both in Temple's critique of Descartes and in the formulation of his own epistemology. At the base of the Cartesian error, Temple contends, is the false separation made between the thinking process and the objects of thought. No such separation is possible for Temple; the subject-object relationship is ultimate. Only such an abstract separation could lead one to believe that *cogito, ergo sum* establishes any more than psychological assurance.

Temple is quite correct that thought is always thought of something. It is, however, questionable whether Descartes challenged such a fact, or that he strived to separate thinking from its objects in the way Temple argues. The question Descartes does raise is: what can a person be certain of when thinking something? His answer is that when one thinks there is a thinker – this is psychological certitude, but based on the logical cogency of the deduction. The distinction here is a significant one: there can be inner certitude about the objects of thought, but the question at issue is the epistemological justification for the psychological assurance.

The second thing which distresses Temple about Descartes' procedure is that he is initiating the quest for knowledge by the method

[3] *Ibid.*, p. 216.
[4] See *Nature, Man and God*, pp. 44, 55.

of artificial doubt. Of course it is artificial in the sense that it is self-imposed doubt; however the purpose is not doubting for doubting's sake, but doubting for the sake of discovering a rational basis for belief to replace the revelational basis of belief emphasized in medieval theology. Descartes is attempting to establish an adequate basis in reason for distinguishing between legitimate and illegitimate beliefs and doubts. The model which Descartes uses to test beliefs about the external world is the logical certainty found in mathematics. Temple's criticism of Descartes' reliance on this model is well taken.

Furthermore, Temple is quite correct that the mind must think objects, some of which, at least, do refer to a state of affairs existing independently of the thinker. If this were not the case, then there would be no reason for either doubting or believing. One can only justify believing certain things if additional experience has supported the belief in them. However, the question Descartes is raising, far from being "nursery make-believe," is the self-conscious posing of the problems of methodology and epistemology. That is, what is at issue is *how* one *knows* that the objects one is thinking actually refer to what they *prima facie* seem to refer? Granted that man begins in a subject-object relationship, all that he can be sure of is himself in relation to something; and what he wants to know is the nature of that to which he is related at any given moment. He wants to know to what extent the objects of his thought, feeling, and willing exist independently of him in the same way in which they appear to him.

To doubt the self-authenticating veracity of particular apprehensions is reasonable doubt for the sake, not of doubt, but knowledge. The basis for building up knowledge is the self and the objects known by the self. As Temple correctly affirms, this self is not isolated from the world; it does think objects which refer beyond itself. But, it is precisely to check the references of one's objects of thought that causes the problem. What Descartes and Temple both fail to see is that the self can only test the references of its ideas by additional *experiences* it has which elicit further objects of thought that *either confirm or negate* the accuracy of the references.

The difficulty with Temple's own epistemology is evident at this point. While criticizing Descartes for imposing doubt artificially on the knowledge venture, Temple imposes belief naïvely and, as a result, fails to take doubt and error seriously. Hence, Temple's proposed synthesis is not really a synthesis: too much is conceded to the thesis. It is true that if man never had any objects given to his mind from beyond himself, he could know nothing of the real world; therefore, the references of all apprehensions cannot be false. But this is an abstract or formal resolution only. What is required is to determine whether any particular apprehension does correctly refer to the world beyond one's thought and whether it exists as described. To this issue Temple's answer is inadequate, and his belief for the sake of understanding degenerates into belief for the sake of believing. The psychological certainty with which he affirms his general belief that knowledge is possible provides no basis for legitimate doubt of specific beliefs.

Temple's handling of the problem of error is likewise inadequate. For Temple it is reality that one knows, not merely one's own ideas. His only concern is that what insight into reality one gains at the moment is related to, and corrected by, what is gained in other moments. Also, though all apprehensions are of reality, not all are equally significant. Error is relegated to a minor place and even serves the positive function of stimulating the quest for a fuller grasp of reality.[5] On this basis there is no way of accounting for error which fosters further misconceptions, that is, error which hinders the quest for truth.

Hence, what is really at stake between Temple and Descartes is two opposing methods for initiating the quest for knowledge. Descartes encourages doubting in order to build a reasonable basis for believing; Temple urges believing in order to provide a reasonable basis for not having to doubt. Both belief and doubt must be joined if a true synthesis is to emerge. What is required is the belief, as Temple correctly argues, that the mind is in interaction with a world beyond itself, making the knowledge venture possible. However, this general belief must be subjected, as Descartes rightly perceives, to particular doubts regarding every apprehension one has until it has been checked by other apprehensions. What Temple fails to acknowledge is the willingness to discard any particular belief not supported by as much of experience as is available.

The issue, therefore, is not whether one believes in order to understand, but whether one continues to believe when understanding does not ensue, and whether the belief that knowledge is possible is itself subject to interpretation resulting from the knowledge that is gained. Temple quite legitimately argues that the knowledge venture can be initiated only if one believes that there is a real world which can be known by man; what is illegitimate is his acceptance of a particular

[5] See *Mens Creatrix*, pp. 274–275, 277–278; also above, Chapters 4 and 10.

interpretation of that reality based on what he believes to be his own encounter with it and which further knowledge can only explicate, never refute. Belief of this nature is not justified on the basis of the error man experiences, and it is not necessary for attaining knowledge of the world.

It is because Temple believes that in Christ the nature of reality is revealed and that in his own experience he is in direct communion with the God revealed in Christ that he is so bold as to claim that he has correctly grasped final truth. The justification for the claim that the God revealed in Christ is the starting point and goal of philosophy must now be evaluated.

C. THE PHILOSOPHIC TASK OF A CHRISTIAN

Describing his own position as theological philosophy or as the attempt to construct a Christocentric metaphysics,[6] Temple claims that it is from the perspective of an experience of personal fellowship with the God revealed in Christ that one can best discern and explain whatever meaning the world has. However, Temple raises doubts about the philosophical legitimacy of his starting point. He justifies it by claiming that a more adequate philosophy is possible by accepting as final the revelation of God in Christ, than by refusing to give priority to it. He states: "While I have less right, philosophically speaking, to my starting-point when I proceed in this way, none the less ... a more comprehensive and therefore philosophically superior scheme can be produced by this method than can be worked out from the other side, and that so far the supposed revelation with which the method started has had its character vindicated and guaranteed."[7]

Temple would seem to have misconceived the relation between philosophy and religion at this point. On the one hand, he too readily concedes that his starting point is not philosophically justified; on the other hand, he too easily affirms that his conclusions are philosophically justified. There is no need to make apology to philosophy for where one begins the philosophic quest so long as the aim is to proceed critically and to render an intelligible account of all the data. The philosopher cannot ask for more than this, but neither can he permit less. Thus, the crux of the issue in terms of Temple's position is whether philosophy

[6] See *Christus Veritas*, p. ix: *Nature, Man and God*, p. 44.

[7] *Christianity in Thought and Practice*, p. 33; also see Temple's *Christ's Revelation of God* (London: SCM Press, 1925), p. 8.

is permitted to consider critically the revelation-claim, and the content ascribed to it, that God is revealed in Christ. The philosopher must be able to evaluate even the starting point of the Christian believer and to modify or reject it, if in the course of applying it to the data of experience a more philosophically coherent hypothesis would result. Hence, the issue is not whether priority can legitimately be granted to one datum of experience, such as the Incarnation, but whether one is willing to accept as the most adequate interpretation both of this datum and of the world whatever hypothesis renders the most adequate account of the data. Indeed, the philosopher has the obligation to accept that hypothesis which relates the data most coherently; the source of the hypothesis is secondary.

Owen Thomas in his study of Temple also contends that Temple has missed the point regarding the proper relation between philosophy and theology.[8] At issue, for Thomas, is Temple's claim that philosophy and religion differ sharply both in temper and in method. Summarizing Temple's view, Thomas states: "The temper of theology is one of assurance, while that of philosophy is inquiry."[9] The separation of the attitudes of assurance and inquiry into the respective fields of theology and philosophy seems unjustified to Thomas. Likewise, Thomas objects to Temple's views that the procedure of philosophy is to comprehend the world without any presupposition concerning the nature of the world other than its rationality and without any existential commitments to a special category of experience for explaining the world by reference to that conception.[10]

According to Thomas, no one can proceed intellectually to understand the universe without many presuppositions that have far-reaching implications. Furthermore, neither the philosopher nor anyone else can completely transcend his own world view so as to get directly at the facts and to evaluate them. "Every philosophical system," Thomas argues, "is founded on the affirmation of some element in the totality of experience as of supreme significance for the interpretation of the whole."[11] Hence, all philosophical systems are based on a key-category, a guiding image, or an organizing principle for which special status is claimed and by means of which all experience can be interpreted. But, if this is the case, then all con-

[8] See Thomas, *William Temple's Philosophy of Religion*, p. 148. Thomas' study is, on the whole, a penetrating analysis and critique of Temple's philosophy of religion.

[9] *Ibid.* In Temple see *Nature, Man and God*, pp. 30f, 35, 44f.

[10] See Thomas, pp. 148–149, 157–158.

[11] *Ibid.*, p. 154.

structive philosophy is apologetic so that the tension is not between philosophy and theology, as Temple believed, but among different world views.[12] The philosophical-theological enterprise, Thomas concludes, consists of a variety of world views, some of which are called religious, some of which are called philosophical. A person may modify his position or even exchange one view for another; the latter is what is meant by conversion. However, "it is impossible to avoid commitment to some world view, although this commitment may be inchoate and by implication."[13]

There is much truth in what Thomas has written. Temple is insufficiently aware of the extent to which his Christian convictions have determined his philosophical conclusions, and that Temple thinks and writes as a Christian philosopher is one of the main contentions of the present study. Also, that Temple is mistakenly concerned about where one starts the philosophic quest has already been noted. Thomas is certainly correct when he writes, "philosophy, like theology, starts by looking at the world of experience from the standpoint or perspective of its organizing principle."[14] However, the philosophical issue does not stop with the recognition that any attempt to explain the World-Process assumes a commitment to some preconceived interpretation of that process. For the concern of the philosopher is not merely with one's initial commitment to a particular organizing principle, but with how one *proceeds* on the basis of that principle to account for the world-process. The fundamental philosophical question is whether or not the principle itself is modified or expanded as demanded by the data of experience so as to render the data intelligible? That is, is the organizing principle itself defined and redefined in the continual attempt to interpret all of experience by reference to it? As Bendall states: "Critical inquiry is essentially self-corrective. And it forbids the treatment of any proposition, no matter how well confirmed or subjectively evident, as infallibly correct or beyond the possibility of need for revision in light of fresh experience and analysis."[15]

Thomas, like Temple, seems insufficiently concerned about what one does with one's commitment to a world view. Furthermore, because everyone has at least an implicit world view does not mean that each position is equally dogmatic or equally adequate. Thus, both

[12] See *Ibid.*, pp. 157–158, 166.
[13] *Ibid.*, p. 166.
[14] *Ibid.*, p. 158.
[15] Bendall and Ferré, p. 107.

Temple and Thomas fail to take seriously enough the demand for theoretical clarity and comprehensive understanding. No doubt only as an individual lives out his commitment to a world view will he know what it means, let alone whether it makes sense of the world. Indeed, it is evident by the present variety of worlds views that different views do "make sense" in the lives of different people. The implications of this view for a conception of truth have been made explicit by John Wild: "The term *truth* is not univocal, and the human truth to which we have access is not one."[16] Nonetheless, what must also be considered is that the living out of one's commitment may *not* make sense of the world, and when this happens one must be willing to alter or to reject the world view to which one has been committed. Life does coerce one to make a commitment as to what is considered to be of supreme value; not to do so becomes a choice by default. Further, a half-hearted commitment avoids the decisiveness of the question and leaves one unsatisfied. In this sense, "critical inquiry is for the sake of life" as Ferré affirms; and Ferré is correct in granting the life-oriented domain priority over theoretical considerations.[17] Nevertheless, effectiveness in the life-oriented domain is inseparable from the theoretical considerations of critical inquiry. Also, error exists in such matters and, though one should commit oneself explicitly and totally to a world view, the commitment should not be absolute or irrevocable. As William A. Christian puts it: "It is possible to adhere wholeheartedly to a suggestion without being absolutely certain about the truth of some proposition one derives from this suggestion."[18] To be intellectually responsible means that one can never relinquish the right and the obligation to change one's commitment in light of the facts of experience.

The proper role and place of both experiential and empirical checks on one's commitment to a particular world view can be seen at this point. That strength and guidance for living be gained from one's commitment to what is considered of supreme value, is a legitimate request. It suggests that any adequate criterion of truth must take into account the experiential facts of one's personal attempt to make sense of life and to find the courage to live when the values one prizes are

[16] John Wild, *Human Freedom and Social Order: An Essay in Christian Philosophy* (Durham, N. C.: Duke University Press, 1959), p. 146. See also Ferré in Bendall and Ferré, pp. 146–148.

[17] See Bendall and Ferré, pp. 139–140.

[18] William A. Christian, *Meaning and Truth in Religion* (Princeton, New Jersey: Princeton University Press, 1964), p. 246.

despised by others. However, this experiential criterion needs to be supplemented by an empirical criterion. The latter suggests that any adequate criterion of truth must make sense of the data of experience as a whole and offer a coherent explanation of all the facts. The success of one's commitment in providing courage and guidance for living is therefore fundamental, but so too is success in providing an intelligible account of the universe as a whole. Success in one of these areas is not an excuse, or a substitute, for failure in the other area. The ultimate test of any position both in theory and in practice, therefore, would be to apply both the experiential and the empirical checks combining them into what may be labeled the experiential-empirical criterion of truth.[19]

The philosophical difficulty with Temple's approach is now evident. It is not that he affirms a particular interpretation of the Christian faith as the starting point for his philosophic quest, but that he does not allow the possibility of moving beyond the place where he starts. To seek to interpret all of experience from the perspective and illumination provided by an event such as the Incarnation is philosophically justified if one is willing in the process to modify the original interpretation of the event as experience requires. However, to take a particular interpretation of the Incarnation as identical with reality so that one refuses to alter the interpretation if and when the facts require is philosophically unjustified.

It is Temple's failure to follow the procedure of relating all the data of experience into a coherent scheme and of modifying his original assumptions in accordance with the facts that excludes him from being described with complete accuracy as a Christian Philosopher and which places him closer to the Christian apologist. What makes this failure on Temple's part to be true to the philosophic task particularly unfortunate and inconsistent is that he describes so well how the philosopher should proceed in what he calls the dialectical method.

The philosophical legitimacy of metaphysical speculation is still being debated, though its justification is gaining support even among some analytic philosophers.[20] The point is that a metaphysical Christian philosophy can be judged illegitimate only if all metaphysical specu-

[19] The role of both experiential and empirical considerations in exploring the problem of God is analyzed in Chapter 18 below. Definite affinities may be noted among the above criterion and the views proposed by John Wild and Frederick Ferré. In Wild, see *Human Freedom and Social Order*, pp. 116–117; in Ferré, see *Basic Modern Philosophy of Religion* (New York: Charles Scribner's Sons, 1967). pp. 353–370, 378–388.

[20] See e.g., P. F. Strawson, *Individuals: An Essay in Descriptive Metaphysics* (New York: Doubleday & Company, Inc., 1963) and James W. Cornman, *Metaphysics, Reference, and Language* (New Haven: Yale University Press, 1966). For a recent defense of metaphysical

lation is shown to be unjustified; for surely the question of whether there can be a metaphysical Christian philosophy is no different philosophically from the question whether there can be a metaphysical naturalistic or an idealistic philosophy.[21] Nonetheless for the Christian metaphysician, the question remains whether or not he is willing to proceed critically from his avowed Christian starting point; to do so is surely one of the major philosophic tasks of the Christian.[22] It is, then, a matter of examining Christian positions to see if the data of the Christian faith and the other data of experience are handled critically. A philosophy is Christian when the key-concepts and inspiration are derived from what is interpreted to be one's encounter with the God revealed in Christ. An exposition of the Christian faith is philosophically justified when the universe is rendered intelligible and guidance for living is provided by the concepts derived from that particular "encounter" with the God Christ revealed and when the interpretation of the encounter is itself continually and critically evaluated in the process of relating it to the facts of experience.

Both Temple's conception of philosophy and his particular exposition of a Christian philosophy, therefore, are not wholly adequate. An excellent analysis of the dialectical method of philosophy is presented by Temple but not adequately followed by him. The nature of reality, he contends, is given in the Christian revelation, and he does not critically relate this conception to the rest of experience. Even the metaphysical task of rendering the universe intelligible is not fully accepted when to do so would require a modification of his conceptions of reality and of intelligibility. Hence, Temple tends to sever understanding the world from personal guidance for living whereas the two should be joined. He is more concerned with providing philosophical support for his Christian convictions than he is with discovering the most intelligible account of experience, if the latter should entail modifying his beliefs. The difficulties with Temple's philosophical approach, then, reside partly in his conception of philosophy and partly in his failure to adhere to the philosophic task as he conceives it.

speculation, see W. H. Walsh, *Metaphysics* (New York: Harcourt, Brace & World, Inc., 1963). James W. Woelfel's, "'Non-Metaphysical' Christian Philosophy and LinguisticPhilosophy" reprinted in Martin E. Marty and Dean G. Peerman, *New Theology No. 2* (New York: The Macmillan Company, 1965), provides a good summary of the issues at stake for Christian philosophy.

[21] Owen Thomas agrees with this position; see pp. 159–160, 165. For an excellent defense of the idea of a Christian philosophy despite objections to it, see Wild, pp. 94–115.

[22] For other tasks of the Christian in philosophy, see John Smith, *Reason and God*, pp. 142–151. Smith does not make explicit the particular task noted above, but it is implied in the tasks he does enumerate.

CHAPTER 17

HUMAN PERSONALITY

The concept of personality is employed by Temple to solve fundamental philosophical problems. How adequately he executes this task needs to be critically examined; however, before that can be done, it is necessary to evaluate Temple's conception of personality. Three issues serve to focalize the main critical points in Temple's conception of personality: (1) the status which personality enjoys in the total scheme of the universe; (2) the type of unity which characterizes the human person; (3) the relation of, and difference between, the person and his psychological personality.

A. THE STATUS OF PERSONALITY IN THE WORLD-PROCESS

In *Nature, Man and God* Temple presents a brief but impressive analysis of the origin and development of personality in the World-Process. The evolution of the distinctive features of the personal level of existence are too often neglected by those affirming a religious philosophy, and Temple is to be commended for striving to discover what insights such an approach affords.[1]

Significant in this connection is Temple's account of the origin of consciousness as rooted in the effort of the organism to adjust to its environment. Thought is rooted in desire and arises so as to facilitate the organism's satisfaction of its needs. Hence, purposefulness characterizes consciousness both at its rudimentary and highest levels; in the latter case purposefulness is reflected in the attempt to alter the world to suit its own ends.[2]

[1] The religio-biological writings of the Jesuit Paleontologist, Pierre Teilhard de Chardin, would have delighted Temple; see e.g., *The Phenomenon of Man* (New York: Harper & Brothers, 1959).

[2] See Temple, *Nature, Man and God*, pp. 111–122, 207, 221; also see above, Chapter 4.

Some of the epistemological conclusions which Temple has drawn from this analysis have been challenged in the previous chapter, but there are important features in his discussion that warrant further comment. Temple professes his reliance on Whitehead at this point. A similar view regarding the origin and characteristics of consciousness is expounded by the biologist Edmund Sinnott who traces consciousness and mind to "the self-regulatory and goal-seeking character of protoplasm."[3] The basic characteristic of all life is a tendency toward goal-seeking which is manifested in the activities of both body and mind. There is a tendency within the organism for bodily development directed to some end, which Sinnott calls a goal. Purpose and desire represent the inward experience of this process of development toward a goal: "The effect of the operation of this goal on the living system is experienced inwardly as a *purpose* if one intends to achieve the goal, or as a *desire* if one is simply attracted toward it."[4] At the higher levels of life the inner experience of protoplasmic purposiveness constitutes conscious purpose.

Hence, the conclusions of Sinnott, the biologist turned philosopher, render additional support to the analysis of Temple, the Christian theist, on the origin and rudimentary characteristics of mind. Unfortunately, however, Temple does not carry on the analysis with sufficient thoroughness. His discussion of matter as inert which he employs most frequently, especially reflected in the distinctions drawn between Thing, Brute, and Person, is antiquated and inconsistent with his own emphasis on the physical world as "continuous becoming."[5] The analysis of life tends to serve only as a transition point from matter to mind and is conceived as hardly more than mind at a rudimentary level.

The distinguishing feature of mind does not arise until it develops a relatively independent status in regard to the environment by forming concepts which are not tied to immediate percepts of existing objects.[6] This conception of "free ideas" is fundamental to Temple's position. It is on the basis of a partial transcendence of the process that mind controls matter, that self-determination is actualized, and that spirit emerges making immortality possible. To hold that mind develops a

[3] Sinnott, *Matter, Mind and Man*, p. 85; see also Edmund W. Sinnott, *The Biology of the Spirit* (New York: The Viking Press, 1955), pp. 49–74.

[4] Sinnott, *The Biology of the Spirit*, p. 53, N. 2.

[5] Temple, *Nature, Man and God*, p. 115. See the criticisms noted by William D. Geoghegan, *Platonism in Recent Religious Thought* (New York: Columbia University Press, 1958), pp. 94–95, 105–106).

[6] See Temple, *Nature, Man and God*, pp. 202, 212, 492; also above, Chapters 4 and 6.

life of its own and at the same time is organically related to the physical organism requires a more complete analysis of the problem in relating mind to body than Temple offers.

The level of personality is attained only when the organism itself determines what goal is to be sought; for Temple this means spirit controls the total nature of man composed of matter, life, mind, and spirit. What, then, is the relation of spirit to the physical organism? To speak of control by spirit, as Temple does, when all the elements of man's nature are organically united needs further clarification than he provides. This issue is best considered in terms of Temple's analysis of the organic unity of man.

B. THE UNIQUE UNITY OF THE HUMAN PERSON

A fruitful evaluation of Temple's views on the mind-body problem and on the problem of the unity and identity of the self can be made by comparing his views with those of Edgar Sheffield Brightman. It is particularly relevant since Temple has been labeled a personal idealist by some interpreters,[7] and Brightman called himself a personal idealist.

Brightman proposes a radically empirical definition of the self. He calls it the datum self and means by it one's present conscious experience. Everything that the self is not aware of, or cannot be aware of, is not-self, no matter how intimate one's relation to it. The self thus refers to consciousness only and must be distinguished from its environment. Brightman states: "Personal consciousness alone is experience, and ... all bodies, brains, and gods are objects of belief."[8]

Brightman, therefore, distinguishes the mind from the body. Body is not the mind or any part of mind, though it is in interaction with mind. Interactionism proposes that both mind and body act on and affect each other. Mind and body act as one, however, and even constitute a "functional unity."[9] Nevertheless, they indicate different realms of experience, just as the brain is not the same as one's awareness. Though closely related, mind and body are not to be considered as one for the following reasons: (1) there is a difference between one's body and one's

[7] See Skelton, p. 137; also, Randolph Crump Miller refers to Temple as closest to Personal Idealism in his article, "Is Temple a Realist?," *Journal of Religion*, XIX (January, 1939), p. 50.

[8] Brightman, *Philosophy of Religion*, (New York: Prentice-Hall, Inc., 1940), p. 349.

[9] Edgar Sheffield Brightman, *Nature and Values* (New York: Abingdon-Cokesbury Press, 1945), p. 55.

experience of his body; (2) cause and effect are not to be identified. Only confusion results when causes and effects are identified. Hence, Brightman states:

> If we are to insist that the causes which are essential to the existence of personality are all a part of it, then the body, the subconsciousness, the air we breathe, the life-giving sun, in fact, the whole of nature, must be parts of every person, and every person is all bodies, all minds, all things.[10]

It is not even accurate to state that the mind is in the body. For if so, then where in the body is it? Mind cannot be located in the body. Mind is what it is experienced to be, namely, personal conscious awareness. Body, interpreted metaphysically, is the activity of the Divine mind with which one is in intimate interaction.[11]

It is Temple's thesis that mind arises within the organism as an extension of organic reaction to environment. Hence, mind and body are one; man is a psycho-physical organism. However, Temple does not identify mind and body, and he refuses to endorse either a panpsychism which would posit a "mind-stuff" at all levels of reality or a view which holds to the activity of thought minus a thinker. These rejections seem inconsistent with Temple's own analysis of mind in its rudimentary forms and point up his failure to provide an adequate analysis of matter and life. At this point Temple is more concerned with emphasizing the distinctive feature of mind at its higher levels. Accordingly, he claims that whatever proves to be the ultimate resolution of the relation between matter and mind, a distinction will remain. Though the mind is immanent in the body and organically related to it, mind transcends the body and is always more than the movements of the body by initiating activity for the sake of what it takes to be some good. Hence, the mind directs the body by means of a purpose it seeks, and the body is the medium for the execution of the purpose.[12]

By distinguishing the activity of the mind from bodily activity, Temple tends to separate mind and body despite his insistence that they are joined. What the actual relation is between body and mind, as the physical activity of the body carries out the non-physical purpose of the mind, is not indicated. A characteristic inadequacy in Temple's analyses of issues comes to the fore in this connection: what aspect of a problem he stresses and what solution he proposes tend to depend

[10] *Ibid.*, pp. 55–56.
[11] See *ibid.*, pp. 124–125.
[12] See *Nature, Man and God*, pp. 201, 282–283, 489.

on the point he is making at the time. When he wishes to distinguish his view from idealism and show the inadequacy of any position that denies the reality of matter, he then points out the emergence of consciousness in the organism and traces its rudimentary analogue at lower levels. In such a case he is content to argue as a critical naturalist or organicist might argue, that is, that mind and body are organically related. But when he wishes to show the inadequacy of materialism and the philosophy of organism, then he stresses the distinctive characteristics of mind as distinct from matter, suggesting an entitative state of mind. In the latter case he willingly employs arguments that are akin to idealism. What is lacking is a thoroughgoing effort to relate systematically these disparate emphases and weave them into a coherent pattern of explanation.

A failure to relate varying emphases on a particular issue characterizes Temple's entire position. In his argument for God he is content to show that philosophical argument supports a theistic position and, then, moves on to the evidence of religious experience which indicates a personal God. Further, the God arrived at through these two avenues of investigation is identified with the God of the Christian faith, but he does not show that one leads to another or attempt to relate the conclusions from the various strands of evidence. It may be that this defect is due to the busy life he led and the hurried manner in which most of his writing was accomplished – in odd half-hours, as he states.[13] It may also indicate that Temple's real concern is not with the development of a systematic philosophy, but with the use of philosophical discourse whenever relevant to support his religious convictions. Whatever the reason, the failure of a philosopher to relate his views so that a coherent pattern is clearly discernible is a major defect. Clarity at the expense of contact with actuality is certainly undesirable, and this Temple rightly condemns; but lack of clarity is no virtue in itself and when inconsistencies are apparent, then failure to make clear what is meant is a serious omission.

Brightman's exposition of this issue, on the other hand, suffers from clarity at the expense of contact with experience. Too sharp a distinction between mind and body is made. It is true that one's conscious awareness is not the same as the physiological processes which occur in the brain; it is also to be granted that a line must be drawn somewhere between cause and effect and that in one sense the whole

[13] See Temple, *Mens Creatrix*, p. vii; also Iremonger, p. 482.

of nature is essential to the existence of mind, but few would be willing to admit the sun as part of anyone's body. It does not follow, however, that the place to draw the line is between mind and body or that the distinction is as clear-cut as Brightman suggests. Indeed, Michael Polanyi argues that all of man's thought processes are rooted in bodily processes: "Our body is the ultimate instrument of all our external knowledge, whether intellectual or practical. In all our waking moments we are *relying* on our awareness of contacts of our body with things outside for *attending* to these things."[14] Also, the fact remains that one's particular bodily organism is more intimately and causally related to one's mind than the sun. My body is experienced as mine in a way that the sun or the air I breathe are not.

C. J. Ducasse indicates the peculiarities which serve as criteria enabling one to identify decisively one's own body.[15] First, one's body is the only physical object in which movements or other bodily changes are directly initiated by one's mind.[16] In only one body does an arm raise when one wills it or does blushing result when one feels ashamed. Second, one's body is the only physical object which when stimulated produces corresponding sensations in one's mind.[17] Thus, though one perceives many hands protruding from under a cloth and observes a pin being stuck in each one, only the pricking of a particular hand produces a feeling of pain and that hand is identified as one's own. Third, in only one body do certain mutilations result in changes in one's conscious mind. For example, the severing of certain nerve tissues in the brain can destroy the capacity of the mind to respond to certain sense stimuli. Fourth, in only one body can certain structural changes be produced – such as establishing specific connections among brain neurons which correspond to certain skills or habits – by the mind's willing the acquisition of these specific skills and habits.

As Ducasse notes, what such evidence suggests is that the relation

[14] Michael Polanyi, *The Tacit Dimension* (New York: Doubleday Anchor Book, 1967), pp. 15–16.

[15] See C. J. Ducasse, *Nature, Mind, and Death* (La Salle, Illinois: The Open Court Publishing Company, 1951), pp. 424–429.

[16] Ducasse qualifies this statement in light of the evidence of psychical research pointing toward PK or psychokinetic effect. Admitting PK effect, Ducasse maintains that there is still only one material object which can be moved more than minutely by one's will, and this object one refers to as *one's* body; see *ibid.*, pp. 426–427.

[17] Again a minor qualification is made by Ducasse on the basis of the evidence for "clairvoyance" in which there is causation by physical events without intermediary stimulation by these events on the sense organs; see *ibid.*, p. 427.

between a mind and "its" body is that of direct causal interaction. Mind and body directly act on each other in a way not characteristic of the relation each shares with other psychical or physical entities. Further, as Whitehead observes and the above evidence implies, the relationship between mind and body is experienced by the self as a unity of mind and body.[18]

However, the question remains of the kind of unity which the mind and body enjoy. Since Temple's position has definite affinities on this issue with the views of Whitehead and Sinnott, a comment on their views is in order. According to Whitehead, the mind's role is to act as coordinator of, and to exercise a unified control over, the multiple organic cells constituting the living organism and the diverse objects potentially capable of being included within the mind's purpose.[19] Sinnott's analysis suggests a similar view: "An *organism* is a mind and body unity."[20] Mind is the integrating and directing agent that sifts the various sensations and controls the possible responses so that unity of conduct is maintained under the guidance of a goal. The advantage of stating the mind-body relation in this way is that the unity of mind and body is clearly indicated; the disadvantage of this approach is that it seems to imply an identification of mind and body. But, if mind and body are identified, then the distinctive characteristics and activities of each are blurred or even eliminated.

Hence, if both the unity of mind and body and the distinctive features of each one are to be maintained in accordance with the evidence, then their relation is best described in terms of interaction and their unity referred to as functional. However, such a conception of functional unity is not the same as proposed by Brightman. The union of mind and body represents a complex unity in which the physical activity of body and the psychical activity of mind directly interact. Thus, the experience one has of his body indicates a more distinct and unique existent than is allowed by Brightman in making body the direct activity of the Divine Mind. At the same time, the uniqueness of mind must be maintained and its activities distinguished from those of the body. Mind and body are distinct, as Brightman argues and they are also uniquely related, as Temple argues; however the relation shared by mind and body cannot be equated with any other relation. It is,

[18] See Alfred North Whitehead, *Modes of Thought* (New York: The Macmillan Company, 1938), pp. 218–228.

[19] See Whitehead, *Process and Reality*, pp. 164–167.

[20] Sinnot, *Matter, Mind and Man*, p. 78.

as J. B. Pratt suggests, *sui generis*, unique.[21] The human mind, though rooted in the body from which it arose, may still act as the agency of control over the body.

The difficult problem of how the activity of mind interacts with bodily activity remains unsolved. However, there is merit in recognizing that there is a unity of mind and body even if the precise relation of the component dimensions cannot be indicated at this stage of the investigation. If the nature of body turns out to be a rudimentary form of mind or self as panpsychism suggests, then the relation between mind and "body" conceived in these terms would prove quite understandable. On the other hand, if the physical and the psychical are coequal, representing "two aspects of the same organized living system,"[22] as Sinnott suggests, then their unique relationship is also rendered intelligible. What the available evidence does suggest at present are two entities with distinctive characteristics causally interacting and uniquely united. What must be resisted, therefore, is the attempt to identify mind and body. Brightman tends to eliminate the body as a distinct existent, while maintaining the unique features of mind and its interaction with a body sustained by God; Temple, while insisting on the unique unity of mind and body, denies interaction and thus blurs the distinctive characteristics of each.

In regard to the problem of the identity of the self a functional view also seems most in accord with the facts. Both Temple and Brightman affirm such a view but differ in that Temple includes the continuity of the physical organism as the basis for, and as part of, the self's identity. Both reject a soul-substance view which posits an underlying ego that persists unchanged through the diversity of experience providing the unity and identity of the self.

For Brightman the unity of the self is the wholeness and individuality of its consciousness, and its identity is the experience of self-identification in immediate experience through memory of the past and anticipation of the future. Temple and Brightman agree that full psychical unity and identity are attained only when all the activities of the self are integrated under the guidance of a purpose. However, for Temple the body is included in this unity when it submits to and expresses the purpose which the self has established; whereas for Brightman the body responds to the self's purpose through the direct activity of God.

[21] See James Bissett Pratt, *Personal Realism* (New York: The Macmillan Company, 1937), p. 269.

[22] Sinnot, *Matter, Mind and Man*, p. 112.

Such a dichotomy of man's unique unity as Brightman asserts seems unnecessary and unwarranted. The unity of the self is complex, sufficiently complex that bodily functionings play their part and must be incorporated into the self's unity and identity.

There is, therefore, cogency in Temple's analysis of the three-fold unity of the self rooted in the physical continuity of the body, manifested on the conscious level by the effort to unify one's impulses, and culminating in a purpose to which the total self is committed and which serves to organize the activities of mind and body. Having stated the unity and identity of the self in this way, the failure on Temple's part to relate these views to his analysis of the mind-body problem, or to his conception of personality is all the more striking.

One thing is clear from this comparison of Temple and Brightman on the nature of the self: Temple is not a personal idealist in regard to this fundamental issue. What label best suits Temple's position is difficult to determine because he has not systematically developed a philosophy, and inconsistencies are apparent. It is not amiss to refer to his philosophical tendencies as being closest to a type of personal realism, not the same metaphysically as that affirmed by Pratt, but having affinities with Pratt's position in regard to epistemology and the mind-body problem.[23] However, any attempt to label Temple's position without taking into account his reliance on the Christian faith is misleading. Temple is a Christian theist who most frequently employs the philosophical arguments of personal realism in order to support and to elucidate the particular issue he is expounding. Personal existence is for Temple the highest reality, and his conception of personality is derived from a Hellenistic-Christian view of God. Further, matter enjoys a relatively independent status in the created universe and serves as the medium through which personal beings execute their purposes. Hence, Temple might be labelled a Christian personalistic realist.

C. THE PERSON AND HIS PERSONALITY

The failure of Temple to relate various strands of his thought and weave them together into a meaningful pattern is nowhere more apparent than in his conception of personality. In his book entitled

[23] See Pratt, *Personal Realism.* Concerning the aim of the book Pratt states: "Its aim is to defend both Realism and the actuality of the individual. ... It is my belief that the only trustworthy defense of the reality of the self, of a metaphysically grounded individualism, must be based upon a realistic epistemology"; p. viii.

The Nature of Personality the analysis is carried on almost entirely in ethical terms. There is a discussion of the distinction between personal and sub-personal levels of existence, but even that involves the ethical concepts of rights and duties. It is significant that Lectures III through VI of *The Nature of Personality* are incorporated almost *verbatim* into the section in *Mens Creatrix* dealing with conduct, Chapters XIII and XIV. In *Nature, Man and God* when the evolution of mind is traced, no attempt is made to relate his analysis of the dimensions of personality arrived at in earlier works, and only in a general way are the levels of existence – matter, life, mind, and spirit – related to the distinctions drawn between thing, brute, and person. Some of the chief characteristics of personality affirmed by Temple do appear in his discussion of the origin of mind in the World-Process, but no attempt is made to point out the relationship and significance of the analysis at this level with the discussion of personality at the human and divine levels.

A major defect in Temple's discussion of personality is the lack of psychological orientation and consideration.[24] William McDougal alone of personality theorists of recognized stature is referred to by Temple and then only to support his own view of the social dimension of personality.[25] No attempt is made by Temple to assess psychological interpretations of personality. Psychoanalysis and psychotherapy as techniques for aiding integration are totally neglected. At one point Temple refers to the field of psychology as an "adolescent science, ... adolescent in the sense that it is still immature, still far from being wholly integrated."[26] He chides: "Regarded as an entity it is suffering badly from what it has itself taught us to call the dis-association of personality and, consequently, from a certain self-consciousness or self-assertion."[27] Considering that these statements were made in 1936, they are not altogether unfair. Temple does show familiarity with psychological concepts and insights, but there is no indication that he had made a serious study of the field.

In terms of psychological theories of personality, Temple's theory would seem to be closest to the Social Psychological theories of Alfred Adler and Harry Stack Sullivan and Gordon Allport's "Psychology of the Individual."[28] Allport defines personality as "the dynamic

[24] Note the similar observation in Fletcher, *William Temple*, p. 306, n. 90.

[25] See Temple, *Nature of Personality*, pp. 46–49.

[26] William Temple, *The Church and Its Teaching Today* (New York: The Macmillan Company, 1936), p. 30.

[27] *Ibid.*

[28] See Calvin S. Hall and Gardner Lindzey, *Theories of Personality* (New York: John

organization within the individual of those psychophysical systems that determine his characteristic behavior and thought."[29] Temple also views the person as a self-organizing system and roots the initial unity and direction of the self in the physiological organism. Temple states: "The concrete person is a self-organising system of impulses, instincts, sentiments, emotions, ideas, and all the rest which psychological analysis may set out."[30]

However, Temple shares only incidental affinities with these psychologists, since his interests and aims were quite distinct from theirs. Further, as the above quotation indicates, Temple does not make clear whether he means to distinguish between person and personality. At times he uses the terms interchangeably. At other times he confines the term person to the notion of spirit, indicating that spirit is the distinctive element in personality. In the latter case, personality would presumably refer to the entire psychophysical organism. It is this interpretation which Temple would seem to mean, but there is no attempt to make these issues clear. Indeed, it might fairly be concluded in the light of Temple's analysis of the mind-body problem that the term person, or personal being, refers to the entire organism, physical and psychic. In this case personality might be used to signify the mode of adjustment which the person develops in interaction with the environment. Temple makes no such distinction though it would be consistent with his position and would have facilitated matters if he had.

In terms of Temple's conception of personality, the fundamental problem lies not so much in what is or is not stated, but in a failure to deal thoroughly and systematically with personality so that a coherent interpretation results. Somewhere in his various writings many of the important elements are noted, but nowhere is a conception of personality explicitly developed in a way that relates to his entire position.

Wiley & Sons, Inc., 1957), pp. 116–127, 134–151, 257–393; Also, see Fletcher, William Temple, p. 46.

[29] Gordon W. Allport, *Pattern and Growth in Personality* (New York: Holt, Rinehard and Winston, 1961), p. 28; see also Allport's earlier edition, *Personality: A Psychological Interpretation* (New York: Henry Holt and Company, 1937), p. 48.

[30] Temple, *Nature, Man and God*, p. 231.

CHAPTER 18

THE CATEGORY OF THE PERSONAL AND THE PROBLEM OF GOD

A. PERSONALITY AS A METAPHYSICAL PRINCIPLE OF EXPLANATION

The centrality of the concept of personality in Temple's philosophy is particularly apparent in the use he makes of personality as a metaphysical principle of explanation. Two points need to be evaluated in Temple's analysis: (1) the justification for using purpose as the only adequate explanatory principle; (2) the adequacy of Temple's approach in arriving at the nature of the Supreme Being whose purpose is held to explain the universe.

1. Purpose as a guiding image for metaphysical speculation

Temple argues that when an account of the World-Process itself is sought, the only principle offered in human experience which really explains it is the principle of purpose. A teleological explanation of the world alone is held to be self-explanatory, and for Temple this means purposive will determined by good.

Temple has been criticized for the approach which he follows in explaining the World-Process by reference to purpose. Some interpreters of Temple contend that in earlier writings Temple appealed more to the self-evident explanatory character of Divine purpose and that in his later writings he stressed more the need of faith in accepting God. Dorothy Emmet seems to have been instrumental in perpetuating this notion. She writes:

> Does Temple assume too easily the unique explanatory value of the category of Purpose when it is applied not only to certain kinds of activity within the world, but to the world as a whole? And does he tend to assume that, if an explanation in terms of Purpose would satisfy our minds, then such an explanation there must be? In his earlier works he does often seem to be saying just this. But

increasingly in his later work he puts forward the idea of a Divine Purpose for Good as a venture of faith, supported though not demonstrated by reason and experience.[1]

Another criticism has been levied against Temple's method for the opposite reason. Mc Garvey claims that modernistic tendencies in the form of an appeal to the empirical evidence and language of science become evident in Temple's later writings.[2] At issue, Mc Garvey contends, are two contrasting conceptions of the intelligibility of the world – the philosophical (or personal) and the scientific (or impersonal). Man, it is held, is so created that he seeks to understand the world in which he finds himself. Science attempts only to orient man in terms of the relations among particular objects in space and time. Philosophy is not content until the question why the universe is as it is has been answered, not simply how it happened. The two ideals of intelligibility are apparent in these different approaches. Mc Garvey goes on to affirm that the only way to terminate the philosophic quest is to discover a self-authenticating reality acknowledged to be significant and meaningful.[3] It is from the perspective of this kind of reality in providing the meaning of intelligibility that Temple is criticized.

In one sense these criticisms cancel out one another. Mc Garvey is critical of Temple's failure to follow in later years an *a priori* approach rooted in religious experience, and Emmet claims that Temple increasingly makes explicit his reliance on faith. However, evidence may be suggested for the conclusion that both have partially misconceived Temple's approach.

Emmet, and those two follow her lead,[4] fail to take into account that in all his attempts to offer a metaphysical explanation of the world Temple appeals ultimately to faith and not to reason, to inner assurance and practical guidance as the tests of adequacy and not to rational coherence alone. This issue concerns the unity of Temple's thought and has been explored already in the first chapter. Hence, some brief references to Temple's writings will suffice at this point. In *The Faith and Modern Thought,* Temple's first book published in 1910, he argues that the religious experience of a Power supporting one and the rational

[1] Dorothy Emmet, "The Philosopher," in Iremonger, p. 527.

[2] See Mc Garvey "Modernism in Archbishop Temple's Metaphysics and Value Theory," pp. 29–31.

[3] See *ibid.*, pp. 125–127.

[4] See Skelton, "The Problem of Evil in the Works of William Temple," p. 137; also John W. Carlton, "The Reach and Limits of Natural Theology in the Formulation of William Temple's Christology" (unpublished Ph. D. dissertation, School of Arts and Sciences, Duke University, 1955).

demand for understanding the world as a whole meet and are satisfied by the view that the world is operated by a Purpose rooted in will.[5] Christ is held to supply the clue to the content of the nature of the Supreme Power. Also in *Mens Creatrix* (1917), Temple explicitly states that ultimate certainty resides in faith and not in knowledge.[6]

Mc Garvey's contention would seem to be supported by what has been noted. However, he fails to recognize that there is a continuity throughout all of Temple's writings. Temple's position in *Nature, Man and God* (1934) does not represent a break with earlier writings; nor can his views be so readily identified with those of Whitehead as Mc Garvey suggests. Indeed, it is Temple's own uncriticized assumption of the validity of the Christian faith as he interprets it, indicated even in the Gifford Lectures, that renders his views philosophically suspect, rather than too much reliance on empirical evidence. *Nature, Man and God* ends with the emphasis on the hunger of natural theology for a specific and final revelation which it can neither produce nor evaluate but must accept on faith in order to render the world intelligible. It must never be forgotten that as a committed Christian Temple strives to set forth as best he can a philosophically intelligible exposition and defense of his faith.

What must be critically evaluated is Temple's contention that in purpose alone a self-explanatory principle is found. Temple argues that one may choose not to ask for an explanation of the World-Process, and it is conceivable that there is none in the sense of explaining why the world is as it is, but that it is questionable whether this is as intelligible an account of the facts as the attempt to discover an explanation of the whole. Hence, although a refusal to raise the question is not self-contradictory, if a self-explanatory principle of the universe is sought, then purpose does supply what is required. To explain something by purpose is to provide an intelligible reason for its being where and what it is; it is to suggest that the reason why an object is the way it is serves some end which is inherent in the object itself or that the object is a means to an end which has been imposed upon it. Thus, purpose is held to be explanatory in a way that no other principle known to man is, and, for this reason, purpose serves as the ideal of explanation for the World-Process.

Temple seems guilty here, as Miss Emmet suggests, of assuming too readily that purpose *alone* is an adequate explanatory principle

5 *Faith and Modern Thought*, pp. 20–22, 25–27; also see above, Chapters 6 and 9.
6 *Mens Creatrix*, p. 4.

of the World-Process and that the only alternative to it is scepticism, or giving up the quest for an explanation. What seems justified in Temple's contention is that purpose deserves serious consideration as a guiding image, or a pregnant root metaphor, that may enable the metaphysician to render intelligible the World-Process. But in any complete philosophical treatment, other alternative guiding images, or root metaphors, deserve the same kind of careful consideration that Temple provides only for his category of purpose.[7] Also, even if purpose serves as an ideal of explanation, it does not follow that such an explanation has been demonstrated. Of course, Temple makes no such assumption: his view of the world as best rendered intelligible through recourse to purposive will determined by good is a venture of faith, rationally and empirically supported. Hence, Temple correctly recognized, though he did not formulate it in this way, that the crucial issue is the choice of one's guiding image and that this issue is determined more by one's faith, or life-orientation, than it is by the conclusions of philosophical argument.

Today the philosopher would need to go further and justify the metaphysical enterprise itself; but even assuming its legitimacy does not guarantee that one alternative can be shown to be sufficiently adequate to eliminate all other contenders. Indeed, the opposite conclusion seems to follow: no one metaphysical hypothesis can be demonstrated to be true though this does not mean that all are equal in their adequacy or inadequacy.

> Some metaphysical theories break down under comparatively little critical inquiry. Others hold their own much better under dialectical scrutiny. Some metaphysicians believe that they have found the one hypothesis that requires no revision. But alternative hypotheses cannot be tested so as to eliminate all but one, leaving that one perfect hypothesis standing.[8]

The current scepticism regarding metaphysical speculation has surely taught philosophers an important lesson: no definitive answers are possible in metaphysics and the claim to have found them is misleading in the extreme.

At issue, then, is not merely Temple's reliance on purpose alone as self-explanatory, but also the method by which he arrives at his claim that the purpose must transcend the world and be embodied in a

[7] Stephen C. Pepper proposes as equally adequate four metaphysical theories based on four root metaphors; see *World Hypotheses: A Study in Evidence* (Berkeley and Los Angeles: University of California Press, 1961), esp. p. 330.

[8] Lewis White Beck and Robert L. Holmes, *Philosophic Inquiry: An Introduction to Philosophy* (2nd ed.: Englewood Cliffs, New Jersey: Prentice-Hall, Inc., 1968), p. 285.

conscious being whose nature is perfect goodness and absolute power. This view of God does not seem empirically justified and will be examined later in the chapter and more fully in Chapter 20. What warrants careful examination now is the *approach* Temple employed to arrive at his conception of God.

2. *An experiential-empirical approach to the problem of God*

Temple's analyses of the world and of man leading to the positing of God as the ground of the universe do seem at first blush to be empirically grounded. Particularly in *Nature, Man and God* the epistemological argument for God combined with the intimations of a personal mind provided by the quest for truth, beauty, and goodness seems rooted in an interpretation of the empirical facts. However, Temple is never content to remain with such empirical evidence alone and he explicitly states that he does not begin there. Temple willingly employs the evidence of experience until it leads him to posit a Supreme Intelligence as Creator and Sustainer of nature and man. Having reached this point on the basis of a cogent empirical argument, he then makes a "leap of faith" and equates the Supreme Mind with the God of the Christian tradition.

However, as we have seen, it is misleading to suggest even that Temple follows the empirical evidence up to a point and then switches to a reliance on faith because his faith provides the motivation and goal for the quest itself. His approach is that of theological philosophy. Whenever the empirical evidence conflicts with the insights of religious faith as expressed in traditional Christianity, Temple ends up either by resolving the contradiction as being apparent only or by simply abandoning the evidence at that point in favor of his religious faith. Examples of this approach have been noted at various points throughout the present study; it is sufficient to recall some of them. Temple's conception of God as self-sufficient and as exercising complete supremacy over history despite the contradictions involved is one such case.[9] The resolution of the problem of evil by Temple offers a clear example of sacrificing empirical evidence for the absolutistic ideal of God as Perfect Being. Admitting that intrinsic evil involved in much suffering is not accounted for on the basis of the instrumental value of suffering in producing character, Temple frankly appeals to religious faith for

[9] A more complete criticism of this point is presented in Chapter 20.

courage and to eternity for hope. Also, the notion of a triune God is a clear case of forsaking human experience of personality; man is asked to accept what on the human level would be the activities of three persons within the unity of a personal being, though to combine them is contradictory for man.

It should be recalled that Temple justifies beginning with the assumption of the finality of a particular Christian world view on the basis that the data of experience can be interpreted more adequately by this approach. But when faced with concrete problems of experience which conflict with his Christian world view and which this world view fails to illuminate, Temple chooses to surrender the goal of rendering the data of experience intelligible rather than modify his world view. Thus, Temple fails to offer a coherent interpretation of experience from the perspective of the Christian faith even though it is on the condition of providing such an account that he justifies assuming the finality of the Christian faith. Temple's failure, once again, to be true to the philosophic enterprise is not that he begins his investigation of experience with clues drawn from a Christian world view, but that he fails to modify his position in accordance with the facts and thereby relinquishes the philosophic task of rendering human experience intelligible from the perspective of his Christian world view. The situation has not changed much since Temple's time. As John E. Smith states: "There is a curious inconsistency at present in the works of theologians who, on the one hand, reject philosophical mediation in theology, but who then go on to argue that a religious view is validated because it alone 'makes sense' out of life as no other view does. This 'making sense' is precisely the appeal to intelligibility."[10]

Temple's method for understanding God may best be described as an ontological-experiential approach. This is not to suggest that he relies on the traditional ontological *argument* for God; what is meant is that Temple begins with an ideal conception of God as a being perfect in goodness and absolute in power and employs the ideal to interpret the empirical facts of the natural order. As was noted in the first chapter, his father (Archbishop Frederick Temple), the Church of England, and Bishop Gore, all exercised major influences on the development of Temple's own theological position and in each case God was conceived in an absolutistic sense; furthermore, the same

[10] John E. Smith, *Experience and God* (New York: Oxford University Press, 1968), p. 155, footnote †. In Temple, see *Christianity in Thought and Practice*, p. 33; also *Mens Creatrix*, p. 253; and above, Chapters 5 and 10.

view of God was confirmed by his own religious experience. The *approach* Temple uses may, therefore, be called ontological-experiential in that his conception of the nature of God is based both on the classical Christian view of God and his own religious experience. This ontological-experiential approach may be distinguished from a cosmological-empirical approach in which God is *inferred* on the basis of evidence derived from an investigation of nature and man. No priority is granted either to religious tradition or to religious experience as offering unique or certain knowledge of God in a cosmological-empirical approach.[11] Temple does not employ the latter approach in the sense of inferring from certain characteristics of the natural order the most coherent hypothesis of God to account for the order of nature and human experience; the cosmological-empirical approach *is* used by Temple to explicate his ideal conception of God and to determine to what extent reason and experience support such an ideal. Thus, for Temple, religious tradition and religious experience combine to initiate the quest for God and to indicate that God is personal; Christ, in turn, reveals the full personal nature of God. However, since one can be deceived, it is necessary to discover independent support for the reality of the object of religious experience. The argument for philosophical theism supplies this support according to Temple. No attempt is made to correlate the type of God arrived at by the two approaches. Temple simply identifies the God of philosophical theism with the God of the Christian faith. The living God cannot be inferred; He can only be experienced. The God of philosophy is not the God of religion, and the latter alone is definite and rich enough to explain the facts of experience and to meet the needs of man. An evaluation of these contentions is necessary.

In Chapter 9 it was pointed out that Temple's approach is ambiguous and empirically suspect. To argue philosophically that the hypothesis of God best explains the facts of experience is not the same as justifying philosophically the object of one's religious experience or the God of the Christian tradition.[12] However, such an assumption

[11] A similar interpretation of these two approaches – referred to as ontological-religious and cosmological-scientific, respectively – and the recognition of the need to synthesize them are presented by John E. Smith, "The Present Status of Natural Theology," *The Journal of Philosophy*, LV, No. 22 (October 23, 1958), 925–936, reprinted in *Reason and God*, pp. 157–172; more recently Smith has developed further his own analysis of the argument about God in *Experience and God*, Chapter V. Cf. also the article by Paul Tillich, "The Two Types of Philosophy of Religion," *Union Seminary Quarterly*, I, No. 4 (May, 1946), 3–13, reprinted in *Theology of Culture*, ed. Robert E. Kimball (New York: Oxford University Press, 1959), pp. 10–29.

[12] See the excellent analysis of these issues in Smith, *Experience and God*, pp. 140–145.

is made by Temple. The error is further compounded by Temple's admission that the conception of God in each case is different, though he must assume their identity to provide real cogency to the argument.

Temple's intuition at this point may have been better than his reason, and his failure to argue in a strictly empirical sense for the existence and nature of God is not without justification, though not entirely the justification he offers. The difficulty confronted by any specific argument for the existence of God has been shown in Kant's famous refutation of the classical statement of the ontological argument. It is not possible to move from the concept of something to the existence of that same object. God either exists or He does not; no one can argue Him into existence. Kierkegaard's suggestive illustration concerning a detective attempting to solve a crime conveys the point admirably.[13] A detective does not set out on the basis of certain clues discovered at the scene of a crime to demonstrate that a person exists who committed the crime, but rather he assumes the existence of such a person and then strives to discover the type of person who did the deed.

So far so good: existence is not produced; it is experienced. However, granted that neither the existence of God nor the criminal's existence is really being argued, this does not make less significant the necessity of arguing for the reasonable possibility and nature of each. That is, there is still the need for interpreting the empirical evidence and formulating an hypothesis to explain it. The brunt even of the traditional arguments for God is not merely that God exists but that it is reasonable to believe He exists and what it is reasonable to believe He is like. F. R. Tennant's wider teleological argument, for example, is an attempt to show what the nature of reality is like and to justify calling this reality God. This aspect of the argument is both valid and essential and is insufficiently acknowledged by Kierkegaard and his contemporary disciples who repudiate natural theology, or any effort to gain insight into God based on reason and human experience. Temple acknowledges the relevance of philosophical reflection but fails to employ it sufficiently for gaining insight into the nature of God. Philosophical argument plays more a psychologically supportive role for the conception of reality of which Temple is convinced than a role of providing empirical clues to the nature of reality.

The relation between religious tradition and religious experience,

[13] See Kierkegaard, *Philosophical Fragments*, pp. 31–35.

on the one hand, and philosophical argument, on the other hand, in determining the *reality*[14] and *nature* of God needs to be re examined. Both are necessary and should be combined more than is usually recognized. It is not a case of philosophical argument confirming what religious experience has revealed to be certain, or of religious experience confirming what philosophical discourse has shown to be most probable. Religious experience and philosophical reflection supply both cognitive insight and psychological assurance, and the insights drawn from one need to be checked and modified by the insights drawn from the other.

The attempt to argue for God is most frequently initiated by an experience believed to be an experience of God. Hence, religious experience is often the incentive for the search for reasonable grounds of belief while providing psychologically, and to some extent epistemologically, some clues to what is sought. But at the same time the experience of God, or rather what is claimed to be an experience of God, is not itself adequate to justify the claim. To interpret an experience one has had as an encounter with God is to assert a truth-claim which is subject to the same philosophical scrutiny as all other truth-claims about reality. That is, insofar as a religious experience has occurred, it, perhaps, cannot be fully communicated and can only be understood by someone who has had such an experience. But when in the experience insight is claimed regarding the subject to whom one is related as being ultimately real or claiming for the relationship ultimate reality, then this interpretation of the experience has become a claim for truth and as such must be related to other claims and brought into a meaningful whole with them. Hence, religious experience is not self-authenticating, though without some such experience claimed to be an experience of God, it is doubtful if any argument however reasonable would convince one of God's reality, let alone convert one to the status of believer. An argument can show to one's satisfaction the reasonableness of a particular interpretation of reality, but the justification for worshipping this reality as God cannot be so demonstrated. Arguments for God are as ineffective on the latter point as arguments for the fact of redness are to one who is color-blind. Perhaps a better analogy is an argument for the sincerity and genuine friendliness of a person to

14 In light of the restricted use of the word "to exist" both in ordinary usage and in modern philosophy to mean, as Charles Sanders Pierce stated, "to be part of a system," it seems less confusing to refer to the reality, rather than the existence, of God. See Smith's analysis, *Experience and God*, pp. 108, 118–120.

a paranoid. Apart from direct experience of such a reality, one can only affirm or deny its possibility. If one claims to have no experience of God, that is, that God is not necessary in order to understand any of the experiences he has had, then for such a person the reality of God must be denied. Argument can at best only make the possibility of God's reality a reasonable possibility. But granting direct experience of a reality for which the term God seems appropriate, it does not follow that the experience is unmediated or that it carries its own authenticity. That is, the experience of God may be interpreted as direct but mediated, as John Smith notes: "Without some form of presence in personal experience, God can have no meaning for an individual, but from this fact it does not follow that God or the religious object is *identical* with any finite experience."[15]

It is at this point that the arguments for the reality of God serve a twofold function. They can serve to eliminate through rational discourse a philosophical predisposition one might have against the legitimacy of a religious world view, and hence make reasonable a religious interpretation of reality. Though the context is somewhat different, Ninian Smart's observation on the relevancy of arguments in producing changes in religious reasonings is still pertinent:

> It must be remembered that rarely do religious reasonings persuade individuals to change their faith. But this does not mean that they are useless. For without reasons and evidences there cannot be such a thing as truth; and without truth there can be no belief. Moreover, we find that, as in aesthetics and in philosophy, reasonings have a longterm effect. What occurs is a kind of social dialogue. In the course of time certain views seem to gather persuasiveness while others fade into implausibility. Reasonings are by no means irrelevant to this process.[16]

Further, such arguments when rooted in an analysis of the structure of the universe, can provide clues to the nature of reality. These clues need to be related to the clues derived from religious experience, and a synthesis of some kind formulated.

What is being suggested is, on the one hand, the need for insisting on religious experience and tradition as necessary factors in any attempt to establish the reality of God and, on the other hand, the need for insisting on the relevance and role of philosophical reflection to justify belief in a particular conception of God. Both are necessary

[15] *Ibid.*, p. 48; see also *ibid.*, pp. 47–48, 52–53, 83, 122–134, 140–145, 149–157. Also in Smith, see *Reason and God*, pp. 170, 181.

[16] Roderick Ninian Smart, "The Relation Between Christianity and the Other Great Religions," in A. R. Vidler (ed.), *Soundings: Essays Concerning Christian Understanding* (Cambridge: Cambridge University Press, 1964), p. 118.

to supplement and modify each other, if the total man is to be satisfied. It is true, as the defenders of the ontological-cxperiential approach have contended, that one does not begin the quest for God without an idea of God based on some religious tradition or without some experience of the world that leads one to believe in the kind of reality to whom the term God is addressed. But it is also true, as the defenders of the cosmological-empirical approach have maintained, that only by analyzing the evidence derived from man and the natural order can a reasonable basis be provided for belief in God. Furthermore, because one starts with an idea of God does not mean one should end up with the same conception. The analysis of the facts of experience may require modifying or enhancing one's conception, and only a constant relating of the two approaches, even maintaining an unresolved tension between them, can avoid the errors of each taken alone. At issue here is the perennial question of the proper relation between faith and reason. John Wild correctly argues that they should be held in a "flexible, dialectical tension with each other. Like the two sides of the arch, each is dependent on the other, and yet at the same time independent, making its own contribution in its own way."[17] What is necessary then is what might be called an experiential-empirical approach to the problem of God.[18]

Temple is, therefore, correct in insisting that if the reality of God is to be affirmed, then one's own religious tradition and one's own religious experience should initiate the quest for God. However, Temple errs in failing to take seriously enough the analysis of the World-Process which he has presented as offering insight into the nature of God. No small part of the difficulty is due to Temple's brand of realistic epistemology in which he assumes that in religious ex-

[17] John Wild, *Human Freedom and Social Order*, p. 91.

[18] Still another example of the experiential-empirical approach to God, though not identified as such, is offered by T. Alec Burkill in *God and Reality in Modern Thought* (Englewood Cliffs, N. J.: Prentice-Hall, Inc., 1963). Burkill concludes his chapter on "The justification of Religion" with the following statement: "The ultimate claim of religion when purged of the naive anthropomorphisms of its liturgy and theology, is that God exists as a cosmic power that nevertheless responds to man's deepest quest for an ideal commonwealth evincing more perfect harmonies than any hitherto achieved. God transcends the finitude of man's spiritual life, yet He informs and sustains it. And if our interpretation is sound, secondary metaphysics accords with the claim that constitutes the primary metaphysics of religion. For it issues in the conception of a universe of continuous creativity in which man is involved not as a mere mechanical production, but as an active agent through whom the future shape of the cosmos, whose past is focalized in him, is being partially decided. The positive principle of reality finds relatively successful exemplification in the evolution of human life, and human organization as an example of the artistry of nature gives some indication of the wealth of reality's potentialities in the way of creative achievement" p. 185.

perience the *feeling* one has of a non-human presence and power is *known* to be an encounter with the God revealed in Christ. Thus, Temple fails to distinguish between a *direct experience* of a power and a presence not one's own and *unmediated knowledge* that the source of this experience is the Christian God.

The experiential and empirical approaches are both required and need to be constantly set one against the other. The idea of God one has based on personal religious experience must be subjected to the criticisms of philosophical reflection. What legitimate inferences about the nature of reality can be drawn from our understanding of man and nature, and how are they related to the conception of God one has as a result of one's religious experience and one's religious heritage? At the same time one's conception of God is brought to bear on the data of experience for the sake of rendering them intelligible.

The ultimate test of the adequacy of one's conception of God involves, therefore, references both to experiential and to empirical criteria. In terms of the experiential factors, the test of adequacy would be to live by one's conception of God and to see if it makes sense of life by providing strength and guidance for living. The criterion employed by the empirical approach would be the acceptance of that hypothesis that best renders intelligible the data of experience with a minimum of mystery. In this way both theoretical and pragmatic criteria are employed: the intellectual need for theoretical clarity and comprehensive understanding is combined with the emotional need for inner assurance and practical guidance for living.

One begins to make sense of life when one finds inner assurance and guidance for living from one's own encounter with the mysterious source and sustainer of life, but only by critically analyzing the evidence derived from the natural order can that encounter be made clear and a reasonable basis for it provided. Temple's dialectical method suggests such an approach, and in his proposal that critical philosophy be employed as a check on theological philosophy he affirms a form of the experiential-empirical method.[19] However, Temple does not actually put the method to use in arriving at any of his own beliefs regarding the nature of God.

[19] See *Nature, Man and God*, p. 44; also see above, Chapter 2

B. THE CATEGORY OF THE PERSONAL AS A BASIC PHILOSOPHICAL CONCEPT

In the present study it has become evident that personality is the primary concept in the philosophy of William Temple. The basis for this claim may now be summarized. There is also a need to evaluate the legitimacy of Temple's use of personality as the fundamental philosophical principle of explanation.

1. Personality as the primary concept in Temple's philosophy

There can be no doubt about the significance of personality in the Christian philosophy of William Temple. Personal existence represents the highest level of reality that the World-Process has produced. Only at the level of persons does knowledge take on an independent status so that it is sought as an end in itself and not merely as a means of aiding the organism to adjust to its environment; only in persons capable of responding appreciatively to their environment does value become actualized.

The arenas of personal and social ethics are constituted by the relations persons share one with another both individually and collectively and the relation they share with the natural order. Furthermore, only persons who are aware of their existence have to strive to orient themselves in this world. Human history needs to be understood, and an attempt needs to be made to discern the significance of history for man and of man for history. Persons arising in the historical process provide some clue to the meaning of that process. Since persons make a distinctive contribution to the world through their individuality and value-realization, they possess the capacity for survival beyond history.

Finally, only persons feel related to the source of the World-Process and only persons seek to comprehend the universe as a whole. As was argued in Chapters 6 and 7, the fact that persons appear in the process suggests that there is a perfect person who is completely self-determined, who is guided by a purpose which totally integrates His being, who knows the actual good and who expends Himself in realizing it by means of disinterested love of others. It is such a Personal Being who offers the satisfactory explanation of the universe. Hence, the universe which gives rise to persons as the highest level of existence is explained by reference to a Divine Person who created and sustains the world for the sake of the development of human personality and the fellowship shared among persons, human and divine. It is by persons that the problems of philosophy are posed, and it is in personality that a principle is provided which offers a clue to the solution of these problems.

2. *Justification of personal categories as basic philosophical principles*

If the problems of philosophy are posed by persons and persons represent the highest level of reality yet attained, then why not seek the clue to an explanation of these problems in personality? Such is Temple's reasoning for employing personality as the principle of explanation. His own religious experience of a personal relation shared with a Personal Being confirms this approach as applied to an explanation of the World-Process.

An evaluation of Temple's solution to some of the problems of moral and social philosophy, and of philosophy of history will be made in the chapters to follow. At this point, a word is in order regarding the use of personality as a philosophical principle of explanation. At the levels of personal and social morality the significance of personal development is not seriously challenged. The development of human personality, even if not the personality of those now existing, is the concern of most moral and social philosophers. History too centers on human persons in terms of what meaning, if any, history has for man and what, if anything, lies beyond history for man. However, in the case of a metaphysical explanation of the universe the thesis that personality supplies the key to reality is severely challenged;[20] indeed, as already noted, any attempt to offer a metaphysical hypothesis to account for the World-Process is currently suspect.

In terms of Temple's position the justification of a teleological explanation of the World-Process has already been criticized. Purpose to be philosophically legitimate, should be viewed as one viable guiding image for metaphysical speculation. The other characteristics of personality need to be examined. Fellowship signifying the inherent social nature of personality is extensively and persuasively argued by Temple at the level of human personality, but at the level of Divine Personality Temple wavers between affirming the need of God to express Himself and of God's total independence of everything He creates. The only basis for asserting the self-sufficiency of God would seem to be that

[20] For a recent defense of the conception of God as personal against the criticisms of science and theology, which follows Temple's thesis, see Trueblood, *Philosophy of Religion*, pp. 259–274. Also, William Hordern, *Speaking of God: The Nature and Purpose of Theological Language*, offers a defense of the traditional belief in a personal God against the challenge of analytical philosophy.

this conforms to the most perfect ideal of personality conceivable. But even if this is granted, for an ideal to be relevant to the facts of experience and to be justified as a principle of explanation, it must account for the facts of experience without self-contradiction and without explaining away the facts. To affirm the self-sufficiency of God while arguing that the universe can be explained by reference to His purpose for fellowship with persons in the world and for fostering the development of persons is both self-contradictory and contrary to the facts of human experience. Thus, on Temple's own view, God should be conceived as requiring another for the full development and expression of His nature. Further, the ideal of God as the supreme and perfect person should be replaced by the ideal of God as signifying the wealth of reality's potentialities for creative achievement. In T. Alec Burkill's words: "It is these potentialities that afford cosmic sanction for man's aspirations after a more perfect commonwealth of distanced value. For the religious person such sanction is divine or worshipful ...."[21]

The love of God is also unclear in Temple for much the same reasons. The notion of totally disinterested love is inconceivable in human terms and must, therefore, be rejected. The mutual response of affection among persons and concern for the welfare of others even at the expense of great sacrifice for oneself are sufficiently high ideals to challenge both man and God.

There is cogency in Temple's choice of personality as a pregnant root-metaphor which offers the metaphysician the possibility of explaining the problems of human existence; although it would be preferable to employ the terms "personal categories" and thereby avoid the connotation that personality ultimately refers to a Divine Person. The fact that persons are the highest level of existence offers *prima facie* evidence, at least, of the legitimacy of employing personal categories as philosophical principles of explanation. John Macmurray in his Gifford Lectures, 1953–1954, offers a penetrating critique of attempts to unify experience on the basis of mathematical (or mechanical) and organic forms and proposes instead the "form of the personal" as the most adequate category for unifying experience.[22] Also, although Frederick Ferré sees the present time as "between models" for himself and others, he does acknowledge the valuational

[21] Burkill, p. 233.

[22] See John Macmurray, *The Self as Agent* (New York: Harper & Brothers, 1957) and *Persons in Relation* (New York: Harper & Brothers, 1961).

adequacy of theistic imagery: "Personal concepts can without straining include organic or other impersonal ones more easily, in fact, than mechanomorphic or biomorphic imagery can include personal values without distortion or reduction."[23]

Essential to this approach, however, is the origin and development of the personal categories in the World-Process. How personality arose offers some clues to its relation to, and supremacy over, the process and, therefore, clues to an understanding of the personal categories employed as adequate to explain all that occurs. Just as the problem of explaining the higher by the lower is that the lower categories may not be rich enough to account for the qualities of experience exhibited by the higher, so too the highest level can be so abstracted from its context in the World-Process that it fails to render an empirically oriented account of the lower levels. The personal categories one employs to explain the process must be varied enough to account for all that occurs and not so qualitatively different from what does appear in the process as to be unable to account for the lower levels and hence be empirically unjustified.

It is not, therefore, so much a question of whether or not personal categories employed as principles of explanation are justified, as it is a question of whether or not the particular categories of personality employed are justified. As we have seen, philosophy is not as concerned about where one begins to philosophize as it is how one advances from the starting place to the conclusions. The question at issue, then, regarding the use of personality as a basic philosophical principle may be formulated as follows: Are the categories of personality derived from an analysis of experience, or, at least, are they modified by reference to the facts of experience?

That there are dimensions to experience that are inadequately explained by reference to impersonal categories and, therefore, that the universe may be conceived as grounded in a reality that can best be interpreted as personal or in personal categories, is, at times, persuasively argued by Temple. However, Temple goes further than this. For him the universe is grounded in a purposive will and purposive will is embodied in the most perfect being conceivable. Thus, Temple simply accepts his own religious experience and the orthodox doctrines of the Christian faith as offering definitive interpretations of the nature of reality without subjecting these interpretations to critical scrutiny.

[23] Ferré, *Basic Modern Philosophy of Religion*, p. 358. But see also *ibid.*, pp. 444–451.

Hence, the concept of personality he employs as a metaphysical principle of explanation is neither derived from, nor modified by, the facts of experience and to this extent is philosophically unjustified.

One's encounter with reality may lead to the formulation of an hypothesis to interpret reality, and the choice of personality – that is, personal categories – as offering a likely key to reality is philosophically justifiable. The only things at issue philosophically are whether or not the content that is given to the category of the personal is empirically based, whether by employing it the facts of experience are rendered intelligible, and whether courage and guidance for living are provided. Only in the case of fundamental social principles and their relevance to social problems does Temple exemplify these demands. As we shall see in the next chapter, his conception of personality as derived from the Christian faith and from his own personal religious experience is modified in accordance with empirical demands to solve pressing problems of society. Unfortunately, the same reference to empirical facts is not true of Temple's conception of personality itself; nor is it sufficiently true of the application he makes of personality to the other philosophical problems.

CHAPTER 19

THE PERSON IN RELATION TO SOCIETY

Temple's moral and social philosophy taken together serve to point up both the merits and defects of his philosophical approach as an examination of the following issues will substantiate: (1) the relation of potentially valuable objects independent of man to man's experience of them; (2) the significance and efficacy of human will in man's quest for ethical goodness; (3) the role that the foreseeable consequences of an act play in deciding one's obligation in a given situation; (4) the application of fundamental Christian social principles to the existing political and economic orders.

A. VALUE-POSSIBILITIES AND VALUE-EXPERIENCE

As indicated in Chapter 11 Temple's theory of value is ambiguous. He seems to want to maintain at one and the same time an objectivist conception of value in which value exists independent of man's appreciation, and a subjectivist view which holds that value is actualized only when mind finds satisfaction in an object.

Temple could have clarified the issue if he had explicitly distinguished between value-possibilities and the actualization of these possibilities in the value-experience of persons. Temple does imply such a distinction but does not develop it in relation to his theory of value.[1] There are value-possibilities in the world which man does not create and which do not depend for their potential valuableness on anyone's knowing them. However, as Peter Bertocci has noted, such objects exist as potentially valuable until someone does choose them thereby actualizing their value potential.[2]

[1] See Temple, *Nature, Man and God*, pp. 154, 165, 208, 364.

[2] These distinctions are further elaborated by Bertocci, *Introduction to the Philosophy of Religion*, pp. 255–267; see also, Peter A. Bertocci and Richard M. Millard, *Personality and the*

In terms of Temple's position this means that the satisfaction one receives from the experience of kinship with an object constitutes value-experience, and the object to which one is related exists independently of him as a value-possibility.

B. INDIVIDUAL INTEGRITY AND MORAL WORTH

Few philosophers have stated the moral dilemma of man with greater perceptivity than Temple. He correctly diagnoses as fundamental issues the problems of motivation and direction. Man needs not only to know what he should do, but also how he can gain the power necessary to do it. The self's bondage is to itself and the limited vision and inner strength which it has. At the same time the source of what moral values are to be realized in the world can only come through the wisdom and efforts of man.

Temple's solution to the major practical problem of ethics also provides much illumination, but fails to shed adequate light on the road which man should take. Temple tends to set up an ideal state for man in which man is truly free and completely good only when the freedom exercised and the good achieved are not consciously sought by him or acknowledged to be his. Man is to love others spontaneously with no thought of himself. Such disinterested love God alone through Christ can elicit in man. Hence, man's total being has to be converted in a way which admits no conscious choice or effort on man's part lest he be proud of his own achievement. He must be possessed by God and of himself possess nothing but the need to be possessed. Scientific ethics is inadequate for the task.

It is quite true that only an act of God could effect what Temple proposes to be the ideal for man. But is the ideal justified? Perhaps it should be candidly admitted and courageously accepted that man can attain only a human affection toward his fellowman and a limited circle of loyalty toward the best he knows with the recognition that the self is involved in all efforts of love and loyalty. Perfection in either one is not man's to attain; he can hope only for a continued opportunity for perfectibility. It is in the quest itself for the best possible realization of perfection that moral goodness resides and not in an experienced state of perfection. Man can never be absolutely certain that his love is truly disinterested or his loyalty complete; nor can he be

Good: Psychological and Ethical Perspectives (New York: David McKay Company, Inc., 1963), pp. 318–321.

certain that the objects of his love and loyalty are the most worthy ones. Such uncertainty in regard to ethical goodness is necessary if man's integrity and individuality are not to be sacrificed, which would be too high a price to pay even for the certainty of God's grace.

In terms of Temple's position this means that man does recognize his dependency on the source of the universe and continually strives to avoid arbitrary exclusiveness which elevates his interests, goals, and prized objects to an unwarranted status of importance in the scheme of things. Temple affirms such a view, but he goes further. In order to insure the self's concern for universal objects and the self's sacrifice of itself, Temple moves toward a position which annihilates the self as a moral agent. The individual Temple wished to save is lost by the method proposed for his salvation. Such an interpretation cannot be reconciled with Temple's own conception of the nature of man and the prominence played by personality in his Christian philosophy.[3]

The self alone can be the agent of his actions, but the objects to which his efforts are directed need not be, and should not become, the self alone. Though man is always and necessarily self-*centered*, he is not always or necessarily sel*fish*. Hence, it is quite correct that the Spirit of the Whole should become the motivation for the self's efforts and the goal toward which the self strives. At the same time, it is the self who must choose the whole and the self who must realize the values which are available. To eliminate the self as an active moral agent does not solve the problem of what values he is to realize; it eliminates the problem and the possibility of any values being realized.

Temple's account of freedom is instructive but defective at this point. What man cannot do, Temple argues, is what he must do: will to love others and forget himself. But such a view is true only if an abstract account of the self is maintained; for the self to concentrate on forgetting himself is indeed absurd, but the self can concentrate on another so as not to be concerned with his own concentration. Man can will that the reality he calls God become the motivation and goal of his life; he cannot always will to abide by his commitment nor is he always willing to commit himself. More fundamental, the self cannot will that he cease to will; he cannot will that as a self he cease to be the

[3] See above, Chapters 6, 7, and 12. A similar observation is made by a recent interpreter of Temple's social thought; see Robert Craig, *Social Concern in the Thought of William Temple*, p. 79.

locus of his own activities and thereby achieve identification with God. But is such identification possible or even desirable?

The will of the individual must always be operative in determining what course is taken. This is true even in regard to the self accepting what he may come to believe is offered to him by God through Christ. Not to maintain the efficacy of self-will in choosing is to eliminate the self as a personal and moral being. Though Temple indicates that he is not arguing for the destruction of the self, his position does lead to the self's annihilation as a center of value-realization. There is a fundamental contradiction here with Temple's argument for personal immortality which rests on each individual's unique value-contribution.

Man must always will to cooperate with another – be it God or fellowman – in the performance of an act or the acceptance of a gift if individual integrity and moral worth are to be maintained. At the same time, the other person – God or fellowman – must also choose to cooperate. However, the issue is more profound than the analysis so far suggests, and there can be no doubt that Temple recognized this fact. To dissect the relationship of person to person, as has been done above, as if all that is involved are two separate individuals is partially to misconceive the relationship and its effect on the persons involved. For in any relationship of love each person in the relationship both chooses and is chosen, but these activities are experienced as a single event.[4] The two acts of choosing and being chosen are distinguished only outside the relationship; within the relationship the two merge in a single, shared experience. Furthermore, the power to choose growing out of such a relationship is certainly not to be identified with individual self-assertion apart from such a shared experience. To do something for another with whom one shares a relationship of love is far different from doing something to meet the demands of a legal contract. Theologically, the difference is between justification by works and justification by faith as Martin Luther rightly perceived; psychologically, the difference is between deficit motivation and growth motivation as Abraham Maslow has recently proclaimed.[5] Ethically, the point is that neither the self as moral agent nor the efficacy of the will of the person-in-relationship can be minimized.

Temple is to be commended for insisting on the ethical significance

[4] See Buber, *I and Thou*, pp. 11, 58–61.

[5] See Abraham Maslow, *Motivation and Personality* (New York: Harper & Brothers, 1954), pp. 213–214, 256–257, 296; see also Gordon Allport, *Becoming* (New Haven: Yale University Press, 1955), p. 68.

of a shared relationship of love, or in more traditional theological terms, the ethical significance of grace. However, if the Pelagian heresy is to overemphasize the self's role in response to God's will, Temple's error is to underestimate the self's response when acting out of a relationship of love. Such an act of choice is more complex than sometimes thought. Man cannot simply by willing lift himself up by his own bootstraps without causing himself to fall down again; but neither can he be lifted up by another apart from his willing it without being sacrificed as a moral agent. But the alternatives taken separately do not exhaust the options, for there is a qualitative difference between what one can will as a result of participating in a meaningful relationship and what can be willed by a separate self alone. The self as a moral agent is operative in both instances, but the locus and efficacy of the self's power to will are not the same.

C. THE OBLIGATION TO WILL THE BEST POSSIBLE CONSEQUENCES

In emphasizing vocation as the solution to the major theoretical problem of ethics, Temple assumes that man can know what his vocation is and that the clue is contained in the logic of his being. One's conscience is his guide, though he is to evaluate the act by the consequences which result. As noted in Chapter 12, Temple seems to be unaware that in relying on conscience as determinative in the decisions one has to make he has moved from a non-cognitive to a cognitive interpretation of the experience of obligation. A non-cognitive theory is affirmed by Temple when he attributes absolute obligation to the will only and not to any particular act. However, not content to stop with the formal guidance this provides, Temple goes on to affirm that one can discern what God's will is for him and hence *know* what it is right for him to do. The consequences of an action are considered in evaluating the goodness of the action. Temple apparently fails to recognize that in claiming one can discover the specific will of God in a given context, he has moved to a cognitive theory of moral obligation and a specific theory of value and value-knowledge.

There is insufficient justification for this shift to a cognitive theory of obligation in Temple's position, though it is in accord with his realistic epistemology. Also, Temple has proposed a false dichotomy between right and good at the time an action is decided upon by restricting obligation to what is right (will) and goodness to the consequences resulting (act). The same problem arises in discerning what is right to do as in discovering what is a true apprehension: one can be wrong in both cases. If it is conceded, as Temple does, that one may be misled by his conscience and should check the consequences of his act, then why not include the consideration of consequences in the decision to act? Temple's objection that it is impossible to determine beforehand all the consequences of an act can be removed if the individual is held morally responsible for considering the *foreseeable* consequences of his act.[6] The right and the good are in this way merged in the decision to act and not only in the relation of the decision to the evaluation of the action taken.

There is, then, a necessity for calculating the consequences of one's action before deciding what action to take. Do the foreseeable consequences promote the good that one desires to achieve? In terms of any particular experience of obligation this may mean modifying what one feels ought to be done in light of the expected consequences that will result. Although a legitimate abstraction from one's total experience of obligation, the feeling of obligation is rarely, if ever, a bare feeling that one ought to do what is right; rather in a given situation one feels that he ought to do, or not to do, a certain act. Because one feels a certain way, however, does not itself make it right or good for one to go ahead and act on the basis of the feeling. A consideration of the consequences serves as an objective check on one's subjective and at times irrational feelings of ought. The standard that one should employ in making a decision is the extent to which a given act will promote the best possible consequences in that particular situation.

Stating one's obligation in this way brings together Temple's notion of right – in regard to the will to act – and good – in regard to the consequences of the act. One is obligated to do what promotes the best results that are possible of being attained in a given situation. This removes the obligation to do the impossible, but sets before one the ideal of always striving to realize the best possible. Also, it encourages the individual to recognize the extenuating circumstances peculiar to a given situation and asks him to achieve the best possible in that situation. Hence, the strategy for dealing with the experience of obligation is to recognize that one's obligation, in principle, is to will the best possible realization of the ideal life as one conceives it.[7] In a given

[6] See Bertocci and Millard, *Personality and the Good,* Chapter 22; also see Fletcher, *William Temple,* p. 327, note 178.

[7] See the interpretation of the experience of moral obligation in Bertocci and Millard, chapter 9.

situation what one experiences as the best thing to do should be critically examined in terms of the foreseeable consequences of the act. Once an act is performed, it can then be reevaluated in regard to what the actual consequences were and serve as a guide for future decisions.

Such a consideration is consistent with Temple's total position and would bring together more coherently than he does the view of absolute moral obligation as applying to the will only and of one's particular obligation as involving the act as well. However, Temple's concern may well lie in another direction, viz., that of the ethical deontologist. Implicit in his discussion is the recognition of the urgency to act in certain situations and the fear that one will become so involved in calculating consequences that the decisiveness of action will be lost or that prudential factors will prevail. These fears are not without foundation. However, risks are necessary if subjective fanaticism is to be avoided, and certainly unreasoned hasty decisions offer risks of their own. Also, as we have seen, Temple recognizes the teleologist's concern in his affirmation of the optimific principle in which right is viewed in terms of good results. Perhaps a way can be outlined by which the ethical issues at stake in the deontological-teleological controversy can be made resolvable. To the extent that the deontologist is concerned that the rightness of an act not be determined merely by prudential consideration of consequences but include a concern for the value of the act itself and the teleologist is concerned that the consequences be considered in any determination of the rightness of an act, the controversy can be partially resolved by distinguishing between ideal consequences (deontological considerations) and factual consequences (teleological considerations). This view of ideal consequences is analogous to John Rawls' view of a rule as at times defining a practice.[8]

The kind of choice sometimes faced is not merely between particular acts the specific consequences of which exhaust the basis of the choice; one may be called upon to choose between actions that mean adhering to or forsaking an *ideal* one takes to be obligatory. Hence, a specific course of action may be viewed as embodying that ideal and failure to act in that way as forsaking the ideal. In such a situation the ideal one acknowledges to be obligatory may be of such overriding importance that the consequences resulting from forsaking the ideal are held to be worse than the specific consequences resulting from the choice to

[8] See John Rawls' essay, "Two Concepts of Rules," reprinted in Philippa Foot (ed.), *Theories of Ethics* (New York: Oxford University Press, 1967), p. 162; see also Brand Blanshard, *Reason and Goodness*, pp. 326–329.

be loyal to the ideal. Socrates' choice of the hemlock and Jesus' choice of the cross are illustrations of individuals who abided by their ideals despite the dangerous consequences for themselves and others. Each interpreted his mission in life as of such importance that to forsake the mission would be more disastrous than death and destruction resulting from adherence to it. Actual consequences were considered, but the ideal which each felt obligated to realize and the consequences which it entailed were held to be more significant whether realized by him in that situation or not. Loyalty to an ideal in such a case retains the value and efficacy of the ideal so that its significance is not lost and the possibility of its realization at another time remains.

There is a place then for "noble recklessness"[9] in which after weighing consequences carefully one still chooses to risk everything for the ideal itself. The deontologist's concern for ideal consequences is given priority in this case over the teleologist's concern for factual consequences; in most choices, however, an ideal is not at issue and the teleologist's concern for factual consequences should prevail. Therefore, what would seem to be Temple's concern to foster forthrightness and boldness of action is well-taken, though his means of preserving them by neglecting consideration of consequences in forming one's decision to act is unwarranted.

D. TOWARD A CHRISTIAN CIVILIZATION

Throughout the present study it has been necessary to call Temple to task for holding to an ideal, sometimes acknowledged and sometimes unacknowledged, on a particular issue to the extent that he employs it as a standard for criticizing other views without subjecting the ideal to modification when applied to problems of human existence. Temple's social thought is avowedly Christian. The ideals of man and society operating in his thinking are derived from his conception of God and the fact that God is held to be the creator of the natural world and of man. An evaluation of his conception of God has already been made. However, at this point what is significant is that in his social thought his ideal conceptions of God and man are modified where necessary to cope with the empirical situation. That Temple succeeded in making Christian principles relevant to problems of contemporary society is confirmed in the following words of Reinhold Niebuhr: "The real fact is

[9] See Edgar Sheffield Brightman, *Moral Laws* (New York: The Abingdon Press, 1933), p. 149.

that Dr. Temple was able to relate the ultimate insights of religion about the human situation to the immediate necessities of political justice and the proximate possibilities of a just social order more vitally and creatively than any other modern Christian leader."[10]

It is in Temple's social thought, then, that he most closely approximates the role of the Christian philosopher as it has been interpreted in the present study. Some illustrations of this point in regard to his social thought are in order.

In Chapters 7 and 11, love was held to be a dimension of human personality that represents its highest expression. In expressing love for another and receiving love expressed by another, human personality best approximates its own fulfillment. It would not be surprising to expect that Temple would, as a result of the sacrificial conception of love he espouses in his conception of personality and his ethical theory, elevate self-sacrifice to the key position in his social thought. But, as a matter of fact, in his later writings Temple rejects sacrifice as a basic social principle, though he retains it as an ideal which should be set before men.[11] Service to others is required, but not self-sacrifice. One should seek the welfare of others, but this does not mean ignoring or relinquishing one's own legitimate interests and aims. Temple recognizes that sacrificing one's own interests for those of another could readily be interpreted as weakness by another; rather than eliciting a response of love, it might encourage the other person to take further advantage of him and then both individuals suffer and no one gains. When groups are involved the most one should strive for is an equitable compromise of conflicting interests. To expect either management or labor to sacrifice their interests without the assurance of comparable concessions on the part of the other group is to encourage selfishness and irrelevant sacrifice.

Justice has its role in making the expression of love empirically relevant. Hence, whereas the self as an initiating center of value-realization is sacrificed to God's grace in Temple's ethics, self-sacrifice is forsaken and replaced by the challenge that all should serve society in his social philosophy. Temple recognizes that the social order is largely composed of competing centers of power and that it is of no avail to condemn individual sin in the hope of eliminating the power blocks. Conflicts of power cannot and should not be eliminated, and

[10] Quoted in Craig, *Social Concern in the Thought of William Temple*, p. 9. Craig's book is itself an eloquent presentation of the continuing relevance of Temple's social thought.

[11] See Temple, *Christianity and the Social Order*, pp. 72–74, and above, Chapter 13.

to strive to do so is to miss the point of group relations; a lesser but equally significant goal must be sought: "what has to be aimed at is such a distribution and balance of power that a measure of justice may be achieved even among those who are actuated in the main by egoistic and sinful impulses. It is a modest aim, but observance of political life leaves no doubt that this must be its primary concern."[12]

The ideal of brotherly love remains to challenge everyone, but it must be recognized that justice in the sense of an equitable resolution of competing interests may be the best possible realization of love in a given situation. Though Temple does not refer to the standard he is employing as that of willing the best possible consequences, it is fair to conclude that such a standard is operating in his analysis at this point. Temple's concern is not with the withering away of the power of the state or of the capitalist economic order; he is concerned with putting to the best possible use the power necessary for both political stability, which fosters individual freedom, and economic productivity, which promotes spiritual development. To achieve this goal radical changes are viewed as necessary particularly in the economic realm.

It is not a sentimental conception of personality development which dominates Temple's social thought. The power of the state to command its citizens to fight in times of aggression is accepted, though the right to refuse on grounds of conscience is stoutly upheld. The ambiguity which characterizes the Christian's role in society is correctly diagnosed without loss of the ideal toward which he is called to work. Since Christ is held to be the center of history and the Kingdom of God the goal of history, the Christian strives to achieve whatever embodiment of the Kingdom of God can be attained on earth. Indeed the Christian is called upon to work toward the construction of a Christian civilization; that is "a civilization in which the Christian standards of value are accepted as those by which both persons and policies are to be judged, and in which there is a steady effort to guide policy by Christian principles."[13]

Temple's social thought represents a coherent application of his Christian ideal of personality and its primacy to the actual existing social order of his day. He comes closest to constructing a systematic position at this point: A general theory of value is proposed and a conception of personal and social morality developed. Weaknesses in

[12] Temple, "What Christians Stand for in the Secular World," reprinted in *Religious Experience* . . ., p. 252.

[13] Temple, *The Hope of a New World*, p. 65.

regard to his value theory and his system of ethics have already been noted. Further, the ideal of personality, both human and divine, which Temple employs in his social thought has been challenged in the present study and his conception of history will be challenged below. Certainly many of the specific proposals Temple made for social reconstruction are no longer relevant. Hence, the social philosophy Temple has set forth is not without flaws; nor is his position especially original. Many of his theoretical views, such as those on the origin of the state and the purpose of the economic order, were derived from recognized thinkers in the respective fields, such as MacIver and Tawney. But in terms of the social principles he has formulated and the general application of them to the political and economic orders – with which the present study has alone been concerned in Temple's social philosophy – a significant contribution has been made toward the task of defining and implementing a Christian civilization. The full impact of Temple's Christian commitment and philosophically oriented mind were brought to bear upon the fundamental social issues of the day with cogency and clarity, even though the philosophical basis for his understanding of the Christian faith is not as clear and as cogent as he believes. W. G. Peck aptly summarizes Temple's contribution toward the formulation of a distinctively Christian philosophy of society: "Whether his conclusions are ultimately substantiated or not, his perception of the necessity of this approach to the chaotic problems of our time and his valiant attempts to reach a statement of Christian social doctrine will doubtless prove to have been amongst the most significant intellectual labours of our epoch."[14]

[14] "William Temple as Social Thinker," in W. R. Matthews and Others, p. 59. See also the estimates by Geoghegan, *Platonism in Recent Religious Thought*, p. 108, and by Craig, *Social Concern in the Thought of William Temple*, pp. 10, 152–156.

CHAPTER 20

GOD AND THE MEANING OF HISTORY

In contrast to Temple's social philosophy, his philosophy of history points up the defects of his position. The task which Temple set for himself in formulating a philosophy of history is certainly a formidable one, namely, to bring together all of the basic truths which traditional Christianity has taught regarding God and history: (1) the complete supremacy of God over history while claiming that man is free; (2) the reality of history and belief in progress; (3) finally, the eschatological expectation of Christians who anticipate the day when God will usher in His new kingdom. Has Temple succeeded in bringing together these facets of Christian tradition and demonstrating their cogency for rendering history intelligible? Concerning Temple's ambitious endeavor, W. R. Matthews writes: "We are persuaded, while we read, that in principle the problem is solved, but subsequent reflection awakens doubt whether the solution may not be partly verbal."[1] The justification for this negative judgment can be indicated by reference to two fundamental issues: (1) the relation of God to history and history to God; (2) the meaning of human history and the grounds for belief in the survival of human personality beyond history.

A. THE HISTORICITY OF GOD

W. R. Matthews' comment on Temple is especially appropriate with regard to Temple's emphasis on the complete supremacy of God over history. Temple praises the first view of history for its advocacy of God's complete supremacy and criticizes the second and third views because they fail to assert His complete supremacy.[2] Nowhere in the entire discussion, however, does Temple attempt to justify, on the

[1] "William Temple as Thinker," in W. R. Matthews and Others, p. 21.

[2] See Temple, *Nature, Man and God*, pp. 434–441; also above, Chapter 16.

basis of a coherent interpretation of history, that God is completely supreme. In fact, the very argument which Temple employs to reject the second view – in which Eternity is conceived as "the integral totality of Time" – namely, that what seems bad now will prove to be good when viewed in relation to the whole, is the same reasoning he employs in arguing for the alteration of values in time and to solve the problem of evil. On the latter point he writes: "The presence of evil can enhance the excellence of what on the whole is good, and the event or act which in isolation is evil can be itself an integral and contributing part of a whole which, as a whole, is good."[3] It is equally arguable that what is at present good may turn out to be evil; moreover, man's supposed freedom and responsibility prove to be merely fictitious.

This point must be belabored because it is the fundamental fallacy which Temple makes throughout his presentation of the relation of God to history. The tenuous basis on which Temple asserts God's complete supremacy over history and independence of it is most evident in regard to Temple's view of time and foreknowledge. From the standpoint of God's immanence in the historical process God is limited by time, and hence future choices by man are unknown to him, but as transcendent Being, God is omniscient. Temple's argument at this point is merely verbal. First of all, to distinguish God as transcendent from God as immanent as Temple does is either to succumb to the fallacy of logical abstraction or else to posit a separate and distinct being. What Temple is positing is, in effect, a substratum substance or a sort of "pure being" regarding God, though he has rejected a soul-substance view of human personality. But is it possible for a part of God to operate in the world without affecting all of God? Neither Temple's conception of personality nor his interpretation of revelation support such a view. What man encounters in revelation, according to Temple, "*is not truth concerning God but the living God Himself.*"[4] Occam's razor is needed at this point to cut away some of the rounded edges of Temple's reasoning. Hence, the notion of God as existing distinct from His activity in the World-Process is beyond man's comprehension and also demands accounting for the immanent Person in the process, or the process itself becomes fictitious. God as a transcendent being may be logically distinguished from God as immanent, but neither one has ontological reality apart from the other. Temple

[3] Temple, *Nature, Man and God*, p. 358.
[4] *Ibid.*, p. 322.

fails to give due consideration to a view of God's self-identity as what endures through the activity, though he affirms this view in regard to human personality.

The fallacy of logical abstraction is evident in the analogy which Temple employs also. He argues that just as the dramatist is not personally within the play, though the play depends on him, so too God is not Himself within the time process, though what happens in time depends on God.[5] The point is, however, that the dramatist (or God) is personally within the play when he is writing it. He is at that moment primarily a dramatist, and only secondarily a husband, citizen, or anyone else. The fact that he can combine many roles is due to the unity-in-variety of his present conscious experience which includes memory and anticipation. In short, in the moment of writing the entire personality of the dramatist is involved; nothing is "totally other" and what endures through it all is his self-identity. Moreover, the analogy of the dramatist breaks down at a very crucial point in regard to God's relation to man, namely, the fact that man is alive and is endowed with freedom; whereas the characters have no existence and no actual freedom. Further, if either God or the dramatist entirely separates himself from his creation, such as the dramatist's arbitrarily ending the play, then the freedom of their creatures ends and the creatures no longer exist. However, so long as man (or the characters) exists and his freedom is real, then God (or the dramatist) is intimately involved in the choices which are made, is limited by them, and is not capable of knowing in any absolute sense what the choices will be.

Hence, even if one accepts Temple's view of God as the Supreme Person, it seems necessary to conclude that God is limited by the historical process, or else human freedom is an illusion and the entire process becomes meaningless. Further, there must be at least as much succession in God as there is succession in history if history is to have meaning for the Eternal. In a word, time must be real. Temple wants God related to history and yet fundamentally unaffected by it and in so doing has sacrificed both God and history. If history is to make a difference to God, then the temporal process which is of the essence of history must also make a difference to God. W. R. Matthews, while retaining the view of God as personal, perceptively analyzes the problem with Temple's position and proposes a reasonable alternative to it: "The difficulty arises from the conception of God as self-sufficient.

[5] See Temple, *Nature, Man and God*, pp. 444–445; also above, Chapter 16.

Why not try the hypothesis, suggested by the Gospels, that God is not self-sufficient?"[6]

The basis of Temple's problem is his aversion to departing from an orthodox or absolutistic conception of the omnipotency of God. Temple is here clinging to an ideal conception of God as the Supreme Personality, perfect in power and in goodness, even when the facts of experience require a revision, and when to persist in affirming the ideal necessitates at the same time affirming contradictory propositions.[7] If the difficulties inherent in Temple's position are to be avoided and the empirical facts of temporal process are to be explained, then the incomplete supremacy of God over history must be acknowledged, even by one who affirms a view of God as the Supreme Person. If God is the ground of history, then history to have meaning must actually affect God, not just a part of Him but His total personal nature. God is, then, in a real sense limited by historical process including irrational factors in history, temporal sequence, and man's freedom.

However, perhaps, what is called for is a more radical reconceptualization of belief in God and God's relation to history such as has been proposed by Leslie Dewart.[8] The place to begin any attempt to integrate Christian theism with the contemporary experience of man, Dewart argues, is by separating the Christian belief in God from the hellenistic view of Being. The Reality and Presence of God replace the hellenistic concepts of Being and Existence. Furthermore, God is not himself a person, but both man's relations to God and God's relations with man are personal, because we are persons. The so-called divine attributes must also be reconceptualized in non-hellenic terms. "Omnipotence" no longer means what God can and cannot do to nature and man, but what can and cannot happen "once God and man enter into personal relations."[9] Thus, for Dewart, "God's 'omnipotence' not only means that all history is possible, it also means that all history is free."[10] Since eternity means self-identity in Scholastic thought, the problem of God's relation to history has plagued Christian thought

[6] "William Temple as Thinker," in W. R. Matthews and Others, p. 21. See also Matthew's criticism of God as self-sufficient, including Temple's position, in *The Purpose of God* (New York: Charles Scribner's Sons, 1936), pp. 173–176.

[7] This issue is perceptively analyzed from different perspectives in Brightman, *A Philosophy of Religion*, pp. 305–341, and in Burkill, *God and Reality in Modern Thought*, pp. 143–157. Burkill descriptively labels the kind of theistic position Temple advocates, "theistic orthodoxy"; Brightman calls it, "theistic absolutism."

[8] Leslie Dewart, *The Future of Belief: Theism in a World Come of Age* (New York: Herder and Herder, 1966).

[9] *Ibid.*, p. 190.

[10] *Ibid.*, p. 196.

unnecessarily; but once God is not conceptualized in hellenic terms, then eternity is no longer necessary or adequate. God, for Christians, must be conceived as historical or not at all.

God's reality is held by Dewart to have real (ontic), not supernatural or metaphysical, import for man, and requires a re-examination of man's relations with God. The relations between God and man on the hellenistic model was conceived in terms of ascendance-submission, since God was viewed as the acme of metaphysical supremacy. But if the hellenistic hierarchical model of the universe is discarded, the superiority-inferiority conception of interpersonal relations is no longer adequate, even between God and man. Man still, of course, has primary obligations to God, who rules by the principle of *noblesse oblige* and enters freely into interpersonal cooperation with man in the historical process. Hence, "God is not charitable; he *is* charity."[11] Finally, the Christian concept of God as Supernatural Being is no longer useful for Christian theism. This does not mean that God is to be thought of as natural in the hellenic sense of nature; the concept of nature too requires reconceptualization. In any case, Dewart contends, it is the doctrine of *grace* that is fundamental for Christian theism. If nature is held to be essentially contingent, then grace and nature are not opposed. "God's grace may be understood as the self-bestowal of the ultimate reality, hence as the source of faith and inspiration, and of existence and creativity, no longer God's cornucopia of immaterial plenty, but the *alpha* and *omega* of consciousness and *praxis*, existence and life."[12]

No definitive statement of, or judgment on, Dewart's views is being proposed. What is significant is that Dewart, like Temple, takes Christian theism seriously, but challenges precisely the kind of Christian-hellenistic interpretation of nature, man, history, and God that characterizes Temple's position. Indeed, Temple seems quite unaware that Christianity might be expressed in other than its historic hellenistic cultural form. Dewart has, thus, rendered a significant service by cogently arguing that the future development of Christian theism requires the formulation of alternatives to the dominant hellenistic Scholastic version of Christian theism. Also, his own attempt at a radical reconception of the philosophical basis of Christianity provides one such alternative.

[11] *Ibid.*, p. 206.
[12] *Ibid.*, p. 212.

B. THE MEANING OF HISTORY WITHIN HISTORY

Temple's suggestion that history is incomplete and that at any stage it points beyond itself for its own fulfillment needs to be examined. He suggests that there is evidence for a progressive upward movement of history in certain areas of life, but not evidence that history itself contains sufficient inherent power to overcome all the conflicts and evils it produces. Even if these conclusions be granted, and they are debatable, to posit another order beyond history as necessary to render the present historical order meaningful does not follow. Nor does it follow that immortality is required to give meaning to the lives of those who died before the result of history, whatever it may be. Once again an ideal Temple has in mind is determining the solution which he accepts as adequate without sufficient concern for the requirements of experience. There is no doubt that if there is another order beyond history for which the present one is preparatory, then this does provide a kind of meaning for history and for the individuals who share in the new order. But it is not the only meaning that either history or man can have.

If in history there is some evidence of progress along technological lines and even a movement from self-interest to enlightened self- interest, then history cannot be claimed to be without meaning unless the only kind of meaning one accepts is that of a state of perfection. Further, if ethical goodness resides in the quest for perfectability and not in a perfect state, then so long as history provides the opportunity for growth and development there is some meaning for the individual. The individual shares in the "eternal" significance of history to the extent that he realizes his own potentialities and fosters the personal development of others. Although this does not remove the tragedy of history for the vast majority of people who throughout the ages have not had even the opportunity for full personal development, neither is the tragedy removed by positing another order beyond history. To claim that the meaning of history resides in a non-historical order does not make the historical order any more meaningful unless that meaning can be discovered in, and made relevant to, the present order; and if it is discovered and is made relevant, then to that extent history is meaningful whatever lies beyond. If the meaning of history is not found in history, then it has no meaning for one in history. This is true whatever awaits one upon death.

Temple's argument for eternal life rests fundamentally on faith in the goodness of God and, for the most part, he develops the case clearly and cogently, granting his assumptions. Waiving the latter for the present, there are still some ambiguities and defects in the way Temple states the case for eternal life. The meaning of resurrection and how it differs from immortality is never clarified. Though Temple could have developed the point more fully, he does indicate the basis for immortality in the capacity of man to transcend his physiological organism and the historical order in the quest of truth, beauty, and goodness. However, Temple weakens the case in his theory of value by wavering in the interpretation of man's role in realizing values in the world. Also, his stress on the supremacy of God and man's utter incapacity before God does not support the notion that God needs man in any real sense, or that He is sufficiently concerned with the values man realizes to continue man's existence for the sake of mutual fellowship.

In any case, the argument for life eternal based on the goodness of God is extremely precarious. Concisely stated the argument runs as follows: If God is conceived as the Eternal conserver of values and persons alone realize the values of life, then God is committed to the preservation of persons. Even on the basis of this argument Temple hesitates to conclude what alone seems warranted, namely, conditional immortality. Man has the capacity for immortality, but Temple denies that man is immortal by nature; his immortality is dependent on the goodness of God and on the unique value-contribution of each individual. Thus, if an individual fails to develop his value-potential, then it would seem that there is no basis for his surviving death.

However, a more fundamental difficulty is the recognition of the conditional nature of the religious argument for eternal life. As Ducasse points out, there are a number of "ifs" involved in the argument: "*If* there is a God ... *if* he is good and sufficiently powerful ... *if* the existence of evil is reconcilable with the goodness and power of God ... *if* value is metaphysically structural in the universe ... etc."[13] Hence, the argument represents an attempt to deduce what should follow from the nature of God, if there is a God and if the nature of God has been correctly interpreted from the evidence of human experience. But man may be wrong about any of the "ifs" and, then, the entire argument is weakened or even rendered invalid. When the close union of mind and body is affirmed, as Temple asserts, then the issue is further

[13] Ducasse, *Nature, Mind, and Death*, p. 448.

complicated. Nor does Temple help matters by rejecting psychical research, which offers possible empirical evidence for personal survival.

However, if the religious argument for immortality is indecisive, so is the case against any form of survival. The case against survival of death rests on the paucity of positive empirical evidence for survival and on both the physiological argument and the argument of psychological monism against it. When the absence of direct evidence for actual survival of human personality is combined with the positive evidence for the mind's dependence on and union with the body, then immortality is held to be an illusion.

According to the physiological argument against survival, conscious experience is only observed to exist in direct interaction with a properly functioning physiological organism. Thus, when the organism is impaired, due to blows on the head or the administering of drugs, consciousness is correspondingly affected; and when the organism is destroyed, all the usual evidence of consciousness also ceases. Therefore, when the body dies, the basis of consciousness is eliminated and survival is impossible.

Essentially accepting the physiological argument, but adding to it evidence from biological evolution and certain recent developments in psychology, Corliss Lamont claims that the dualism of mind and body is refuted and survival beyond death disproved.[14] Lamont affirms that monistic psychology has sufficiently established the indissoluble union of mind and body, rendering impermissible and unintelligible any attempt to conceive of the mind existing independent of the body.[15] Personality (or mind) is held to be the function of the body; hence, body is primary and mind is derivative both temporally and substantially. Lamont develops his case at great length, but the evidence for the functional relationship is summarized in the following four points:

first, that in the evolutionary process the power and versatility of living forms increase concomitantly with the development and complexity of their bodies in general and their central nervous systems in particular; second, that the genes or other factors from the germ cells of the parents determine the individual's inherent physical characteristics and inherent mental capacities; third, that during the existence of a human being from childhood to youth and from adulthood to old age, the mind and personality grow and change, always in conjunction with environmental influences, as the body grows and changes; and fourth, that specific alterations in the physical structure and condition of the

[14] Corliss Lamont, *The Illusion of Immortality* (3rd. ed., New York: Wisdom Library, 1959), see esp. Chapter III, pp. 123–126. A shorter statement is contained in Lamont's, *The Philosophy of Humanism* (5th. ed., New York: Frederick Ungar Publishing Co., 1965), Chapter III.

[15] See Lamont, *The Illusion of Immortality*, p. 108.

body, especially in the brain and its cerebral cortex, bring about specific alterations in the mental and emotional life of a man, and conversely that specific alterations in his mental and emotional life result in specific alterations in his bodily condition.[16]

Thus, Lamont concludes: "All in all, such a close and far-reaching functional relationship has been proven to exist between personality and body that we can hardly conceive of them as other than an inseparable unity."[17]

Despite Lamont's confidence that he has "disproved the notion of an immortal soul,"[18] the arguments against man surviving death in some form are not decisive. Granted that consciousness as we know it is dependent on bodily processes and that head injuries seem to extinguish consciousness temporarily, it does not follow, as Ducasse notes, that consciousness is totally extinguished: "the strict fact is only that the usual bodily signs of consciousness are then absent. But they are also absent when a person is asleep; and yet, at the same time, dreams, which are states of consciousness, may be occurring."[19] Nor is the fact that we have no memory of conscious states when drugged or injured conclusive, since we have few memories of most of our waking lives in the past: "if absence of memories relating to a given period proved unconsciousness for that period, this would force us to conclude that we were unconscious during the first few years of our lives, and indeed have been so most of the time since; for the fact is that we have no memories whatever of most of our days."[20] Furthermore, that death extinguishes mind since the usual manifestations of it cease is to ignore the evidence of psychical research which will be examined below.

Although it is true that certain states of consciousness (e.g., sensations) can be caused by stimulating the body, it is equally true that mental states can cause various bodily events: merely by willing it one's arm may be raised; imagining food can cause a hungry person's mouth to water; feelings of rage, fear, or excitement can hinder or stop digestion; anxiety alters the quantity and quality of milk of a nursing mother; certain vivid images may suffice to produce tears, blushing, or even fainting. In terms of the relation of mind and body, what the evidence points to is mutual interaction. Lamont acknowledges this

[16] *Ibid.*, p. 109.
[17] *Ibid.*
[18] *Ibid.*, pp. 123–124.
[19] Ducasse, *Nature, Mind, and Death*, p. 454.
[20] *Ibid.*

fact, but fails to draw the inference that the efficacy of mind on body is evidence for the *partial* independence of mind from body and certainly not evidence for the kind of exclusive reliance of mind on body required by his position. Lamont's argument clearly establishes the unity of mind and body and a certain dependency of mind on body, but not their identity or the complete dependency of mind on body.

Some comments are in order concerning the correlation of the development of the nervous system with the growth of mind and the degree of intelligence. It is quite true, as Lamont claims, that one hypothesis warranted by these facts is epiphenomenalism, the view that mind is the product of the nervous system; however, another hypothesis equally justified is hypophenomenalism, the view that "an obscurely felt need for greater intelligence in the circumstances the animal faced brought about the variations which eventually resulted in a more adequate nervous organization."[21] In any case, it is evident that in the development of the individual certain structural changes in the body can be produced by the person willing the acquisition of specific skills and habits. Thus, highly complex nerve connections are established in the brain of a skilled pianist or athlete, for example, as a result of willing these skills over a period of years.

Finally, both the physiological argument and the argument of psychological monism against surviving death are, like the religious arguments, conditional and rest ultimately on a metaphysical bias. What is being claimed is that conscious experience not only interacts with a body but is totally dependent on the body; but unity is neither identity nor complete dependency. Also, as Ducasse has shown, implicit in the two arguments is the *metaphysical assumption* "that *to be real is to be material*; and to be material ... is to be some process or part of the perceptually public world."[22] Such an assumption is quite legitimate for the investigation of the physical world, but its legitimacy is relative to that purpose. When one has a different purpose in mind – e.g., the possibility of the mind, or some parts of it, surviving death – then it is illegitimate to carry over automatically the metaphysical bias that only what is perceived to be part of the physical world is actually real. Ignored in this approach are precisely the facts of mind based on introspection that one is concerned to investigate. Hence, only *if* mind is identical with, or completely dependent on, body, and only *if* the

[21] *Ibid.*, pp. 456–457.
[22] *Ibid.*, p. 458.

material world alone is real, does it follow that the mind cannot *possibly* survive bodily death.

The task remains, nonetheless, to propose evidence for the possibility of survival. The place to begin, as noted above, is with an examination of mind, its activities and relations to the physical world, as introspectively observable. What the introspective experience of mind and its relation to the body reveals is that there is direct interaction, but not identity or complete dependence of mind on body. Thus, ideas and meanings of the mind are not to be identified with bodily events despite the close connections. We have ideas that refer to objects which are green or two feet long, but none of our ideas are colored or spatially extended in this way. Likewise, man responds to the meanings of stimuli and of events and not simply to certain specific sensory signs. A dog may become so accustomed to walking with its master whenever the latter gets the dog's leash that the dog will respond accordingly even if this series of events occurs in the middle of the night during a blinding snow storm with the master dressed in pajamas.[23] A partial independence of mind from the body is further illustrated by the ability to concentrate attention on an object to the extent that one is unaware of bodily disturbances of pain or hunger, or of environmental surroundings. Not to be ignored either is the experience of moral obligation which on occasion calls for sacrifices contrary to the interests of one's physical well-being.

Hence, conscious experience enables one to transcend partially the natural order through the formation of concepts or "free ideas"; that is, the mind can contemplate an object not present in one's sensory experience.[24] At the basis of human consciousness is the ability of man to gain what might be called psychical distance from the objects, ideas, and values given by the environment and to see them in a new perspective by relating them to what they are not. Evident here is man's capacity to be guided by ideals; that is, the ability to project himself into the future and to envisage a type of experience he has not had but would like to have and to guide his actions in the present so as to realize it. Thus, man not only responds to meaning he demonstrates his freedom by creating "a new world of meaning around a chosen project."[25]

[23] See Beck and Holmes, *Philosophic Inquiry*, p. 328.

[24] See Brand Blanshard, *The Nature of Thought* (New York: The Macmillan Company, 1939), Vol. I, 257–259, 528–549.

[25] John Wild, *Existence and the World of Freedom* (Englewood Cliffs, N. J.: Prentice-Hall, Inc., 1963), p. 146; see also *Ibid.*, p. 110.

Added to these direct experiences of the conscious life indicating the relative independence of mind from body is the empirical evidence for the possibility of survival based on allegedly paranormal capacities of the mind. Ducasse summarizes the evidence for survival disclosed by psychical research, and some statements from his writings suffice for our purposes. Two categories of evidence are noted. The first concerns "apparitions of a person dying or having just died but not known to have been ill or in danger."[26] In some instances the apparition conveys information not known by the percipient until that time. One famous case reported by Ducasse concerns a father, who sometime after his death, "appeared" to one of his sons and conveyed information specifying the location of a second will which was then found as indicated. A second type of empirical evidence for survival "consists of communications purporting to come from the dead, made through persons commonly called sensitives, mediums, or automatists."[27] The facts communicated in many instances were unknown to the medium and, more crucial, in some cases the facts were also unknown by the sitter or even unknown by any living person. Most impressive are those cases known as "cross correspondences" in which, for example, "two mediums sometimes thousands of miles apart give each a different communication, neither of which is intelligible by itself, but when put together they are found to constitute an unmistakable allusion to an obscure passage in some work of classical literature."[28]

Apart from explaining away these facts as fraudulent, two hypotheses have been proposed to explain them. One is to accept the survival hypothesis and to grant that the communications come from minds that have survived death in some form. Another alternative is the hypothesis of telepathy in which the medium directly collects the information from others. In some cases this requires that the medium be able to tap the minds of persons far away in both space and time and even tap subconscious processes of the mind, including events which the individual himself cannot consciously recall. Even, then, there remains those cases "where the facts communicated were not known to any living person."[29]

On the basis of the introspective evidence of the nature of mind

[26] Ducasse, *Nature, Mind, and Death*, p. 473.
[27] *Ibid.*, p. 475.
[28] *Ibid.*, p. 476.
[29] *Ibid.*, p. 478.

and the evidence from psychical research Ducasse concludes that survival in the sense of the continuation of some psycho-psychical capacities of the human mind beyond bodily death is *theoretically* possible, and that there is strong *prima facie* evidence for belief that some mental capacities *actually* survive. It seems unlikely to Ducasse that the total personality survives death. In any event the evidence only conclusively establishes the theoretical possibility of partial survival; it does not establish that there actually is survival of death.[30]

The issue of personal survival of death remains, therefore, unsettled; neither the arguments for nor the arguments against are decisive. The arguments for survival fail to establish that it actually occurs, but, on the other hand, the arguments against survival amount to no more than the same thing – namely, a denial that survival has been demonstrated to have actually occurred. Hence, the *theoretical* possibility of life in some form after bodily death, far from impossible, would seem to be established. This means that the nature of mind admits the possibility of detachment from the body such as survival of death requires, but whether such detachment actually occurs is at present not empirically established, though belief in its occurrence does not represent an unfounded faith.

Any hypothesis offered about life after death is, of course, highly tentative and largely speculative. Man knows not if anyone lives beyond earthly existence; at best he knows only that there is the possibility of survival, and that if it occurs it will probably be an extension in some form of a kind of conscious state he now experiences. Hence, this earthly life is, at least, the primary determining factor both in terms of life on earth and in terms of the possibility of life beyond. Therefore, whatever may or may not lie beyond history, man is thrown back to an understanding of the present historical realm in order to discern the meaning of human existence; and he is called upon to commit himself to the present order by devoting himself to realizing within history what meaning he has discovered or can himself create.

C. A CONCLUDING COMMENT

It would not be justified or accurate to end this extensive analysis and critique of Temple's contribution to philosophy in general and to Christian philosophy in particular on the primarily negative note con-

[30] See *ibid.*, pp. 479–483.

tained in the above criticisms of his Christian philosophy of history. It is certainly true that the ideal of a coherent and systematic Christian philosophy was not achieved. However, at no point did Temple fail to provide provocative analyses of the philosophical problems he discussed or to offer suggestive solutions, even though at only one point – viz., his social philosophy – did he deal thoroughly and systematically with an issue.

Temple's merit lies more in the suggestions he proposed to possible solutions, which need to be worked out more critically and systematically than he did, than it does in offering definitive solutions to philosophical problems. Indeed, his writings reflect this approach and are appropriately labeled essays or lectures aimed at outlining possible positions but not at developing a system of thought. Such an approach no doubt reflects not only Temple's scepticism toward such a completed system of thought but also the simple fact that he never thought out completely a systematic philosophy. But then in terms of temperament, social concerns, and the mission to which he felt called, it is doubtful if a life of thought would have been the most fruitful use of his life. The words of W. R. Matthews reflect a similar estimate and provide a fitting conclusion:

> Temple once remarked that we required a new *Summa* but that probably the time was not ripe for it. There were few men of our time who had greater qualifications for writing a new and reasoned system of Christian theology. ... In some moods we may regret that he did not devote his life to this supreme task, but doubtless we are wrong. He did what was laid upon him to do, and we must be grateful for the contribution to Christian thought which he has made. I do not think he could have passed his years in studious reflection; his temperament would not have allowed him to remain a spectator of the conflict, and it may well be that the sense of the actual life of the Church and community, which is so valuable a characteristic of his thought, derives its strength from his constant immersion in the conduct of affairs.[31]

[31] "William Temple as Thinker," in W. R. Matthews and Others, p. 23.

BIBLIOGRAPHY

The following lists include only those writings by and about William Temple that are referred to in the present work. An extensive bibliography of Temple's writings can be found in Fletcher, *William Temple: Twentieth-Century Christian*, pp. 349–365. Critical reviews of Temple's three major works are listed in Thomas, *William Temple's Philosophy of Religion*, pp. 171–172.

I. BOOKS, ESSAYS, ARTICLES, AND PARTS OF BOOKS BY WILLIAM TEMPLE

Christian Faith and Life.
New York: The Macmillan Company, 1931.

Christianity and the Social Order.
Harmondsworth, Middlesex: Penguin Books, Ltd., 1942.

Christianity and the State.
London: Macmillan and Co., Ltd., 1928.

"Christianity as an Interpretation of History" (1944), reprinted in *Religious Experience and Other Essays and Addresses.*
London: James Clarke & Co., Ltd., 1958.

Christianity in Thought and Practice.
London: Student Christian Movement Press, 1936.

Christ's Revelation of God.
London: S. C. M. Press, 1925.

Christus Veritas.
London: Macmillan and Company, Ltd., 1924.

The Church and Its Teaching Today.
New York: The Macmillan Company, 1936.

The Church Looks Forward.
New York: The Macmillan Company, 1944.

Church and Nation.
London: Macmillan and Co., 1915.

Citizen and Churchman.
London: Etyre & Spottiswoode, Ltd., 1941.

"The Divinity of Christ," in B. H. Streeter, William Temple and Others, *Foundations, A Statement of Christian Belief in Terms of Modern Thought: By Seven Oxford Men.*
London: Macmillan and Co., Ltd., 1913.

Doctrine in the Church of England.
London: Macmillan and Co., 1938.

Essays in Christian Politics and Kindred Subjects.
London: Longmans, Green and Co., 1927.

The Faith and Modern Thought.
London: Macmillan and Co., Ltd., 1910.
Fellowship with God.
London: Macmillan and Co., 1920.
"The Godhead of Jesus" (1922), reprinted in *Religious Experience and Other Essays and Addresses.*
London: James Clarke & Co., Ltd., 1958.
The Hope of a New World.
New York: The Macmillan Company, 1942.
"In the Beginning – God" (1939), reprinted in *Religious Experience and Other Essays and Addresses.*
London: James Clarke & Co., Ltd., 1958.
"The Idea of Immortality in Relation to Religion and Ethics" (1931), reprinted in *Religious Experience and Other Essays and Addresses.*
London: James Clarke & Co., Ltd., 1958.
The Kingdom of God.
London: Macmillan and Co., Ltd., 1912.
Mens Creatrix.
London: Macmillan and Co., Ltd., 1917.
"My Point of View" (1930), reprinted in *Religious Experience and other Essays and Addresses.*
London: James Clarke & Co., Ltd., 1958.
Nature, Man and God.
London: Macmillan and Co., Ltd., 1934.
The Nature of Personality.
London: Macmillan and Co., Ltd., 1911.
Personal Religion and the Life of Fellowship.
London: Longmans, Green and Co., Ltd., 1926.
Plato and Christianity.
London: Macmillan and Co., Ltd., 1916.
Readings in St. John's Gospel. First and Second Series.
London: Macmillan and Co., Ltd., 1945.
"Religious Experience" (1914), reprinted in *Religious Experience and Other Essays and Addresses.*
London: James Clarke & Co., Ltd., 1958.
Religious Experience and Other Essays and Addresses. Collected and edited with an Introduction by Canon A. E. Baker.
London: James Clarke & Co., Ltd., 1958.
Repton School Sermons: Studies in the Religion of the Incarnation.
London: Macmillan and Co., 1913.
"Some Implications of Theism," in J. H. Muirhead (ed.), *Contemporary British Philosophy,* Volume I.
New York: The Macmillan Company, 1924.
Studies in the Spirit and Truth of Christianity.
London: Macmillan and Co., 1914.
"Symbolism as a Metaphysical Principle" (1928), reprinted in *Religious Experience and other Essays and Addresses.*
London: James Clarke & Co., Ltd., 1958.
"Theology To-day," reprinted in *Thoughts in War-Time.*
London: Macmillan & Co., Ltd., 1940.
Thoughts in War-Time.
London: Macmillan & Co., Ltd., 1940.

The Universality of Christ.
London: Student Christian Movement, 1921.
"What Christians Stand For in the Secular World" (1944), reprinted in *Religious Experience and Other Essays and Addresses.*
London: James Clarke & Co., Ltd., 1958.

2. BOOKS, DISSERTATIONS, AND ARTICLES ABOUT WILLIAM TEMPLE

Baker, A. E. (ed.)
William Temple and His Message.
Harmondsworth, Middlesex: Penguin Books, 1946.
— (ed.)
William Temple's *Teaching.*
Philadelphia: The Westminster Press, 1951.
Bell, G. K. A.
"Memoir," in *William Temple and His Message*, edited by A. E. Baker.
Harmondsworth, Middlesex: Penguin Books, 1946.
Carlton, John W.
"The Reach and Limits of Natural Theology in the Formulation of William Temple's Christology."
Unpublished Ph. D. dissertation, School of Arts and Sciences, Duke University, 1955.
Carmichael, John D. and Howard S. Goodwin
William Temple's Political Legacy: A Critical Assessment.
Naperville, Illinois: Alec R. Allenson, Inc., 1963.
Craig, Robert.
Social Concern in Thought of William Temple.
London: The Camelot Press, Ltd., 1963.
Fletcher, Joseph
William Temple: Twentieth-Century Christian
London: Oxford University Press, 1948.
Geoghegan, William D.
Platonism in Recent Religious Thought.
New York: Columbia University Press, 1958.
Iremonger, F. A.
William Temple, Archbishop of Canterbury: His Life and Letters.
London: Oxford University Press, 1948.
Lowry, Charles W., Jr.
"William Temple, Archbishop of Canterbury."
Christendom, VIII (Winter, 1943), 26–41.
Matthews, W. R.
"William Temple as Thinker," in *William Temple: An Estimate and an Appreciation*, by W. R. Matthews and Others.
London: James Clarke & Co., Ltd., 1946.
Matthew, W. R. and Others.
William Temple: An Estimate and an Appreciation.
London: James Clarke & Co., Ltd., 1946.
Mc Garvey, John P.
"Modernism in Archbishop Temple's Metaphysics and Value Theory."
Unpublished Ph. D. dissertation, School of Theology, Temple University, (1951).
Miller, Randolph Crump
"Is Temple a Realist?"
Journal of Religion, XIX (January, 1939), 44–54.

Page, Robert J.
New Directions in Anglican Theology: A Survey from Temple to Robinson.
New York: The Seabury Press, 1956.
Peck, W. G.
"William Temple as Social Thinker," in *William Temple: An Estimate and an Appreciation,* by W. R. Matthews and Others.
London: James Clarke & Co., Ltd., 1946.
Ramsey, Arthur Michael
An Era in Anglican Theology: From Gore to Temple.
New York: Charles Scribner's Sons, 1960.
Skelton, Eugene
"The Problem of Evil in the Works of William Temple." Unpublished Ph. D. dissertation, School of Theology.
Southwestern Baptist Theological Seminary, 1951.
Thomas, Owen
William Temple's Philosophy of Religion.
New York: The Seabury Press, 1961.

INDEX